CAVING BASICS

A Comprehensive Manual for Beginning Cavers
New Revised Edition

1982 Editor Jerry Hassemer
1987 Editor Tom Rea

Production by NSS Special Publications Committee
1982 Edition Linda Starr
1987 Edition David McClurg

NATIONAL SPELEOLOGICAL SOCIETY
CAVE AVENUE
HUNTSVILLE, ALABAMA 35810
USA

Caving Basics, Second Edition

Published by
National Speleological Society, Inc.
Cave Avenue
Huntsville, Alabama 35810

Library of Congress Catalog Card No. 82-061922

ISBN No. 0-9615093-1-7

Cover photograph by David and Janet McClurg: *Two young cavers peer into the darkness beyond at the entrance to Bat Cave, a lava tube in the Medicine Lake Highlands of Northern California.*

The techniques and practices described in this manual must be discussed and practiced with knowledgeable, experienced cavers above ground before you attempt to use them in caving. The place to make your mistakes and discover any misunderstandings is with qualified instructors **before** you enter a cave.

Liability Disclaimer. Warning: Serious injury or death could result from using the techniques, practices, or equipment described in this book. It is your responsibility to get qualified instruction in safe caving for yourself. This book is sold with no liability, expressed or implied, to the authors, the editors, or the National Speleological Society, in case of injury or death to the purchaser or reader.

CONTENTS

APPENDIXES

FOREWORD

In 1976, the NSS decided to develop course material to be used by its local grottos to instruct new members. it was intended that these new members first be exposed to certain basic information. Then this could be combined with practical experience with seasoned cavers to give them the background necessary to negotiate the typical cave.

I think you'll agree that the resulting material well satisfies the needs of both the new caver and the caving instructor. It provides a standardized, authoritative guide to be followed in a logically developed training. sequence Each chapter has been authored by an "expert" in that field. Besides covering the basics of caving, references to sources of advanced information are included.

Of special interest in this revised edition, are the new chapters on caving electronics, women in caving, and getting started with an experienced group. Revised chapters cover carbide vs electric lighting, fitness and nutrition, and newly updated references on first aid

Besides functioning as the basis of a grotto training course, this manual will also serve to introduce new members to caving and the Society.

The original edition and this new revision were written primarily for newer cavers. However, it will appeal to all cavers as a basic reference book on a variety of caving topics. I hope you will find it as useful as I have.

Paul Stevens 1982 Executive Vice President
1987 President
National Speleological Society

PREFACE

This Manual

Caving is the sport of exploring and studying caves. It is a growing sport, not only in the United States, but around the world. People who explore caves are cavers. There are proper and safe caving methods and there are improper and unsafe methods of caving. This manual explains how to cave properly. From it you will be able to learn about lights, helmets, packs, conservation and much more.

Twenty experienced cavers contributed the material which follows. Their combined experience totals about 400 years. Many of the authors are recognized authorities in their field and are constantly developing new theories and improving techniques to make caving safer and more enjoyable for the rest of us. A short section following this preface gives information about these people.

Each chapter of this manual was written independently. Each author has his own style of writing and his own ideas of what is important. This individuality was preserved as much as possible but has resulted in some items and ideas being mentioned in more than one chapter. The chapter sequence was arranged in an order that the editor felt coincides with the natural way a person becomes comfortable in the cave environment. First, one needs a light, not just one, but at least three of them. Then one needs a helmet, cave clothing and a pack. A caver will then develop a greater respect for the cave itself, the things he finds there, the land above it and its owner.

What is included here is only an introduction for a beginning caver or one who does not care to become a specialist in any one aspect of caving. Topics such as cave photography and cave surveying are not addressed. This, then, is a "basic" manual intended only to develop the basis for further exploration by the reader.

The techniques and practices described in this manual must be discussed and practiced with knowledgeable, experienced cavers above ground, before you attempt to use them in caving. The place to make mistakes and discover misunderstanding is **before** you enter a cave.

The NSS

The National Speleological Society (NSS) is the only national caving organization whose membership is made up not only of sport cavers (those who cave just for the fun of it) but also cave conservationists and speleologists (those who study caves). The present membership is over 5000. The goals of the NSS are to promote the study, exploration and conservation of caves. The NSS has a permanent office in Huntsville, Alabama and also owns several caves. The address of the NSS office is:

National Speleological Society
Cave Avenue
Huntsville, Alabama 35810
Phone: 205/852-1300

NSS members in the same area generally form a cave club and apply to become a chapter of the NSS. Such a group is usually called a grotto; currently there are about 140. Several grottos may join together to form a region. Functions of grottos and regions vary greatly, but each provides an organization in which the novice caver can learn about caving and can find others to go caving. If you do not know of a grotto in your area, write to the NSS office for the address of the grottos near you.

Any person interested in caves should join the NSS as well as the local grotto. Membership in the NSS provides you with the monthly *NSS News* and the quarterly *NSS Bulletin*. The *NSS News* usually contains one or two cave trip reports on some outstanding cave or cave system; a calendar of caving events around the country; notes on the meetings and actions of the Society; book reviews; reports of equipment testing; accident reports and analysis thereof and much more.

The *NSS Bulletin* is the scientific publication of the NSS. It is the only journal in the U.S. devoted to speleology. Current ideas on cave development, cave minerals, the evolution of cave life and other topics are reported.

Just how valuable these benefits are to you depends on how you use them. They can go from the mail box to the files. Or you can dig into them to see how the articles in the *News* and *Bulletin* relate to your type of caving and how these different ideas can be used to broaden your caving experience. To be a caver is to be flexible in your ideas, equipment, techniques and practices.

Brand Names

The use of specific brand names of various products in this manual is for clarity and convenience only. It would be very hard to talk about underground lights without using their names. However, the use of these names does not imply any endorsement of the use of these products by the National Speleological Society, the particular author or the editor.

Jerry Hassemer, Chairman
Caver Training Committee

ABOUT THE AUTHORS

Hugh W. Blanchard
South Pasadena, Calilfornia

Caving Liability
Hugh served as Chairman of the NSS Legal Committee for many years. He started caving in New York and Massachusetts in 1957. Hugh lived in Alabama for several years and was active in the Birmingham Grotto. In 1967, he moved to Los Angeles and joined the Southern California Grotto where he edited *The Explorer*, the Southern California Grotto newsletter.

Langford G. Brod, Jr.
Tucson, Arizona

Reading Cave Maps
Lang joined the Middle Mississippi Valley Grotto in 1959. He has served as chairman of the Missouri Speleological Survey and as a director of the NSS. Lang maps small caves as well as large ones. He is well-known for his efforts in Missouri's 16-mile long Berome-Moore Cave System. Lang moved to Arizona in 1969 and he is currently a member of Escabrosa Grotto and the Arizona Speleological Association.

Roger W. Brucker
Yellow Springs, Ohio

Moving Through A Cave
Roger is an Honorary Member of the NSS. He was a founder, and later President, of the Cave Research Foundation. Roger helped organize the week-long 1954 C-3 Expedition, and NSS project in Floyd Collins Crystal Cave, Kentucky. He is co-author of three books on caves: *The Caves Beyond* and *The Longest Cave* (both on Mammoth Cave System), and *Trapped!* (a biography of Floyd Collins).

Eileen Carol, RN, FNP, MN
Santa Rosa, California

First Aid
Eileen joined the Southern California Grotto in 1971. She has taught several courses on caving first aid and helped develop a spine board for moving persons with neck and spinal injuries. Eileen has given talks on rabies and other infectious diseases cavers may encounter. She has made many caving trips to Mexico.

Ray Cole
Alexandria, Virginia

Caving Safety
Vertical Caving Checklist
Ray joined the District of Columbia Grotto in 1970 and since then has held a variety of offices in that Grotto, including chairman. Since 1947 he has served as co-chairman of the Organ Cave Survey. Ray is currently a director of the Appalachian Search and Rescue Conference. He has also been an active member of the NSS Safety and Techniques Committee.

Donald Davis
Parachute, Colorado

Carbide or Electric Lighting?
The Carbide Lamp
Donald discovered the connection passage in Spanish Cave, Colorado in 1959. He has explored and studied caves throughout the western U.S. He worked as a naturalist at Carlsbad Caverns National Park and is an active carbide lamp collector and dealer.

William R. Elliott
Austin, Texas

An Introduction to Biospeleology
Bill joined the University of Texas Grotto in 1967. He received an M.S. and PhD in Biology from Texas Tech. His graduate research was on topics related to cave biology. Bill has studied and described cave life from caves in Texas, New Mexico, California, and Mexico. During 1977 and 1978 Bill conducted an ecological transplant of harvestmen from a cave to a mine for the U.S. Army Corps of Engineers at the New Melones Lake project in California. He has served as chairman of the Texas Speleological Association and chaired the biology session at annual NSS conventions.

Bernice Gottschalk
Brewerton, New York

Women in Caving
Bernice is a long-time Northeastern caver. She was one of the original members of the NSS Women's Section and has served as chair of that Section.

Louise Hose
Baton Rouge, Louisiana

Fitness and Nutrition
Louise has a B.A. in Physical Education and an M.S. in Geology. She started caving with the Outing Club of California State University, Los Angeles. She has served as chairperson of the Escabrosa Grotto in Arizona. Louise wrote her master's thesis on the geology of the Sistema Purificacion, Mexico's longest cave.

Kyle Isenhart
Little Hocking, Ohio

The Selection, Use and Care of Ropes for Vertical Caving
Kyle joined the NSS in 1970. He is a charter member of the Vertical Section of the NSS and served as its chairman for two years. Kyle is active in developing vertical equipment and new types of rope. He does most of his vertical caving in the tri-state area of Tennessee, Alabama, and Georgia.

Tom Kaye
Alexandria, Virginia

Electric Light Systems for Caving
Tom joined the District of Columbia Grotto in 1975 and has served as its vice-chairman. In 1981 Tom became editor of the NSS Caving Information Series. He is active in the Organ Cave Survey and generally caves in West Virginia.

Ed LaRock
Denver, Colorado

General Equipment for Each Caver
Ed joined the Philadelphia Grotto in 1970. He served as chairman of the Commander Cody Caving Club, an NSS chapter in Newark, Delaware. He is the author of Caves of Snyder County, Pennsylvania (MAR Bulletin 10). Ed was active in mapping efforts in the Friars Hole System, West Virginia.

Mary Looney
Colcord, Oklahoma

Clothing for the Caver
Mary has a caving family. From 1949 to 1965, she caved with her husband, Murray, and her two sons, Joe and Nick. In 1965, all four Looneys joined the NSS. Mary edited Oklahoma Underground for five years. The Looneys live next to the entrance of Stansberry-January Cave, a wet 6100-foot-long cave which they own.

David McClurg
Carlsbad, New Mexico

Why You Should Join an Organized Caving Club
An NSS member since 1958 and still a very active caver, David has written three books on caving techniques, the latest being *Adventure of Caving*. He has also served the NSS as Administrative Vice President, Board Member, chair of Public Relations, Program and Activities, and the Vertical Section, and chair and co-chair of two NSS conventions, Sequoia Park, California (1966) and Angels Camp, California (1975). He is currently Special Publications chair.

Jim Pisarowicz
Denver, Colorado

Additional Light Sources
Caving Helmets
Jim joined Colorado Grotto in 1974. He has served as chairman of both Colorado Grotto and Colorado Mines Grotto. He is a former editor of Depths of the Rockies and CINTHER. Jim is an active cave diver and dove Spring Cave's fourth sump in 1978.

Frank Reid
Bloomington, Indiana

Electronics in Caving
Frank began caving in Kentucky in 1961. He is a specialist in cave radio and cave rescue communications and a co-founder of the NSS Electronics and Communications Section. He holds a Bachelor of Science in Electrical Engineering and has amateur-radio and commercial-pilot's licenses.

Bill Steele
San Antonio, Texas

On the Ups and Downs of Vertical Caving
Bill is an accomplished vertical caver and a recipient of the NSS Lew Bicking Award. He has served as a Director to the NSS. His favorite caving area is Mexico, but he has also been active in exploring alpine karst and caves in Montana. Bill was an organizer for the 1979 AMCS-NSS expedition to Huautla, Mexico.

Tom Strong
Lakewood, Colorado

Cave Conservation
Tom was chairperson of the NSS Conservation Committee from 1977 to 1979. He has also served as officers of NSS chapters in Arizona, California and Colorado. Tom was chairman of the Congress of Grottos for two years. He worked one summer as a seasonal guide at Lehman Caves National Monument, Nevada.

Guy Turenne
Gaithersburg, Maryland

Landowner Relations
Guy joined VPI Grotto in 1968. He served as chairman of the NSS Landowner Relations Committee from 1972 to 1974. Guy was vice-chairman of Virginia Region in 1972 and 1973. He also served as a director of the Virginia Speleological Survey for five years. Guy actively explores and maps caves in Virginia.

William B. White
University Park, Pennsylvania

The Geology of Caves
Will has studied caves in Pennsylvania, Virginia, West Virginia, and elsewhere for almost 30 years. He has served as Executive Vice-President of the NSS and as Earth Sciences Editor of the NSS Bulletin. Will is a professor of geology at Penn State. He is the author of many articles on cave geology.

Alan Williams
Denver, Colorado

Cave Packs
Alan started caving in 1966 in Arizona. He has explored caves in the U.S.A., Canada and Mexico. Alan served as an officer in NSS grottos in Arizona, Utah, and Colorado. Recently he has been active in mapping Groaning Cave in Colorado. He is also an accomplished cave photographer and cartoonist.

ACKNOWLEDGEMENTS

The authors of the following chapters are the ones who have made this manual possible. They, and many more cavers like them, are the ones who have made caving what it is today—safe, enjoyable, interesting and challenging. Many thanks are due to them for their continuing efforts.

Six persons reviewed the first completed draft and made many comments and corrections that greatly improved this manual. These six were Paul Stevens, Don Davison, Norman Pace, Jim Powers, William Mixon and Pamela Young. Reviewers of the second draft for the Board of Governors of the National Speleological Society were Bob Addis, Mike Dyas, Bill Mixon, Emily Davis-Mobley, Rob Stitt and Paul Stevens. Bonnie Butler made many grammatical corrections to the entire text.

Also the entire membership of both the Colorado Grotto and the Colorado Mines Grotto have had input at an early stage. As each chapter was received from its author, copies were given to members of these grottos for their comment as to whether or not that particular subject matter was covered in such a way that a novice could understand it. Many thanks to them.

The drawings are the work of Alan Williams and Kathy Grossman. Everyone enjoys a break in the text every now and then. Alan and Kathy have provided those breaks. Snoopy Caver is by Fritz.

Tom Thornberry proofread the galleys. Linda Starr, as the Special Publications Committee Chairperson, took on the final task of having this manual printed and published. Adobe Press helped with typesetting and advice on production.

Jerry H. Hassemer, Editor

CARBIDE OR ELECTRIC LIGHTING?

Donald G. Davis
NSS 4956F

Carbide lamps came into use just before 1900 and by 1915 were used extensively in mines. Portable electric lamps were not used to any extent before 1908. Soon thereafter, however, improved electric models of essentially modern design appeared (Pilley in 1911, General Electric in 1912, Edison in 1913).

In spite of the fact that efficiency was low by present standards, electric lighting steadily gained adherents. By the mid 1930's carbide was losing its position as the standard miner's light. By the mid 1940's, its use was considered obsolete except in small operations, prospecting, and exploration (Young, 1946). Carbide lighting seems to have reached its peak of efficiency long ago, while electric lighting still has great potential for improvement, particularly in regard to more compact energy sources.

Why, then, do most American cavers still use carbide lamps as their primary light source? Caving is an aesthetic pursuit, so perhaps there is certain atavistic pleasure in lighting one's way underground by fire—even so sophisticated a fire as the acetylene flame produced by the carbide lamp. There are however, more concrete reasons: caving is not mining, and neither method of lighting has yet been established as superior under all conditions. Most mining is systematic and relatively predictable. In such a case, procedures can be tailored to take full advantage of the convenience of electric lights. They are clean, safe, and need little routine attention. And the brilliant spot-beam obtainable with electric point-source light cannot be duplicated by the line-source light of acetylene. Electric lights are also better adapted for intermittent use, as carbide lamps do not switch on and off instantly. An electric headpiece, where the battery is carried elsewhere, is lighter on the helmet than a self-contained carbide lamp.

Carbide lighting, however, tends to be more versatile under the varied demands of caving (except in cave diving or climbing under waterfalls). In the usual form, the lamp and fuel are lighter and less cumbersome than most electric assemblies and need no vulnerable cord. The light is even and diffuse, minimizing the hazard of stepping in unseen holes. Fuel supply can be determined at a glance, and consumption regulated as needed.

Carbide light has a special advantage for expeditions of more than one day, since it does not depend on the availability of chargers or expensive sets of extra batteries. The lamp can serve as a heat source in emergencies, or the carbide itself can be dampened to make an open fire. The lamp may warn of dangerous CO_2 concentrations by burning poorly or going out.

Perhaps most important, their simple mechanical functioning makes them less apt to develop malfunctions that cannot be repaired underground. However, even good quality carbide lamps have minor operating problems more often. Electric lights that are as reliable under the mud, dust, wetness, and hard knocks of caving are still much more expensive. Total costs are lower with carbide than electric lighting except perhaps on a very long-term basis.

An actual example of the performance obtainable with a good carbide system and careful management occurred on a two-day trip several years ago. Using an Auto-Lite with a four-inch parabolic Justrite reflector, I averaged about 7 1/2 hours per charge of carbide. The lamp was in actual use for 38 hours. The flame was kept at 1/2 to one inch (adequate with a parabolic reflector in normal passages) and only five 2 1/2 ounce charges were used. Weights involved were as follows:

Empty lamp	8 oz
Carbide used	12 1/2 oz
Water used	16 oz

Total weight was about 2 1/2 pounds. Carbide containers and spare parts were of negligible weight. Canteen weight is not counted since the canteen was necessary for drinking water in any case. Weight of the lamp water itself could have been neglected as it was freely available in this as in many other caves. Carbide was obtained in bulk for about 50 cents per pound (1987) for an operating cost of about one cent per hour of light. Since most people seem to get only about three hours from a charge of carbide, the operating cost then would be about 2 5/8 cents per hour and the weight of the carbide used would be nearly two pounds.

It is not easy to compare carbide and electric light directly in terms of brightness and burning time per unit weight. Most electric lights are focused to a spot beam, much brighter than carbide directly ahead, but dimmer to the sides. It is possible, however, to alter an electric light reflector to give a light pattern resembling carbide's (Plummer, 1961; 1962). An electric light using a PR-2 flashlight bulb (1.2 watt, 2.4 volt, 0.5 ampere), is roughly comparable in light output to a carbide lamp with a 1/2 inch flame.

With four nickel-cadmium cells (eight ampere-hour size) this electric light weighs about 2 1/2 pounds and should burn 32 hours (Plummer, pers. comm., 1970). This is performance somewhat inferior to the carbide example. Using fresh alkaline cells of the same bulk, however, this electric light should burn two or three times as long as with the nickel cadmium cells. This is considerably longer than a carbide flame of similar intensity on a fuel supply of equal weight.

In actual practice electric assemblies usually do weigh more and burn for a shorter time than carbide lamps. But this is because brighter bulbs (up to six watts or more) or inefficient batteries or heavy casings are commonly used. As a source of light energy, carbide (including the weight of the water required) has some efficiency advantage over nickel-cadmium batteries in terms of watt-hours per pound but is considerably inferior to alkaline batteries of modern design.

I should emphasize that I do not advocate total reliance on any one mode of lighting. Cavers should diversify their light sources (at least three) to meet the unexpected. A carbide caver will be wise to carry a waterproof electric light with a lamp bracket for helmet mounting as a secondary light source. An electric caver would be wise to carry a backup carbide lamp.

Some technically advanced cavers are using a twin carbide/electric system involving two helmet brackets—one with a carbide lamp, used in routine caving to conserve power, and the other with an electric headpiece to be used only for swimming, waterfall work, lead spotting, or route finding.

References

Plummer, B. (1961) Electric Cave Lamp Reflector, Baltimore Grotto News, Vol 4, pp 94-96 and Speleo Digest 1961: Section 3, pp 18-21.

------------- (1962) Quantitative Comparison of Cave Lamps, Baltimore Grotto News, Vol 5, pp 184-188 and Speleo Digest 1962, Section 3, pp 1-5.

Young, G.J. (1946), Elements of Mining, McGraw Hill, New York and London, 755 p.

THE CARBIDE LAMP

Donald G. Davis
NSS 4956F

Abstract

The acetylene lamp was introduced into mine use about 1897 and had become standard for mining around 1915. About 1940 electric headlamps had supplanted carbide lighting in more mines. Yet today, the main light source used by most cavers is the carbide lamp. Carbide lamps afford versatility and ruggedness at low expense under most cave conditions. The advantages and disadvantages that led to these generalizations are analyzed; and the merits of different carbide lamp styles are discussed and the four most common makes compared. Practical aspects of techniques, parts, accessories and maintenance are considered in detail.

How Acetylene Lamps Function

Miners' or cavers' carbide lamps (Fig. 1) normally consist of two chambers, a water tank above and a removable carbide canister below, with a connection valve to permit controlled seepage of water into the calcium carbide. The carbide and water react to generate calcium hydroxide and acetylene gas. This reaction is usually written as follows:

$$CaC_2 + 2H_2O \rightarrow Ca(OH)_2 + C_2H_2\uparrow + \text{heat}$$

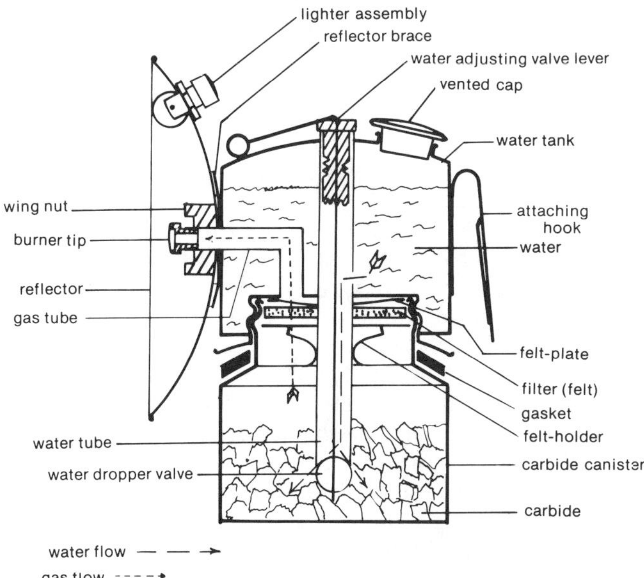

Fig. 1. A generalized carbide lamp suitable for mounting on a helmet. Shown are the main parts and the water and gas flows.

The gas passes through a filter into a tube and through a tiny burner-tip orifice designed for the optimum mixture of air with acetylene. When ignited, it burns with a brilliant yellow-white flame. (The usual brightness of the flame is due to incandescence of tiny carbon particles released from the carbon-rich acetylene.) A reflector concentrates the light in the desired direction.

History of the Carbide Miner's Lamp

The invention of the carbide lamp, a great advance in underground illumination, was not as early as many people assume. Acetylene was first produced by Edmond Davy in 1836, but it long remained an academic curiosity as early methods of production were costly. Practical use of the intense light of the acetylene flame was accomplished only through the manufacture of calcium carbide. This compound was described by Wohler in 1862, but its commercial history began in 1892, when it was first made in quantity in the electric furnace. By 1897, portable carbide-fueled acetylene lamps had been devised chiefly for use on bicycles, and the first experiments with their use underground had been made. During the next ten years the new lamps were widely adopted in European mines. In the United States they were slower to displace the traditional candles and oil lamps, but a start was made in 1900 with the patenting and marketing of the early Baldwin lamps. Most carbide lamps of this period had various inadequacies, such as flimsy construction, small and weak reflectors without lighters, unadjustable water feed, and easily-broken "lava" (steatite) burner tips. By 1906 they were rarely used in American mines except by bosses and engineers. About 1912-1916, however, several manufacturers had entered the field, the worst defects had been overcome and the carbide lamp had become popular. In 1919 Justrite alone advertised more than forty models. By the 1930s over forty trade names by more than a dozen makers had appeared.

Carbide lamps were widely used by farmers and outdoorsmen, as well as miners. It may be assumed that cavers were among the early users, though there is little evidence for this other than the appearance of smoked signatures on cave walls in positions where earlier lights could not have placed them!

Carbide Lamp Styles

Carbide lamps are of three standard styles: hand lamps, head lamps with separate generator and cap lamps. Large hand lamps were much used in mining and

Table 1. Comparison of weight and volumes of carbide lamps.

Lamp	*Weight*	*Capacities* Usable H_2O	*Capacities* Carbide Canister
Flat-hook Premier	180g (6.3 oz)	47cc	94cc
Flat-hook Justrite, brass	171g (6.0 oz)	49cc	80cc
Flat-hook Justrite, plastic	140g (4.9 oz)	70cc	80cc(approx)
Flat-hook Auto-Lite	160g (5.6 oz)	53.5cc	87.5cc
Flat-hook Guy's Dropper	160g (5.6 oz)	48cc	82.5cc
Round-hook Butterfly	150g (5.3 oz)	52cc	95cc

are used by cavers today in places having predominantly horizontal caves (notably Australia). They have the virtue of burning for up to 20 or more hours without changing carbide, but generally have been found impractical in American caving since the hands must often be free for climbing and crawling.

Head lamps with a large generator carried at the caver's waist have been widely used in Europe but are rare in America. They are long burning and do not encumber the hands, but the generator and connecting tube are apt to snag in tight spots, and accidental ignition of a gas leak could burn the wearer badly. Belt generators combine the hazards of open flame with the awkwardness and vulnerability of electric headlamps, and it seems remarkable that Europeans have put up with them for so long. Camp lighting is about the only reasonable use for either style of large carbide lamp, and this only where mantle-type lanterns are not practical. When buying such lamps, brass ones are usually best; tinned-steel ones are stronger and slightly cheaper, but rust rapidly in use.

Only standard cap lamps (Fig. 1) will be discussed in detail here. They are self-contained and easily removed from the hat as a unit—a valuable feature, especially for work in tight crawlways. They weigh about ¾ pound when fully charged, and are made with two types of attachments—flat-hook or the wire round-hook. The latter kind is generally furnished with a wire spring-clip for lateral bracing. For some obscure historical reason, round-hook styles have traditionally been advertised for use with soft caps as coal-miners' or hunters' lamps and flat-hook styles for use with hard hats as metal-miners' lamps. The flat-hook type should always be obtained when possible. Many hard hat brackets are not adapted for round-hooks, and round-hooks are harder to handle, more easily knocked loose and more likely to have their side clips damaged.

Characteristics of Available Makes

Carbide cap lamps were once made under many trade names. Some early ones were American Lamp & Splty Co., Arrow, Baldwin, Brite-Lite, Buddy, Defender, Dewar (ITP & Sun-Ray), Elkhorn, Ever-Ready, Fulton, Gee Bee (or Grier Bros.), Gem, Hansen, Lu-Mi-Num, Maple City, Maumee, Milburn, Pathfinder, Pioneer, Scranto, Shanklin Metal Products Co., Squarelite, Springfield, Sure-Light, Union Carbide, Wolf, X-Ray and Zar. Some of these, such as Grier, Hansen and Lu-Mi-Num, were superior in some ways to any now available but their good points were combined with defects in such ways that anyone interested only in good performance need not rush to antique shops looking for any of the above names. Today only five brands—Premier, Justrite, Auto-Lite, Guy's Dropper and Butterfly—survive in sufficient numbers to be in regular American caving use. Of these only Premier, Justrite and Butterfly are still in production. Table 1 provides some measurements on these five lamps taken from representative lamps of recent models, clean and free of dents, with reflectors and rubber grips removed.

Premier. Premier is an English company which still produces carbide lamps in four models. Their products were not marketed in this country until about 1970. Most users have found the Premier quite satisfactory after a few alterations. The carbide capacity is greater than that of the Justrite or Auto-Lite and I have averaged over six hours per charge at a flame level of ⅔ to 1 inch. The lamp comes with a flat-hook which fits American hard hat brackets. The bottom has a bumpergrip. Premier bottoms are often interchangeable with the old-style Justrite, although in some cases the Premier bottom will be a little too tight for a Justrite top. Justrite gaskets and old-style felt assemblies, lighters and reflectors will also interchange with Premiers. Justrite tips can be used in Premiers, but may not hold well unless an adhesive such as gasket cement is used. Original Premier reflectors are of non-magnetic aluminum alloy, a point of possible interest to cave surveyors.

The Premier does have some drawbacks. The felt assembly was poor on the older model but in 1977 improvements were made with a better three-piece felt assembly to reduce tip clogging. The standard reflector is small and will not stay in good condition for very long. I recommend buying the Premier with Justrite four-inch reflector or four-inch parabolic reflector as offered by some suppliers.

The configuration of the hook is such that it sometimes works loose along the solder joint. This possibility is easily forestalled by reinforcing the attachment with a small brass bolt sealed with epoxy or pipe dope. The water valve seems somewhat insensitive, though not so much so as to be seriously troublesome. The wingnut and reflector-brace are not interchangeable with American ones.

Premier has cut costs by minor design and manufacturing changes in recent years; most of these have been slightly detrimental, such as the change to a stamped wingnut in 1976 and to a flat, weak reflector brace about 1980. There have been many complaints about Premier bottoms cracking around the lower edge but reputable dealers will replace parts found to be defective.

Premiers made between 1978 and 1981 have a technical problem. The water valve tube ends about half an inch too high in the carbide chamber, so that special care is needed to see that the carbide charge is large enough to touch the end of the water feed. If it does not, the water will fall as separate drops on the carbide, causing the flame to flare and die rhythmically until the carbide swells enough to contact the feed end. In 1981 Premier redesigned the lamp to correct this.

Despite the above annoyances, Premier is still the best carbide lamp currently in production.

Justrite. Until late 1971 Justrite cap lamps were made of brass. In the 1950s and 1960s their best model for caving was number 2-844 shown in Fig. 2. In general this lamp was acceptably rugged and reliable, and it became the standard U.S. caving light after the demise of competing makes in 1960. In later years quality control was not of the best; leaks, cracks, maladjusted valves, gave occasional cause for complaint. The basic design is slightly deficient in having a flat front and back which reduces bend-resistance, and the reflector brace is flat and weak. A minor annoyance with late brass Justrites is the impossibility of removing the reflector without popping out the 9/32 inch burner tip as the wingnut is unscrewed, though this does make it possible to change tips without tools. Any usable parts of worn-out brass Justrites should be saved as they are obsolete and in demand.

Fig. 2. A Premier lamp (without reflector) on the left and a Justrite, No. 2-844, on the right with standard four-inch reflector.

Late in 1971 Justrite converted totally from the manufacture of metal lamps to new models made primarily of plastic. In the process a completely different body design was adopted, with only the reflector and burner assemblies being interchangeable with the old brass styles. The plastic body is significantly lighter, yet has comparable carbide and larger water capacity (see Table1). Plastic should be free of chemical corrosion by the contents.

However, these minor advantages are overwhelmed by serious defects. The worst problems are as follows:

1. The lamps can be destroyed by their own heat. If the flame is aimed down for a few minutes, the reflector and burner seat may absorb the rising heat until the surrounding plastic melts and the whole assembly falls out. This may be followed by fire or explosion of the body. The same thing may happen if a windguard is used.
2. The body, through rigid to normal blows, may split or shatter if dropped down pits.
3. The plastic hook is weak and apt to break the first time the lamp hits the ceiling (fortunately the hook is readily replaceable).

Other defects are less dramatic but still significant.

4. The design causes thread-fouling and tip-clogging problems. Carbide cannot be emptied without dumping it across the inward-facing screw threads or (unless you are very careful) into the exposed burner tube.
5. The short gas path allows both particles and condensing moisture to clog the burner.
6. Since the carbide chamber is integral with the lamp body, it is impossible to carry charges in extra bottoms for quick changing.
7. The water filling hole is too small and the cap is unattached and easily lost.
8. The water valve has no control notches and is easily knocked out of adjustment. It is also reported that the water valve clogs often, causing surging of the flame.

The user can make some improvements—replace the hook with a homemade sheet-metal one; scratch reference points on the lamp top and valve knob. Unfortunately, there is no home remedy for brittleness and tendency to melt.

The plastic lamps in present form cannot be recommended for caving.

Auto-Lite. The Auto-Lite lamp, made by Universal Lamp Company, Fig. 3, was probably the most popular caving lamp when production was discontinued in 1960. Since then the lamps have come to be regarded as collector's items. They are in many respects the best of the standard brands and it is worthwhile to search antique and second-hand stores for them. In 1978 it was

Fig. 3. A Universal Auto-Lite lamp.

still possible to find good used Auto-Lites (usually of the round-hook style) in many areas at prices averaging $15 to $30.

The lamps are strongly built, and have about 10% larger carbide capacity than Justrites. The Auto-Lite water valve usually seems more precise in its control than those of other brands. After 1930 Universal lamps were furnished with rubber "bumpergrip" bottom protectors. Original Universal tips, with a 15/64 inch end, are narrow enough that reflectors can be removed over them. Threaded Universal parts (bottoms, wingnuts, lighter spring caps and hexnuts) are not freely interchangeable with Justrite lamps, though a rough fit can sometimes be managed.

The only serious defects in Auto-Lite design are in the hooks. After long use, especially if the bracket arrangement allows much flexing, the flat-hook tends to fatigue and break off at the narrow point just above the top rivet. The spring-clip on the round hook style often breaks or loses its attachment screw unless carefully handled.

Guy's Dropper. This brand was produced from about 1914 to the 1930s by the Shanklin Mfg. Company of Springfield, Illinois. In later years it was taken over by Universal, which manufactured it along with Auto-Lite until 1960. The "Dropper" is a good lamp and seems to have special prestige among cavers, perhaps because it is a little less common than Auto-Lite. However, it is doubtful whether it is quite as good as Auto-Lite on most points. Its most distinctive part is the patented rotating-sleeve water valve, which was intended to make cleaning easy, but whose more important effect is to predispose the valve to rapid wear and to make exact control of the water flow difficult. The Dropper's best points are the broad attachment of its flat-hook (even though not riveted, it is less liable to break than Auto-Lites) and its particularly strong bottom shape. All removable parts except the reflector-brace (and the spring-clip on round-hook lamps) are interchangeable with Auto-Lites. In some areas Droppers are about as common in antique shops as Auto-Lites, while in others they seem unaccountably rare. Most late Droppers fortunately have flat-hooks.

Butterfly. The Butterfly lamp (also called Safesport Lamp on the box), imported from Hong Kong by Safesport Mfg. Company of Denver, Colorado and by other importers in the eastern states, is essentially a poor copy of the Guy's Dropper, but without the rotating-sleeve water valve. It is in current production and is available in many surplus and sporting goods stores. It is made with both the round-hook and flat-hook attachment. Its only advantage is an unusually large carbide chamber. It is flimsily built and often leaky at vital joints. Butterfly bottoms and lighter parts will not interchange with other lamps. The thin reflector and its flat, weak brace are especially inferior. The gas tube is frequently soldered out of line with the hole in the bottom of the water chamber allowing gas, water and carbide to mix indiscriminately, rendering the lamp useless. Even when the solder joint is complete, the gas tube pulls out easily because it is cylindrical.

The manufacturer is improving the Butterfly but as yet it is not a dependable lamp and should be avoided.

Reflectors

Whatever lamp is used, proper choice of reflector is very important. Reflectors have been made in many sizes and forms. A common diameter is 2½ inches. The particular focus characteristics of these small reflectors vary depending on their shapes, but all of them tend to waste too much light to the side to be desirable. At the other extreme, the deep seven-inch type used on outdoorsmen's lamps for sharp focus is too cumbersome and fragile for general cave use. The four-inch parabolic, when available, will stand the hardest use and gives the best fuel economy since it focuses well at ½ to one-inch flame levels. The standard Justrite four-inch chromed-steel reflector is less expensive and more widely available; it works best for lighting large spaces but requires about a 1½-inch flame for optimum focus.

Reflectors should be kept clean for maximum brightness. Dirty reflectors should never be scoured with abrasive cleansers; the surface will be scratched or the plating worn off. Toothpaste is the strongest abrasive that should be used, and that sparingly. Black coatings will rub off easily after soaking in vinegar for a few minutes. Unplated reflectors such as the Premier aluminum alloy or the stainless four-inch parabolic can be repolished with a buffing wheel using jeweler's rouge.

Techniques and Efficiency

Basic operation of the lamp is very simple—merely load with carbide and water, turn water valve on slowly, wait until gas is issuing from the burner tip. Then light by cupping one hand briefly over the reflector before striking a spark by quickly sliding the hand over the lighter wheel.

However, getting the most out of the lamp is an art. Many users load the bottom only about half full of carbide, which ensures that the water will flow freely but makes for short charge-life and often lets the used carbide become soupy. With Justrite lamps most cavers average about 2½ to 4½ hours between charges. This can be improved. First, use a charge which fills the bottom ⅔ full, but not more. When the flame begins to burn low, do not change carbide at once but check the water level and turn the water valve further on. If this has no effect, loosen the bottom/top joint half a turn, twist it a few times, tighten and relight. This will open a water passage in the caked carbide and rejuvenate the flame within a few minutes. It may be repeated as necessary until the charge is completely used. Charge life of 4½ to 6½ hours is not uncommon with this technique. This is how the 7½-hour average on one trip, previously described, was obtained.

Troubleshooting

Before using a carbide lamp, take it apart and study it until you are thoroughly familiar with it and are sure it has no defects. If you understand your lamp, keep it clean, use it with reasonable care, and carry a tip cleaner and parts kit, you will rarely, if ever, have trouble that you cannot fix on the spot.

Nearly all malfunctions of carbide lamps can be attributed to one of the following causes.

1. A low flame that decreases on opening the water valve indicates that the lamp needs water.
2. A low flame that increases briefly on opening the water valve indicates that the carbide charge is used up.
3. A short and crooked flame is caused by a clogged tip; this is easily corrected with a tip cleaner.
4. A short flame may also indicate carbide caked around the water valve; correct by loosening the bottom and wiggling it. If these measures fail, check whether the water drips freely; if not, rinse the water tube to remove any dirt. In bad cases of clogging, apply suction to the water tank.
5. A "jumpy" flame indicates a wet filter, which usually results when an expiring charge has become flooded—recharge and change the filter or dry it between layers of clothing. An emergency filter can be made from a piece of thick cloth.
6. Gas bubbling up through the water usually means either a clogged tip or water turned on too high. When associated with a wet filter, this may indicate a leak between the water and carbide chambers. If the leak can be located (it will usually be at the joint of the gas tube), temporary relief may be attempted with candle wax. A lamp thus repaired must be burned at a low level thereafter to avoid melting the seal.
7. Gas leaks around the gasket sometimes appear when a lamp is too loosely screwed together, has a bad gasket, is badly dented, or has threads heavily caked with deposits. If tightening or replacing the gasket does not stop the leak, try turning the gasket over or adding a second gasket. Threads may be cleaned by gouging with a knife, preferably with the leatherpunch blade.

The burner-tip orifice controls the mixture of acetylene with air, and its diameter is critical for brightness and economy. Tips that have been opened too wide by many reamings will produce a thick yellow flame and should be replaced. However, even if a tip is lost and no spare is on hand, the lamp will produce a dim and smoky fire adequate for emergency travel. (This should not be tried with the plastic lamps.) The reflector should be removed in such a case to avoid ruining its finish. Never light a tipless lamp until all air has been displaced from the inside; otherwise it could explode. This is not a hazard with the tip in, as an explosive wave in acetylene mixtures cannot pass through an orifice of less than 0.02 inch diameter (Lewes, 1900, p. 563). This is more than half again the usual width of a tip orifice.

Old burners require more frequent cleaning than new ones, as the pores of the insert become impregnated with benzene and other polymers of acetylene which cannot be totally removed (Lewes, 1900). These residues catalyze further production of such contaminants, which then carbonize around the orifice. The sooting that may occur even on new tips when the flame is allowed to burn out slowly is more superficial. "Carboning" of the tip, in any case, is not as bad a problem as clogging from the inside.

Spare Parts and Accessories

A brush-type tip cleaner should always be carried in a convenient place, preferably tied or clipped to the lamp or lamp bracket, but not where it could jab the wearer. In addition, the cave pack should include a spare parts kit containing the following: at least one individual tip reamer (in case the brush-type is lost), tip, gasket, felt or filter, flint and (if possible) lighter spring, lighter spring cap, wingnut and windguard. Be sure each item will fit the particular kind of lamp used. All of these, except the brush-type cleaner, will fit into a 35-mm film can, with room to spare for a flashlight bulb and a few band aids. A short length of acid-core solder, with the ends heat-sealed, is a recommended addition to the parts kit. It is a good idea to keep a felt holder and felt plate at home, but these need not be taken into caves. A lamp will operate with the entire felt assembly missing, if gently handled so that spent carbide and water do not enter the gas tube.

Some possible improvements or substitutions are worth mentioning. For superior filtering, replace original felts with homemade copies of dense open-cell flexible foam, cut to fit around the side. These can be wrung dry when wet, and will not shrink like commercial felts. The material used must be acetylene-resistant. If standard gaskets for brass lamps are not available when needed, 1½-inch O-rings can be substituted. These are not advised for general use because they do not support the lamp flange against dents. To keep a tip cleaner closed when not in use, unbend the eye enough to slip a ball-point pen coil-spring over the shaft and then rebend the eye to the original shape.

Matches are a vital part of any caver's gear. They are usually carried in "waterproof" cases which, all too often, prove not to be so when actually submerged. An excellent alternative is to tape a few matches to the inside of a container of fresh carbide. Carbide is a dessicant and the matches will remain dry as long as the carbide is good. Tape over the match heads to prevent friction against the carbide chunks. Another alternative is to carry a lighter in a waterproof container.

Hazards

The open acetylene flame is an obvious fire hazard. Carbide lamps should not be used near highly flammable surroundings (including dusty guano caves) or where the possibility of explosive gas or fumes is suspected (including the vicinity of auto gas tanks). When on climbing ropes, a low flame and constant alertness are advisable. With these exceptions, the worst that is apt to result from carelessness is a painful singe. Carbide lamps are very unlikely to explode from excess pressure, as both the water tube and the tip act as safety valves.

If a lamp leaks gas, the leaky spot may burst into flame. Such leaks are usually detectable by the disagreeable odor before they ignite. Leaks should be stopped at once (see Troubleshooting, above) to prevent such fires or small explosions and to avoid possible poisoning. For the same reasons, containers for extra carbide must be strong and waterproof.

The carbide flame itself is exceptionally clean burning and is normally odorless. It gives off no carbon monoxide unless burning in oxygen-deficient air (Lewes, 1900). Its products are almost entirely CO_2 and steam. Carbide lamps are said to use several times less oxygen and to produce several times less CO_2 than candles or oil lamps (Parsons, 1906 and Morrison, 1908). Since a person at moderate work is apt, in breathing, to exchange O_2-CO_2 at about nine times the rate that a carbide lamp does (Paul, 1915), the flame should not be a serious threat to air quality even in small spaces.

Explosive gases, common in coal mines, are very rarely found in natural caves. Several deaths have occurred in caves artificially contaminated with hydrocarbon vapors, in the vicinity of oil or gas fields or where waste petroleum had been dumped (Meador, 1965). Any scent of gas should be the signal to put out flames instantly and withdraw by electric light.

Since an injured person may have difficulty operating a carbide lamp, an accident victim awaiting rescue should not be left alone with a carbide lamp as his only source of light. In fact, for rescue work in general, electric light is preferable. The use of carbide requires time and attention that are needed for other purposes and rescue parties are likely to include persons unfamiliar with the use of carbide.

Lamps in Bad Air

If the carbide lamp flame begins to burn yellow and smoky, or goes out with no apparent cause—and particularly if all lamps in a party are affected—a dangerous displacement of air by carbon dioxide is indicated and quick retreat is in order. Such hazards are very uncommon in natural caves but may exist, especially where organic matter is decaying in stagnant air, as in debris-choked swallow-holes. **Carbide lamps are far from an infallible test for bad air, as they may continue to burn poorly** in still air at a CO_2 level as high as 25%, **well above the human danger point** (Smith, 1913). Labored breathing is experienced at CO_2 levels as low as three percent and is followed by headache, but cavers entering bad air often midjudge their symptoms and attribute them merely to fatigue, until noticing that their flames are extinguished.

Carrying Carbide and Water

Carry a personal reserve of carbide in a strong, airtight, **waterproof** container. Assigning all the carbide to one member of a party has a way of causing trouble. Most cavers prefer plastic baby bottles; the small (four-inch high) size will hold about eight ounces of carbide—enough for three or more charges, while the large (6½-inch high) size holds nearly a pound. Some cavers have used 35-mm film cans (1½ cans per charge). This has the virtue of allowing exact measurement of reserves, but handling many small containers is time consuming, and film cans made in recent years (of aluminum and plastic) are too flimsy for this use. Also the heavy-gauge plastic bottles of toner for duplicating machines are good carbide containers. A caver starting with a full lamp, one extra charge in a spare lamp bottom, and a small baby bottle full should have enough to last 15 to 30 hours in normal use. With lamp, extra bottom and large baby bottle, about 24-48 hours of light are available.

For users of brass lamps, individually prepared charges in spare bottoms are a valuable adjunct to the main carbide supply, as they permit changing carbide merely by switching bottoms. The bulk and expense of such containers make it impractical to carry one's entire supply this way, but it is wise to have at least one extra bottom along. It will pay for itself when you need to change in a tight crawlway, on a rope, in the dark, in emergencies or in any other situation where it is important not to delay the party. Premier bottoms now have a flanged screwcap and gasket for airtight sealing and may fit Justrites and (less often) Universal lamps, being intermediate in thread size. Also various commercial bottles (salad dressings, vitamins, etc.) have caps that will fit. In practical use, these work as well as original caps if the rim of the lamp bottom has not been damaged. The cardboard gaskets in such caps should be replaced by rubber ones for use in wet caves.

A stout canteen or strong plastic bottle can be used to carry water. Allow about three ounces of water per 2½-ounce charge of carbide, or 1½ to two fillings of water per charge. Lamp water is often not a major concern as it may be locally available in most caves; and in emergencies, urine can be used. Its effect on flame quality is insignificant. But one should carry an adequate supply of water as many cave passages contain no water for long distances. Avoid muddy or sandy water. A separate water bottle for lamp water would allow refilling of this supply without contamination of drinking water.

Removing Used Carbide

Spent carbide, a paste of impure hydrated lime, is toxic and unsightly; **good caving practice requires that it be removed from the cave** and discarded out of reach of cattle or other animals—not dumped or buried in the cave. A tough plastic bag is the standard container. When the spare bottom system is used, the bag will be needed only to catch small bits that may fall when the lamp is unscrewed. **Do not close spent carbide containers airtight** except briefly when they must be submerged in water—residual gas should be allowed to seep out. When emptying bottoms, do not pound them on rocks; brass dents easily. Sludge is best loosened by scraping with a blunt pocketknife blade, alternated with gentle tapping of the back of the knife flat across the bottom. Avoid getting carbide into the lamp threads.

A charge emptied while still generating gas freely may melt a plastic bag, as well as creating a fire hazard. Cavers who habitually change before a charge is exhausted may find such bags unsatisfactory. The best solution is to use one's changes more efficiently; failing this, some heavier container will be needed.

Outdoor Use

Carbide lamps, where not prohibited due to high fire hazard, are excellent for night hiking and backpacking. The diffuse light is ideal for walking, the lamp is a good handwarmer, the flame will light campfires in wet weather, and the problems of keeping batteries charged in the wilds are avoided. Lamps used outdoors (or underground in winds over 15 mph) must be provided with a windguard (or flame-protector) as shown in Fig. 4. A windguard will also give some protection to the flame from water spray near waterfalls. The Justrite windguard is now the only one manufactured, but it can be adapted to the Universal or older style Premier wingnuts by spreading the windguard base.

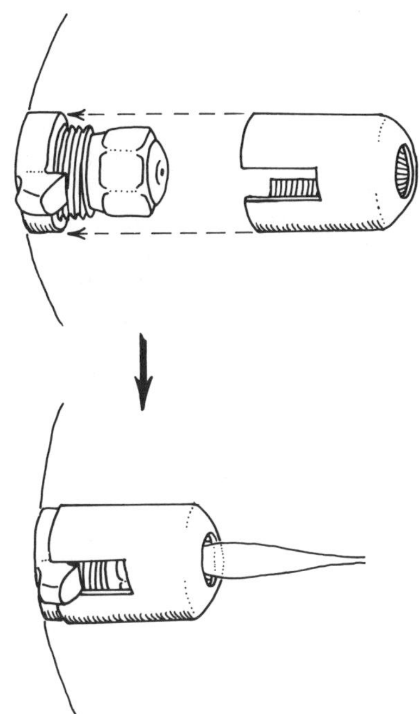

Fig. 4. A carbide lamp windguard.

I have successfully tried carbide lamps as tent lights on winter mountaineering trips in sub-zero weather. Once in operation, the lamp generates enough heat to keep from freezing. However, the **fire hazard becomes considerable** when handling carbide lamps in such close confines, and water and damp used carbide **must not be left to freeze** in the lamp after it is turned off. Even if the water has been poured out, the water valve usually freezes and must be rewarmed before the next use. Rubbing alcohol (70%) is said to be a safe and effective anti-freeze for carbide lamps, though it effectively shortens charge life in proportion to the amount mixed with the lamp water. The following Table 2 of freezing points is adapted from Whiting (1966).

Table 2. Freezing points of alcohol and water mixtures. Liquor (100 proof = 50% ethanol) may be used in lieu of rubbing alcohol.

Approximate Alcohol Percent By Weight	*Freezing Point Degrees F.*
20	14
25	5
33	-10
50	-34

Obtaining Carbide

The major American producers of calcium carbide are Union Carbide and Shawinigan. There seems to be little difference between the two brands; both companies guarantee a minimum yield of 4.5 cu ft of acetylene per pound (or 280 liters per kg) of ½ x ¼ inch, "miner's lamp" size, carbide (this is the standard Federal Specification 0-C-101a). The ¼ x 1/12-inch size, more easily found in bulk, should be of equal yield and will serve well in lamps. The even smaller "rice" size may be used, but it tends to deteriorate faster in storage and to make excessive dust in the lamp. It cannot be screened to recover good lumps. The federal standard for the "rice" size calls for a yield of only 4.3 cu ft per pound, but this is too small a difference to be important. Time and conditions of storage are more significant than brand or size in determining the quality of carbide.

If one buys the two-pound can commonly stocked by hardware and recreational suppliers, carbide costs $1.35 per pound or more. It is better for groups to arrange to purchase 50 or 100-lb drums from industrial supply houses; this may bring the cost down to $0.40 per pound. It is wise not to buy more than will be used within a year or two, as the carbide will deteriorate slowly over a period of several years. However, by transferring the carbide into well-sealed containers, such as bleach bottles, it can be kept for a longer period of time.

Cleaning and Storage of Lamps

One of the common causes of bad performance is the practice of letting lamps sit indefinitely without cleaning. Damp lime clogs parts, corrodes brass and will eventually set like plaster. After each trip, the absolute minimum maintenance procedure is to scrape out the sludge as well as possible and let the carbide and water chambers stand open until completely dry.

Whenever time allows, or when malfunctions have happened, the lamp should be taken apart and washed thoroughly inside and out. Scrape and scrub all residue from the bottom (an old toothbrush helps). Remove the filter assembly and clean all parts. Scrub the threads; rinse and flush the tip and water valve. If hard deposits have developed, soaking for a few hours in vinegar will dissolve or soften them. Replace deteriorating gaskets or filters before they cause trouble. After rinsing, let all parts stand open to the air until entirely dry before reassembly. Lubricating the threads with petroleum jelly assures a smooth seal and reduces the chances of the bottom becoming "frozen" so hard that the lamp can't be readily disassembled. Store in a dry place—dryness is the most vital single aspect of lamp maintenance. When properly treated, lamps should work well for many years.

When removing a burner tip for cleaning, it is advisable to use a properly fitting wrench if possible. Never use vise-grip pliers for this; pressure is very likely to crack the insert.

Repairing and Restoring Lamps

Many lamps are thrown away for want of simple repairs. Missing parts can be replaced. Broken hooks can be duplicated with sheet metal; broken spring-clips can be replaced with coat hanger wire if originals are not available; cracks and punctures in metal lamps can be soldered.

When soldering, clean the metal well with vinegar or other acid followed by sandpaper, steel wool or wire brush; use a small high-heat source of short duration. Beware of overheating the lamp; it is easy to make good joints leaky. To remove dents, take a stiff nail and round the head slightly; bend it suitably, clamp the point in locking pliers, insert the head into the lamp, and lever the dent up. If the dent cannot be reached in this manner, a small hole can be drilled in it, a bent wire inserted, and the dent pulled up. The hole should be closed with solder. A leaky water valve can often be readjusted simply by turning the lever ⅔ toward full open, then directing a torch flame sideways against the top of the valve post while pressing down against the valve-ball until the solder softens, then remove the heat. If an old lamp is only soiled and tarnished, vinegar soaking followed by scouring and polishing often works wonders. (Vinegar attacks brass slowly, so should not be left in contact with the lamp longer than necessary. Several hours will do no harm.) Never use steel wool or abrasives on reflectors.

When buying a used lamp, turn the valve partly on and pull up and down on it to check for vertical play. If there is more than a trace of play, precision in water-flow control is lessened. Worn valve threads are usually impractical to repair, and if the valve is loose enough to rattle, the lamp may be considered worn out no matter how good it looks otherwise.

Summary of Recommendations

In situations calling for intermittent use, very bright, long-range light, highly efficient use of time and/or ability to function underwater, electric lighting is recommended. For versatility, reliability and ruggedness at low cost, and for long expeditions, carbide is superior. As the best carbide lamp system, I recommend a flat-hook Premier, Auto-Lite, Guy's Dropper or brass Justrite cap lamp fitted with a four-inch parabolic reflector or Justrite four-inch reflector, with an extra bottom if available, and spare parts kit including a windguard. Next choices, in order of descending quality, are round-hook lamps of the above brands and the Butterfly. All but the last one will generally give good service if not abused.

Recommended containers for the fuel supply: plastic baby bottle for carbide; spare lamp bottom with cap; heavy plastic bag for used carbide; and canteen or plastic bottle for water. Whatever system is used, learn how everything works, and keep components clean and well maintained.

References

Lewes, V. B. (1900)—Acetylene; A Handbook for the Student and Manufacturer:MacMillan, New York, 977pp.

Meador, T. (1965)—Why not dump it here?:Texas Caver **10**:212-213 and Speleo Digest 1965:section 2, 141-143.

Morrison, A.C. (1908)—Better light and air for miners: Mining World **29**:879.

Parsons, F. W. (1906)—Acetylene lamps for mines:Eng. & Mining Jour. **82**:111.

Paul, J. W. (1915)—Notes on miners' carbide lamps: U.S. Dept. of the Interior, Miners Circular 18, 10pp.

Smith, E. E. (1913)—Acetylene as an illuminant in mines:Mining & Engineering World **39**:1111-1113.

Whiting, D. (1966)—Carbide lamp antifreeze:Wisconsin Speleologist **5**:23-24 and Speleo Digest 1966:section 3, 36-38.

ELECTRIC LIGHT SYSTEMS FOR CAVING

Tom Kaye*
NSS 16356

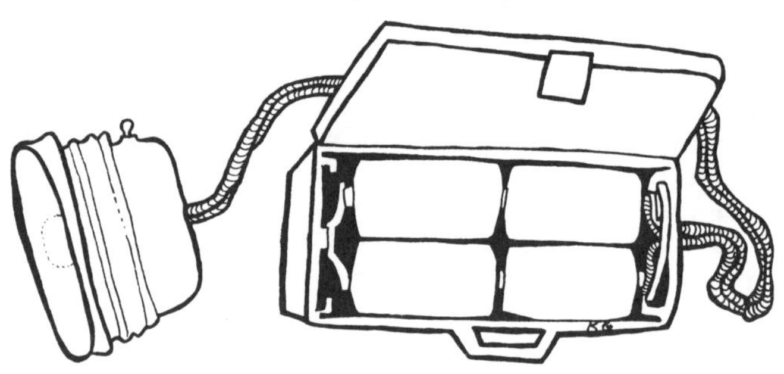

Introduction

The main reasons for using an electric lamp are convenience and versatility. An electric lamp is reliable because its operation depends on only four simple parts: bulb, wire, switch and battery, which means that little can go wrong. It is easy to carry spare bulbs and a small spare wire. Often these can be carried inside parts of the lamp.

Information is provided here about several electric light systems suitable for caving, and the construction and use of battery chargers. Cavers without the necessary mechanical and electrical skills to assemble their own electric system should consider buying one of the commercial miner's lamps complete with charger or a less expensive type such as a Justrite.

Because of the various changes in the battery industry, no specific models of battery or charger are referred to in this article. The one exception is the Wheat Lamp. This lamp and the similar MSA (Mine Safety Appliance) miner's lamp have been around for many years and will probably continue relatively unchanged.

Special Uses of Electric Lamps

Certain aspects of electric lamps make them especially advantageous for several kinds of caving and caving situations. One of the obvious advantages is the non-susceptibility of electric lamps to water, as opposed to the open flame of a carbide lamp. The normal operating voltages of caving batteries of four to six volts are low enough that total submersion will not result in any energy loss. Low water crawls and vertical pitches with spray and flying water droplets are typical situations where electric lamps are advantageous.

The focusable bright beam of the electric lamp makes it valuable in cave surveying. Checking for high leads and getting a good view of large passages are enhanced by the ability to concentrate the light output to a narrow beam. The focused beam is critically important in cave photography which often requires focusing the camera on distant cave features. A bright light cast on the subject is necessary for precise focusing of the lens. Even more important is the ability to illuminate distant features from the camera's viewpoint for compositional planning.

* With descriptions of battery chargers by Ray Cole, NSS 12460

Choosing a Battery

Once you have decided to get an electric system, there are several decisions to be made. The number of possible electric systems that can be constructed, adapted, or purchased ready-made is large. The most significant difference between these systems is the type of battery used. Batteries fall into two categories: rechargeable and non-rechargeable. Rechargeable batteries can be recharged 200 to 2000 times, depending on the type, while non-rechargeable batteries are thrown away after they are discharged. For caving purposes, rechargeable batteries are preferable. Using almost any cost analysis scheme, even the more expensive rechargeable batteries come out cheaper than the cheapest non-rechargeable batteries. Only if you plan to use an electric system once or twice a year or less would it be advisable to avoid purchasing a rechargeable battery. Even though rechargeable batteries are the most cost-effective, cavers often start caving with an electric system based on non-rechargeable batteries.

The next most important consideration in choosing a battery is the capacity requirement. You will need to review your past caving trips and determine the number of hours that you will require your light source to operate per caving trip. For instance, if most of your caving trips are eight to ten hours long, you may want a battery that will provide 12 to 15 hours of light. On the other hand, you may at first be satisfied with a smaller capacity battery for your short trips or for use in vertical pitches with waterfalls.

Types of Rechargeable Batteries

Rechargeable batteries that are suitable for caving can be classified in five basic types: (1) lead-acid wet cell, (2) sealed lead-acid, (3) nickel-cadmium wet cell, (4) nickel-cadmium D-cell and (5) rechargeable manganese. Each of these types has a particular set of characteristics. The following paragraphs provide a brief discussion on the most important aspects of the different types of batteries as related to caving use.

Wet-Cell Batteries. Lead-acid and nickel-cadmium wet cells both require vents of some type for use during the charging phase of the cycle. This is because these batteries will produce water vapor, hydrogen and oxygen gases while they are being charged, especially when they near the state of full charge. To prevent these batteries from exploding during charging, they are designed with open air vents to relieve the pressure. Loss of water vapor through open vents, requires that distilled water must be added from time to time to replace that lost by vaporization and electrolysis. The usual type of vent is a screw cap which must be slightly loosened during charging. The vent caps of wet cell batteries must be protected from damage and accidental unscrewing in the cave, and yet you must be able to open them each time you charge the battery. This situation can be considered a disadvantage of wet cells since it requires that you build a battery case to adapt them to caving use.

Miner's lamps use wet cell batteries, but they are already suitable for caving purposes. Their vents are small holes designed so that even though they are permanently open, the liquid electrolyte cannot be poured out in any position. These batteries can be used in any orientation (such as in crawlways or walking passage) without worry that the electrolyte will spill. Miner's batteries are susceptible, however, to dust entering the vent holes, so these should be covered with electrical tape while caving. A pinhole in the tape for each cell window allows you to omit removing the tape each time the battery is charged. Underwater exposure of these batteries usually requires a little better hole-sealing technique. Such techniques will be discussed in the miner's lamp modification section.

All vented wet cell batteries require extra care in their storage, transport, charging and use because of the chemical harshness of the electrolyte and the possibility of some of it getting out of the battery. The electrolyte of nickel-cadmium batteries is caustic potassium hydroxide solution and is chemically very similar to lye and drain cleaner. Even worse is the sulfuric acid solution electrolyte of lead-acid cells. Both chemicals can corrode rope and clothing among other things, and special care should be taken to avoid proximity problems in the storage and transportation of these batteries. Miner's batteries with their permanently open vent holes should never be transported or charged while upside down or even face down. Even though you can't pour the electrolyte out, vibration and jiggling in a vehicle over a period of time could cause a minute amount to escape the vents if the battery is not upright or lying face up. The best way to transport these batteries is lying down and face up. The battery is then stable and the vents are straight up from the acid. Miner's batteries should not be stored for long periods in a completely enclosed space with rope because the air outside the battery is exposed to the electrolyte and could absorb a minute quantity of acid. Keeping rope and batteries in the same room or clothes closet would be technically safe, but keeping them in the same duffle bag or a car's trunk for several weeks would be inadvisable. The best practice is to keep batteries and caving gear, especially ropes, in separate places at all times, at home and in the vehicle. It is a good practice to always store and transport the battery in the same location so that any spilt acid doesn't get onto other caving gear.

Sealed Batteries. In addition to the wet cell batteries, there are the dry cell and the sealed cell batteries. These can absorb the gases produced during charging so they don't require vents. This is a major advantage for caving use. As opposed to vented wet cells, these batteries do not have the problems of susceptibility to water and dust or the possibility of the electrolyte leaking. They still require at least a carrying case since they do not have provisions for wearing them as do miner's batteries. The Justrite case for D-cells or an army ammunition belt pouch for a sealed lead-acid battery are examples of possible carrying cases for sealed batteries.

Circuit Breaker

All types of rechargeable batteries can put out a large amount of current if shorted. Because of the rigors of the cave environment, a circuit breaker in the system is a good safeguard against a hot lamp cord or damaged equipment. Small circuit breakers, 1½ x ¼ inch, are available from electronics supply dealers such as Poly Paks, Inc., South Lynnfield, MA 01940. Electron-type fuses and fuseholders are more commonly available, but they do not reset and you need to carry a supply of replacement fuses.

Charging and Discharging Differences

The different types of batteries vary widely in terms of recharge cycle life. A rechargeable battery will, after a number of discharge-charge cycles, gradually deliver fewer and fewer hours of service per charge. A wet cell nickel-cadmium battery has the greatest cycle life, with over 2000 useful cycles. A nickel-cadmium D-cell has about 1000 cycles of useful life. Lead-acid wet cells have a lifespan of about 500 cycles and sealed lead-acid cells have about 200 cycles. Rechargeable manganese batteries can only deliver about 40 cycles.

Batteries also differ in their discharge curve characteristics. The discharge curve of a battery shows the output voltage of the battery as it gradually decreases with time to the point at which the battery is considered dead (usually defined as a battery delivering only 80% of its rated voltage).

The discharge curve of the nickel-cadmium battery is almost linear and remains constant throughout the discharge cycle. This type of battery produces a constant voltage and hence a light source of constant intensity. Although this is a desirable characteristic, there is a drawback. When a nickel-cadmium battery reaches its "dead" point, the voltage falls to near zero quite rapidly. This can be quite disconcerting if it happens in a cave. If a nickel-cadmium battery is discharged to this point, it is best to turn the light system off to avoid reverse charging damage to the discharged cells.

Lead-acid batteries have a discharge curve which is rather flat, but is not as horizontal as that of a nickel-cadmium battery. The lead-acid light system will produce a light which decreases gradually and at about the same rate throughout its discharge cycle.

Alkaline (manganese) and other dry cells used for caving have discharge curves which are curved downward, meaning that the light output will decrease more and more rapidly as the battery discharges. The discharge curve of lithium batteries is extremely flat, even more so than that of the nickel-cadmium. The lithium battery also differs in that each cell is three volts instead of the usual 1.5 volts and is very expensive for a non-rechargeable.

Miner's Lamp Modifications

Miner's lamps are increasing in popularity among cavers. They are well built and rugged for mining use and require little or no modification for caving use as opposed to most other electric systems. There are, however, modifications and additions that can be made which will improve their safety and versatility for caving use. The following discussions primarily apply to Koehler Wheat brand miner's lamps. Other miner's lamps are also useful for caving and the modifications can be applied to them as well.

The Wheat Lamp is designed to prevent tampering with while in the mine. This is primarily done to prevent explosions caused by the mine atmosphere coming into contact with electrical contacts. If you buy a miner's lamp, you will want to permanently remove the small cap screw that prevents the lens from being removed. You don't want to be prevented from changing a burned-out bulb while in a cave.

In a few cases, the metal posts that come up through the tops of the cells in a miners's lamp battery have become unglued. This condition allows small amounts of electrolyte to seep out. You may want to occasionally check for this condition and add epoxy or other adhesive if necessary.

Bulb Locking. The lamp bulb of the Wheat Lamp does not lock into its socket like conventional bayonet-base construction but is held in place by the glass lens in front of the headpiece. Although it is not easy to break the lens, the possibility does exist and represents a weak point in the Wheat Lamp. If the glass lens breaks, the bulb cannot be kept in place against the electrical contacts. To prevent the possibility of this happening, the glass lens should be discarded and replaced with a transparent plastic lens.

Vent Hole Protection. Wheat Lamps are often used in underwater exploration as well as in expeditions that cause the battery to be submerged part of the time. The battery design includes vent holes which are necessary during charging. The holes connect to special vent chambers inside each cell which are designed to keep the electrolyte from dripping out when the battery is in a horizontal or upside-down position. The design, however, does not prevent water from entering the vents when the battery is submerged. Both plastic tape and self-tapping no. 8 sheet metal screws made of stainless steel have been used to temporarily seal the vent holes during battery-submerging cave trips. The tape method has not proven entirely satisfactory and the screws may not effect a sufficiently tight seal. Probably the best solution is to use screws in conjunction with rubber washers of the type used for faucet repair. Caution must be exercised, however, to always remove the obstructions from the vent holes when the battery is to be charged. Charging a battery with its vent holes plugged will cause the battery case to crack or even explode.

Short Circuit Protection. A circuit breaker (see section on circuit breakers) is a possible addition to a miner's lamp to protect it and you from short circuit problems. To install one, use a hacksaw to cut the lead band connecting the two cells of the battery under the cap. Solder the circuit breaker leads to the separated parts of the connector band. Completely cover the circuit breaker and all parts of the leads with PC-7 or other epoxy. With a small hacksaw cut, the connection can easily be remade by pressing a rock on it if the circuit breaker fails.

Spare Wire. Another modification of the Wheat Lamp is a fail-safe measure for wire and switch problems in the cave. A length of small gauge speaker wire can be coiled and stored under the metal top of the battery. If the switch or cord should fail for some reason, you can find places in the headpiece where you can attach the leads of the speaker wire to make the bulb operate. You may even want to attach a solder lug to one of the conducting metal parts inside the headpiece to facilitate an emergency connection. If you do step one of the following socket adaptation procedure, you can lead the emergency wire into the interior of the headpiece through the pry notch in the reflector if you enlarge it slightly. Otherwise, you can drill a small hole in the back of the headpiece and refill it with a removable amount of black silicone glue.

Bulb Socket Adapter. Wheat Lamps have a uniquely designed bulb socket which accepts the General Electric bulbs (BM30, BM30A, BM3232, and BM4010) made for use in Wheat Lamps. The lowest amperage bulb available is the BM30A, rated at one amp. The light output of the BM30A is considerably brighter than that of a carbide lamp. There are bulbs, however, that will provide an amount of light near to that of a carbide lamp. The advantage of these bulbs is that when used with a Wheat battery, the light system will provide a steady light for much longer than the normal fifteen hours possible with a BM30A bulb. A No. 41 bulb when used with a Wheat battery will, for example, provide about 24 hours of light that is as bright as that of a carbide lamp. The catch is that the low amperage bulbs have miniature screw bases and require an adapter for use in a Wheat Lamp headpiece. Such an adapter can be built using the following steps:

1. Buy a No. 1157 automobile bulb. The No. 1157 bulb has a double contact index bayonet base like

the Wheat Lamp bulbs.

2. Disassemble the lamp headpiece (you'll need a small allen wrench) sufficiently to remove the sleeve that holds the bulb. On each side of this sleeve is a slit that accepts the guideposts on the sides of the bulb base. Using a needle file, you can lengthen these slits to allow the bulb to be rotated slightly and relax upwards as in a normal bayonet bulb and socket. The bulb can now be locked in place in the Wheat Lamp headpiece without requiring the lens to hold it in.

3. Wrap the bulb in a rag or piece of paper towel and pulverize the glass with a pair of pliers as much as possible, being careful to avoid damaging the brass sleeve excessively. If you are very careful, you can save the piece of opaque glass forming the base of the bulb. If not, salvage the two hemispherical contacts with their one-inch lengths of wire.

4. Buy a miniature screw socket from an electronics supply dealer.

5. Wheat Lamp bulbs have three contacts; two are the contacts on the base of the bulb and the third is the entire brass sleeve. The adapter should be wired so that the bulb works with either switch position of the Wheat Lamp headpiece. First, you must locate the contact on the old No. 1157 bulb that corresponds to the common contact of a Wheat Lamp bulb. Double contact index bulbs like a No. 1157 or a Wheat Lamp bulb have two small brass indexing studs on the sides of the bulb base; one is higher than the other. To make sure the bulb is used in the right position, as you hold the No. 1157 bulb sleeve with the upper indexing stud on your right and the lower on your left, the contact that is to be wired common is the base contact nearest you. Wire the base contact of the miniature screw socket to the one-inch wire connected to the common contact. Wire the threads contact of the miniature screw base socket to both the brass sleeve and the remaining one-inch wire of the No. 1157 bulb.

6. Push the miniature screw socket into the brass sleeve of the No. 1157 bulb, making sure that the contact wires remain visible and not excessively tangled.

7. Screw in a No. 41 bulb into the miniature screw base and arrange the distance between the filament in the bulb and the two contacts at the base of the adapter so that it is equal to the corresponding distance in a Wheat Lamp bulb.

8. Slip pieces of cardboard or other insulating material into appropriate places between the miniature screw base, the brass sleeve, and contact wires to prevent shorting occurring during the rest of the adapter construction process.

9. Check the bulb filament to base contacts distance again and carefully unscrew the No. 41 bulb.

10. Fill the space between the miniature screw base and the brass sleeve with PC-7 or other epoxy cement. A toothpick can be used to force the epoxy into the spaces. Be careful not to get epoxy into the miniature screw socket.

Note: If you don't do step 2, then replace the word "filament" with the word "top" in steps 7 and 9.

A number 13 bulb can also be used in a Wheat Lamp using the adapter. This bulb is lower in current than the number 41 and it will give up to 50 hours of (dimmer) light per charging of the Wheat battery. If this amount of service per cave trip is preferable to the 24 hours of the number 41 bulb, you may want to favor the filament to base distance of the number 13 bulb in the construction of the adapter.

Replacing Miner's Lamp Electrolyte

If you made the mistake of going into a wet cave without plugging the vent holes of a miner's lamp and water enters the cells, or if the electrolyte becomes extremely dirty from dust entering the vents, you need to remove the liquid and replace fresh electrolyte using the following procedure. First, the battery should be charged as completely as possible, leaving the charger connected to the battery for an extra long time. The charging should be done before attempting to remove any liquid from the battery. Be careful of liquid leaking out of the vent holes of an over-filled battery during charging.

After recharging as much as possible, all the liquid should be removed and discarded. This can be done using the plastic hose that fits into the vent holes. The battery should then be partially refilled (80%) with fresh sulfuric acid solution electrolyte (available at automotive supply dealers). After charging the battery again as much as possible, fill the cells to the fill line with electrolyte.

Modifications to Other Electric Lights

Justrite electric lights and other similar types are about 20% of the initial cost of a Wheat Lamp with charger. However, they need several modifications before going underground.

The **elastic** helmet **strap must be replaced** with a lamp bracket for helmet mounting. The elastic strap is not to be depended on. A bracket can either be homemade or a bracket for a carbide lamp can be used.

The electrical cord that is supplied with these lamps is flimsy and must be replaced with a stronger wire and attached in such a manner that any stress on the wire is not transmitted to the conductors or the connections. While making this new wire also make a spare.

The off-on switch should also be replaced with a sturdier one.

Battery Carrying Methods

There are several different methods of carrying a battery for an electric cave light. The most general consideration is where you want to wear your battery.

Usually, it is worn on a belt on your side. This placement conserves your narrowest dimension—front to back. To avoid the tendency of the battery to rotate around to your stomach while in a crawlway, you can run your belt through one of the battery's belt loops, then through one or two of the belt loops on your pants and finally through the other belt loop of the battery. The use of the special miner's lamp belt also helps to prevent sliding around. This kind of belt can be loosened to change battery position and retighten without too much worry about the battery rotating by itself. Europeans seem to prefer to wear their battery on the back on a waist belt. This method probably is less restrictive to leg motion and provides an even balance. You may want to try both methods.

Another point of contention is whether to wear the battery inside or outside your coveralls. The main advantages of wearing the battery inside the coveralls are that the battery is less likely to catch on things and the wire connecting the battery and the helmet can be run inside the coveralls, preventing any catching on rock projections. The main advantage of wearing your battery outside of your clothing is that it can easily be removed for extremely tight places. A compromise encompassing the advantages of removability and streamlining with clothes is to sew a large flap above the battery that can be fastened below.

Miner's batteries already have built-on belt loops so they can be worn on the body. The Justrite battery case for D-cells has a large clip for belt or pocket carrying. Other batteries are not specifically designed for wearing and require you to use a carrying method of your own design. The simplest method is to make belt loops out of heavy wire, such as coathanger wire, and tape them to the battery with about three feet of fiber-reinforced tape. Surprisingly, the tape can last for five to ten caving trips. A much better method is to use the 6 x 3 x 2-inch army surplus belt pouch. Some sealed lead-acid batteries or nickel-cadmium wet cells fit in these packs. For better balance, you may want to remove the belt-connecting strap on the pouch and re-sew it in a higher position on the pouch. Another method especially useful for nickel-cadmium wet cells, which are usually not as solidly constructed as sealed lead-acid batteries, is to build a case out of metal or other strong material and use a potting compound (silicone glue or thick epoxy) to secure the battery inside.

An occasionally seen rig consists of four nickel-cadmium D-cells mounted on the back of the cave helmet using battery-holding clips. Although this system has some obvious advantages, it is limited by the ultimate capacity of the D-cells which is 4-amp-hours per cell. In terms of light output, four 4-amp-hour D-cells will provide about eight hours of light slightly brighter than a carbide lamp. Of course, four extra D-cells can be carried in a cave pack to provide 16 hours of light potential. However, eight 4-amp-hour nickel-cadmium D-cells usually cost more than a Wheat Lamp and much more than a sealed lead-acid battery, both of which provide about 16 hours of bright light.

Battery and Bulb Matching

The output of caving batteries ranges from three to six volts, and each kind has its own type of discharge curve. Each variety of battery will work best with only certain bulbs. Especially if you design your own electric system, you will need to know how to determine which are the most efficient bulbs for use with your battery.

Many electric systems use the Justrite headlamp which has a miniature screw base fixture. Considering all the small bulbs available, the miniature screw configuration provides the widest possible choice. There are approximately 48 different miniature screw base bulbs available for ten volts or less. From these, you will want to choose a main bulb to produce about two candlepower of light (equivalent to a carbide lamp with a flame approximately 1¾ inch long (Varnedoe, 1970)) and one or two efficient low-power bulbs. These low-power bulbs are useful as precautionary equipment in case an extra long caving trip is expected or if the time of a caving trip is unexpectedly increased.

The relative efficiency of different bulb and battery combinations can be evaluated by determining their brightness and expected hours of service per charge. To determine these things, one needs to know the design voltage (DV), design brightness (DB), design life (DL), and design current (DC) of the bulb being used, and the rated voltage and amp-hour capacity (AH) of the battery. Since batteries lose voltage as they are discharged, the calculations should be made using the average voltage (AV) of the battery. The average voltage is the voltage of the battery during the period between the beginning of discharge (use) and the point when the battery's rated amp-hour capacity has been spent. Since each type of battery has its own characteristic discharge curve, the average voltage as a percentage of the battery's rated voltage can be used in designing a system. For the batteries most often used in cave lights, these percentages are:

wet cell lead-acid, 90
sealed lead-acid, 105
wet cell nickel-cadmium, 100
D-cell nickel-cadmium, 99
manganese rechargeable, 80
common alkaline non-rechargeable, 80
common carbon zinc batteries, 80

Table 3
Standard Specifications of Useful Lamp Bulbs for Electric Systems.

Bulb Number	*Design Volts*	*Design Amps*	*Design Brightness*	*Design Life (hrs)*	*Base Designs*
13	3.7	0.3	0.98	15	Min. Sc.
27	4.9	0.3	1.4	30	Min. Sc.
40	6.3	0.52	0.15	3000	Min. Sc.
41	2.5	0.5	0.5	3000	Min. Sc.
42	3.2	0.5	0.35	3000	Min. Sc.
157	5.8	1.1	8.1	50	Min. Sc.
365	3.69	0.5	1.6	15	Min. Sc.
403	4.0	0.3	0.98	30	Min. Sc.
425	5.0	0.5	2.3	15	Min. Sc.
502	5.1	0.15	0.6	100	Min. Sc.
605	6.15	0.5	3.4	15	Min. Sc.
1432	3.2	0.16	0.2	3000	Min. Sc.
1438	3.8	0.43	1.6	·15	Min. Sc.
1482	6.0	0.45	2.2	100	Min. Sc.
1483	6.0	0.04	0.1	500	Min. Sc.
BM30	4.0	1.2	4.9	250x2	D.C. Index
BM30A	4.0	1.0	3.9	250x2	D.C. Index
BM32*	4.0	1.2	4.9	250x2	D.C. Index
BM32A*	4.0	1.0	3.9	250x2	D.C. Index
BM3232	4.0	1.2/2.5	4.5/12	300/60	D.C. Index
BM4010	4.0	1.0/4.0	3.9/ ?	250/60	D.C. Index

All D.C. Index bulbs have two filaments.
*For Mine Safety Lamp

An electric system's average brightness (AB) (measured in mean spherical candlepower), bulb life (L), and the expected number of hours of service per charge (H) are calculated using the following formulas (Catalog of Miniature Lamps, undated):

$$AB = \left(\frac{AV}{DV}\right)^{3.5} DB \qquad L = \left(\frac{DV}{AV}\right)^{12} DL$$

$$H = AH/\text{current} = AH/\left[\left[\left(\frac{AV}{DV}\right)^{0.55}\right]\left(DC\right)\right]$$

Typical criteria for a good electric system are: a minimum of eight hours of service per charge at a minimum of 1.8 candlepower average light output, a minimum of ten hours for the bulb life, and a maximum battery thickness of 2½ inches. The best comparison of different bulb possibilities with the same battery is on the basis of candlepower-hours (CPH). This is the bulb's brightness multiplied by the number of hours per charge with the bulb at the average voltage. Usually there are two or three efficient bulbs with almost the same CPH (although their brightness may differ) while the rest have only half this CPH or less.

Table 3 lists the bulbs most suited for caving along with their industry standard specification. The information in the table can be used to match batteries and bulbs using the bulb equations and characteristic average battery voltages. Table 4 shows such a matching completed for five common types of caving batteries. Both good and poor battery-bulb matches are included with the discriminating CPH ratings. Each battery has one good primary bulb of around two candlepower and a couple of secondary bulbs for long trips or emergency use.

Sources of Batteries and Bulbs

There are several sources of batteries and other electric light system equipment. The most obvious are the familiar caving gear suppliers (see appendix). In

Table 4.
Characteristics of Some Battery-Bulb Matchings for Five Common Batteries

System	*Bulb*	*Hours/Charge*	*Aver. Bright.*	*Bulb Life*	*Bulb Amps*	*CPH*
A	13	49	0.9	21	0.30	44
	365	29	1.5	20	0.49	44
	41	24	1.8	38	0.61	43
	BM30A	15	2.7	550	1.0	41
	BM30	13	3.4	400	1.2	44
	BM3232	13/6	3.4/8.3	300/60	1.2/2.5	44/50
	BM4010	15/3.7	27/?	250/50	1.0/4.0	41/?
B	502	48	1.2	10	0.17	58
	605	16	3.5	14	0.50	56
	157	7	10.2	22	1.14	71
	1482	17	2.5	68	0.46	43
	1483	196	0.1	338	0.4	19.6
C	502	29	0.5	150	0.15	15
	1432	21	0.9	17	0.20	19
	27	14	1.4	29	0.30	20
	425	8	2.2	18	0.50	18
	42	9	2.3	17	0.44	21
	157	4	4.6	360	1.0	18
D	502	85	1.1	14	0.16	94
	31	47	1.8	290	0.30	85
	605	28	3.1	20	0.49	87
	157	12	9.1	33	1.10	109
E	1432	70	0.83	23	0.20	58
	27	47	1.3	38	0.30	61
	425	29	2.0	24	0.49	58
	42	32	2.1	23	0.44	67
	157	14	4.2	480	0.99	59

Explanation for Table 4

System A: Koehler Wheat Lamp rated at four volts, 15 amp hours (14.4 amp hours). Average voltage is 3.6 volts.

System B: Sealed lead-acid battery rated at six volts, eight amp hours. Average voltage is 6.3 volts.

System C: Four nickel-cadmium D-cells rated together at five volts, four amp hours. Average voltage is 4.92 volts.

System D: Five nickel-cadmium wet cells rated together at six volts, 14 amp hours. Average voltage is six volts.

System E: Four nickel-cadmium wet cells rated together at 4.8 volts, 14 amp hours. Average voltage is 4.8 volts.

addition to complete electric systems, they have the Justrite headpiece and some of the varieties of bulbs. Another kind of source is the military and industrial surplus mail-order house. These are especially good for liquid cell and sealed D-cell nickel-cadmium batteries and chargers. Miner's supply stores offer miner's lamps and chargers at good prices. Some of the miniature screw bulbs are difficult to obtain. One supplier, D. H. E. Electric, 1135 Okie St., N.E., Washington, D.C. 20002, seems to have all varieties (in boxes of ten only).

Battery Chargers

Caving battery chargers range from those you buy ready-made to ones that are made from circuit diagrams.

The factory-built ones are usually expensive, especially the ones sold by battery manufacturers for their battery.

The cheapest ready-made charger you can buy is the small plug-in cube-type charger like the ones used with calculators and transistor radios. These chargers do not have the best electrical design for charging the different types of batteries, but they are low enough in power so that they will not normally cause any harm to your batteries. They are usually rated at 0.5 to 0.6 amps (500 to 600 milliamperes) of charging current. Amperages smaller than this are common but are not very useful for charging the typical batteries used for caving because of the excessively long charging times. Be sure that the cube charger you are buying is rated at the proper voltage. The actual output voltage of any charger should be a few percent higher than the rated voltage of the battery to be charged.

Another type of commercially made battery charger that isn't extremely expensive is the motorcycle battery charger available at cycle supply stores. These can be used to charge six-volt batteries and they will usually have about twice the amperage of the cube-type chargers and will charge your battery about twice as fast. One or two small rectifiers can be used in series with a six-volt charger to bring it down to a proper level to charge four-volt lead-acid batteries. The rectifier is better than a resistor since the effected voltage drop remains about the same over a range of charging currents.

Other possibilities include cheap automobile battery chargers with a switch for six-volt operation and component power supplies available from military and industrial surplus outlets.

Of special interest to cavers is the "mobile charger" for using a car battery to charge your caving battery. You may want to make one of these whether or not you have a 110-volt charger at home. There are many occasions when you have access to a car but not 110 volts and you need to recharge your battery, or just bring it up to full potential just before a caving trip. A simple mobile charger is a large power resistor that drops your car's 12 volts to six or four volts to charge your caving battery. These resistors are available from electronics surplus stores for about $0.50. The kind you want to look for is about ¾ inch in diameter and about 4 inches long (about 50 watts rating) that has a resistance of 20 ohms or less and a slide contact for varying the resistance. To drop six volts at one amp, you need to set the resistor at about six ohms. Check the amperage with a meter as you begin to charge a completely discharged battery while the car motor is off. Set the resistor to give an amperage equal to one-tenth the amp-hour rating of your caving battery. After you do this once or twice with a meter, you can put a mark on the resistor where the slide contact will be in the best position. The resistor should be mounted in a minibox or some other container to prevent the warm resistor from coming into direct contact with anything in your car. The only other things you need are spring clips to connect to the caving battery's terminals and a cigarette lighter plug to get 12 volts input. If you don't take advantage of your car's cigarette lighter fuse and want to connect directly to your car's battery, be sure to include a fuse in your mobile charger. An accidentally shorted car battery can pump lots of current into your charger wires!

Battery Charging Time

How long should you charge your battery? This depends on several factors: (1) the type of battery you have, (2) the amperage rating of your battery, (3) the amperage rating of your charger, (4) the length of time the battery was discharged in the cave, and (5) the amperage rating of the bulb(s) used on the cave trip. The calculations using these five variables are not complicated at all, nor are caving batteries extremely sensitive to overcharging. It will help, however, to see exactly how they relate to get a feeling for how much you should be charging your battery.

The type of battery makes a difference in charging because some types are more efficient for storage than others. For the two most common types used for caving, a lead-acid battery needs to be charged with about 110% of the energy (ampere-hours) discharged and a nickel-cadmium battery needs to be charged with about 140% of the energy discharged.

The ampere-hour rating of your battery determines the maximum rate at which you should charge your battery as well as the amount of energy that it actually stores. A good rule of thumb is the 10-hour rate. This is the rate at which a battery would be completely charged in a 10-hour period if it were 100% efficient. In other words, if your battery is rated at six volts and eight amp-hours, you should charge it at a little over six volts and 1/10 x 8 = 0.8 amps. If it was a lead-acid battery, this should take 11 hours and for a nickel-cadmium battery, it would take about 14 hours.

If you are using a cube charger or other small charger that has an amp rating that is less than a tenth of the amp-hour rating of your battery, you have to charge for extra time to replace the energy. For example, if your battery is rated at eight amp-hours and your charger is rated at 0.5 amps, you have to charge for 8.0/0.5 or 16 hours to recharge a completely discharged battery (assuming 100% efficiency).

The amount you have to charge depends on the amount of energy actually discharged. The energy in amp-hours that is discharged is simply the amp rating of the bulb(s) used in the cave multiplied by the number of hours of use. For example, if you go on a 12-hour cave trip using a ½-amp bulb for eight hours and a 0.15-amp bulb for the rest of the time, you use (8 x ½) + (4 x 0.15) = 4 + 0.6 = 4.6 amp-hours. If you charge at a rate of 0.6 amp-hours and the battery is lead-acid type, you need to charge for a minimum of 4.6/0.6 x 1.1 = 8.4 hours. Batteries are not particularly sensitive to overcharging (however, don't use 12 volts to charge a six-volt battery, etc.), so you can charge up to 3 or 4 times as long as the above calculations indicate. Don't make a habit of it, however; it may degrade your battery in time. The most important thing is to be sure your caving battery is fully charged before you depend on it in a cave.

Charging Nickel-Cadmium Batteries

The following information applies only to nickel-cadmium batteries—do not attempt to charge any other type of battery with the following circuit.

Nickel-cadmium batteries can be charged in numerous ways, but the basic problem is determining when they are fully charged. The technique described here avoids this problem by charging the nickel-cadmium batteries at 1/10 their ampere-hour capacity. At this rate most makes can be charged for extended periods with no damage to the cells. By charging at this rate for 16 hours the cells will always be fully charged. Note that it is necessary to replace the energy used with 40 to 60% extra since the cells are not perfect storage devices.

The nickel-cadmium battery charger described here consists of a constant current device that delivers the same amount of current with a wide range of DC supply voltages for charging any number of cells in series.

The circuit is shown in Fig. 5. This simple circuit is made possible by IC_1 which is a voltage-regulating integrated circuit with a low reference voltage of 1.25 volts. LED D_1, R_2 and R_3 are included to indicate that the battery is charging and that all connections are made. This feature can be omitted leaving just R_1 and IC_1. R_3 will have to be chosen experimentally due to variation in component tolerances. Select R_3 so that the LED D_1 is just clearly visible.

The charger will fit into an aluminum minibox measuring 2¾ x 2-1/8 x 1-5/8 inches. IC_1 must be attached to a heat sink or the metal case since it will have to dissipate many watts and will get hot. Use a conductive paste and insulating washer in mounting IC_1. The component placement is not critical. Test the charger by connecting an ammeter across the output terminals. It should read 0.38 to 0.42 amps. If the current is too high, it may be necessary to replace R_1 with a higher value such as 3.15 ohms.

To use the charger, connect it to a DC power source such as your car's electrical system, 12-volt power supply for your CB radio or HAM rig, or a 12-volt battery charger. Any number of cells can be charged in series and as long as the charge-indicating LED is at full brightness you should be O.K. Alternatively, you could insert a series ammeter. To calculate the supply voltage required, use the following equation where Vs is the minimum DC supply voltage and N is the number of cells connected in series:

$$Vs = 4.0 + 1.6N$$

For example: four cells require 10.4 volts while ten cells require 20 volts. You should be able to charge up to six cells in series using your car's electrical system while the car is running, but the charge current will decrease when you stop the engine since the car battery voltage will drop from 13.8 to 12 volts.

The DC voltage applied must be less than 30 volts more than the terminal voltage of the batteries being charged. If a large DC voltage is applied while charging a

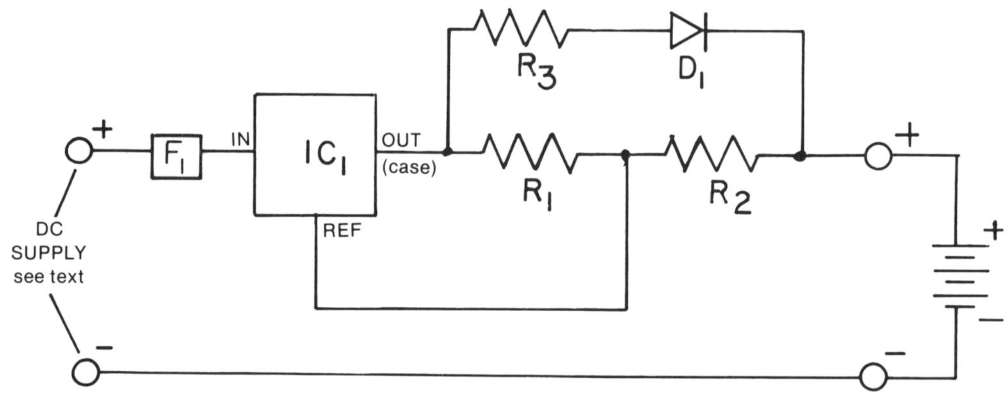

IC_1	National LM 317K, LM317T, or LM350 Integrated Circuit
D_1	Red LED 1.6 volt at 10 milliamps
R_1	three-ohm five-watt resistor 10% tolerance
R_2	one-ohm, one-watt resistor 10% tolerance
R_3	zero- to 20-ohm, ½ watt resistor (see text)
F_1	In-line, one or two amp fuse between DC supply and IN

Fig. 5. Constant current charger for four-amp-hour nickel-cadmium batteries and parts list.

few cells, the charger will get very hot to the touch—it could become dangerously hot. This should not harm the charger since the integrated circuit will cut itself off if it gets too hot, then back on when it cools. Take care that no one, and especially children, come into contact with a hot charger which could cause burns. If you find the charger is too hot it can be built into a larger case or a heat sink can be added to help dissipate the heat.

Parts for any electronic project are difficult to locate. However, most of these are available at a local Radio Shack store. The LM317K has been available from Quest Electronics, P.O. Box 4430, Santa Clara, CA 95054.

To achieve maximum capacity from your battery, it should be charged just prior to use. Nickel-cadmium batteries lose energy quickly compared to non-rechargeable batteries. Avoid only partially charging the batteries, otherwise they might temporarily lose their maximum capacity.

Nickel-cadmium batteries can be damaged if a reverse charge is applied. This can happen if one of the series cells runs down to zero before the others while using your light system. To avoid possible damage to any of the cells turn the light off as soon as possible after it starts to dim.

Miner's Lamp Charger

The miner's style of electric lamps have become popular with cavers due to their ruggedness, light output, large battery capacity, availability and cost. Unfortunately the same cannot be said about the commercially-made chargers. The chargers described here will deliver a constant voltage charge to the battery either from 110 volts AC or DC from an automotive electrical system.

Always charge lead-acid batteries soon after use and leave them in a charged condition when stored. Remember to add distilled water to a battery only after it has been fully charged.

The preferred method of charging a lead-acid battery is to apply a constant voltage at the battery terminals until it is fully charged. The voltage applied will determine the time required for the battery to reach a full charge.

With the 14.4 ampere-hour capacity lead-acid battery used by Koehler, a voltage of 5.2 volts will produce a full charge condition in about ten hours or less if the battery was not completely discharged. Continuous charging at this voltage will not harm the battery but will require distilled water to be added to each cell periodically. The gassing and resulting water usage caused by the overcharging can be reduced by lowering the charge voltage after the battery is fully charged. A low voltage that will keep the battery charged is called the float voltage and for the Koehler lamps appears to be around 4.6 volts. If the lamp will not be needed for some time it can be fully charged at this voltage but that may take several days.

The circuit diagram for the miner's lamp charger is shown in Fig. 6 along with the components. The DC

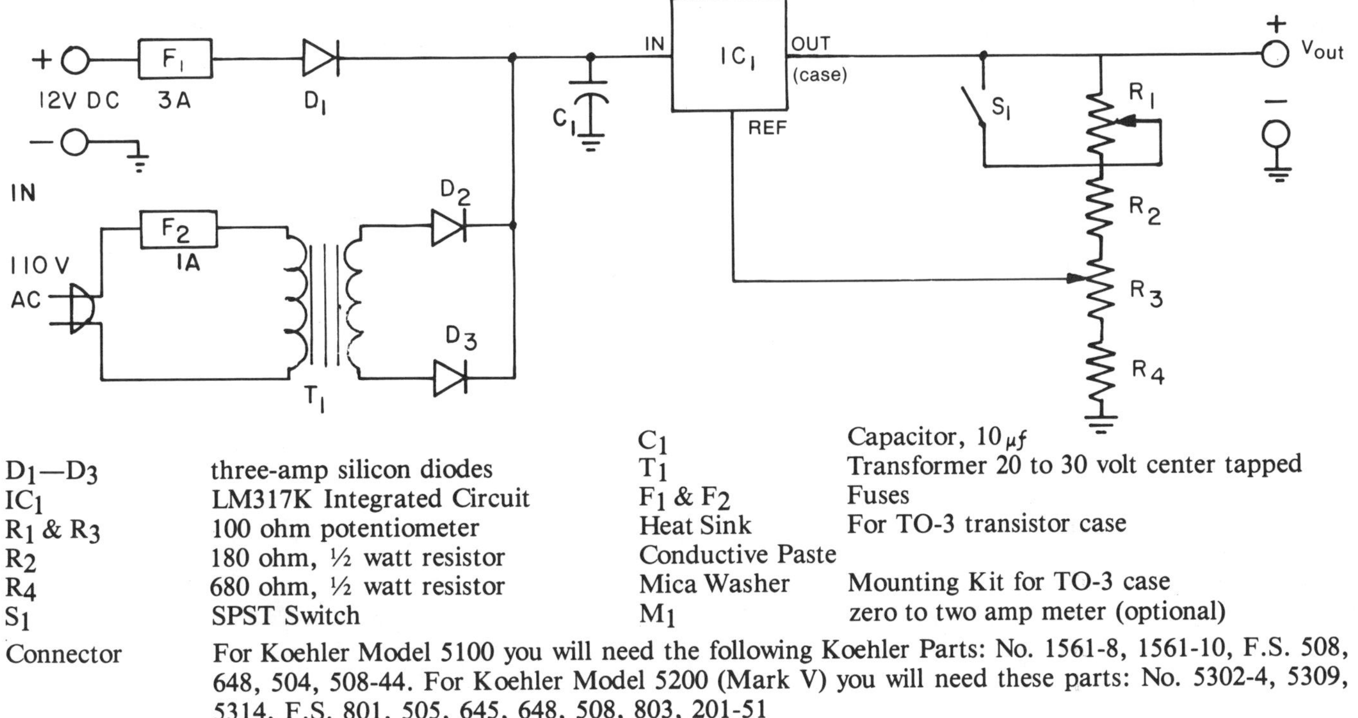

D_1—D_3	three-amp silicon diodes	C_1	Capacitor, $10\mu f$
IC_1	LM317K Integrated Circuit	T_1	Transformer 20 to 30 volt center tapped
R_1 & R_3	100 ohm potentiometer	F_1 & F_2	Fuses
R_2	180 ohm, ½ watt resistor	Heat Sink	For TO-3 transistor case
R_4	680 ohm, ½ watt resistor	Conductive Paste	
S_1	SPST Switch	Mica Washer	Mounting Kit for TO-3 case
		M_1	zero to two amp meter (optional)

Connector — For Koehler Model 5100 you will need the following Koehler Parts: No. 1561-8, 1561-10, F.S. 508, 648, 504, 508-44. For Koehler Model 5200 (Mark V) you will need these parts: No. 5302-4, 5309, 5314, F.S. 801, 505, 645, 648, 508, 803, 201-51

Fig. 6. Miner's lamp charging circuit and parts list.

voltage required can be supplied from a 12-volt car electrical system through a cigarette lighter adapter or other connection, or from 110 volts AC. The 110 volts AC must be converted to DC before it can be used. This is done by T_1 which reduces the AC voltage to around 14 volts which is rectified by D_1 and D_2. Electrolytic capacitor C_1 produces a smooth DC voltage. Be sure to observe the polarity on C_1. Since the 12 volts DC is connected through a diode, an OR arrangement results which will automatically select the power source connected to the greater of the two. The resulting DC voltage is then applied to a combination voltage regulator/current limiter consisting primarily of IC_1. The output voltage from IC_1 is determined by the following equation (Catalog of Miniature Lamps, undated):

With S_1 closed for charge

$$V_{out} = \frac{1.2\,(R_2 + R_3 + R_4)}{R_2 + \text{part of } R_3}$$

With S_1 open for float

$$V_{out} = \frac{1.2\,(R_1 + R_2 + R_3 + R_4)}{R_1 + R_2 + \text{part of } R_3}$$

The part of R_3 referred to in the above equations is the portion from the center contact to R_2.

With S_1 on, R_1 is adjusted for 5.2 volts for fast charge and with S_1 off, R_2 is adjusted for 4.6 volts for the float voltage.

The components will fit in a 5 x 10 x 3-inch aluminum chassis. Component placement is not critical. Since the case of IC_1 is at the output potential, it must be insulated from the case and heat sink with a mica washer using heat conductive paste.

The type of connectors used to attach the electric lamps depend on the model of miner's lamp used.

More than one lamp can be charged at once but the total charging time may be increased. See Fig. 7 for connecting an optional ammeter and connectors for additional lamps. The initial charge current will be about 1.5 to 2.5 amps on charge and as the battery reaches full charge this current will drop to below 100 milliamps, depending on the battery condition.

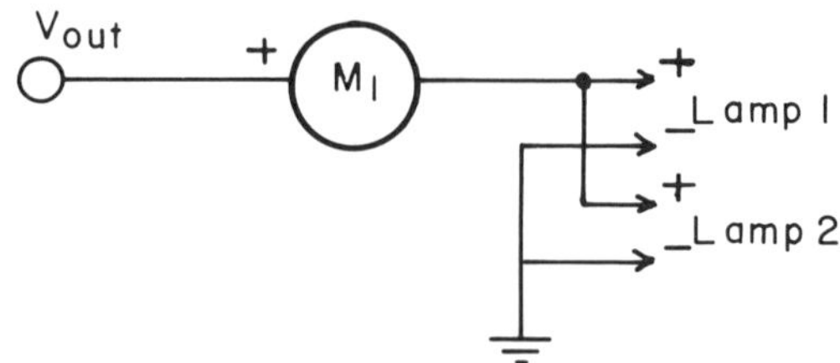

Fig. 7. Connecting multiple lamps and ammeter.

Again, most of these parts can be gotten at a local Radio Shack store. The LM317K, again, is available from Quest Electronics, P.O. Box 4430, Santa Clara, CA 95054.

References

Chicago Miniature Lamp Works (undated)—Catalog no. 7000: Miniature lamps, 33pp.

Varnedoe, Jr., W. W. (1970)—Some engineering characteristics of small portable electric lights for caving: NSS Bull. **70**:71-87.

ADDITIONAL LIGHT SOURCES

Jim Pisarowicz
NSS 16872

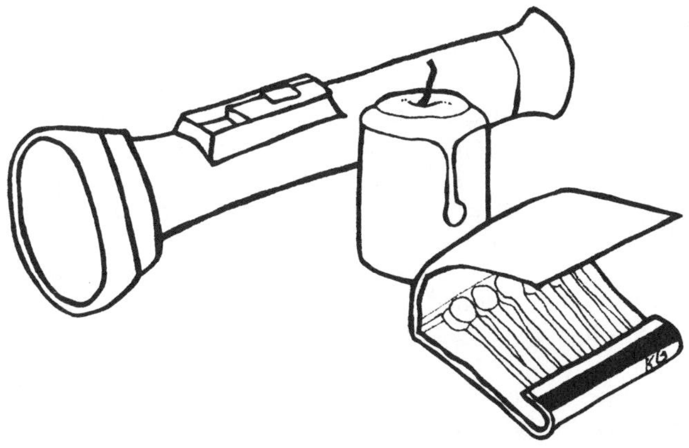

Introduction

When it comes to light sources, the magic number is three. This usually works out to be a carbide or electric headlamp for general caving applications plus two additional sources of light for backup use in case the primary light source fails. Until recently, the two additional light sources carried by many cavers were a standard flashlight plus a candle and matches. With some recent advances in technology, the caver now has the option of several other sources of light which can supplement the primary light source.

Whatever backup lights are carried, remember that these will furnish the light that a caver must use when the primary light fails. **A caver must be able to safely exit a cave using backup lights!**

Before considering the many available secondary sources of light, consider why the standard carbide or electric headlamp, flashlight and candle lighting combination has worked so well, for so many cavers, over the years. This combination of light sources has proven itself over time because each source of light is relatively independent of the others. Consider the caver who chooses to carry three carbide lamps along on a caving trip and ends up losing his carbide container far into a cave. This single loss adversely affects not only his primary lighting source, but his backup sources as well.

There is a growing trend toward taking four light sources as caving trips become longer and more difficult. One of the "extra" three could be a duplication and totally independent of the primary light.

Flashlights

The most common secondary light carried by cavers is the standard flashlight. Most cavers prefer the smaller types, those using two C-cells or two or four AA-cells. Since this light is to be used primarily as a backup to a carbide or electric headlamp, the smaller capacity of C- or AA-cells when compared to the standard D-cell seems negligible. By using alkaline batteries and carrying extra batteries and bulbs, a more than sufficient margin of safety can be achieved.

Several strong points can be made for both C and AA battery flashlights. First, both are small and light, an important consideration to every caver. In fact, all the AA-cell flashlights in general, and the Mallory brand in particular, are so small that they may be easily carried in the mouth in an emergency, thereby freeing both hands for climbing. Another important feature of these lights are that they are inexpensive. In fact, the Radio Shack version of the AA flashlight is often given away free or for a nominal charge at store promotions. Finally, both these flashlights, along with their components (bulbs and batteries) can generally be found almost anywhere in the United States (and in other parts of the world as well).

Although many cavers merely purchase one of these flashlights, supply it with batteries, and toss it into their caving pack, several suggestions can be made regarding caving and its relation to backup flashlights. One suggestion is that before you toss your emergency light into your pack or pocket, you reverse one of the batteries so that if the switch is accidentally turned on, the batteries do not drain. Another method, but not as foolproof, is to tape the switch in the off position. There is probably nothing so disheartening as to run into that situation where you actually do need your backup light, only to find that the batteries are dead. In this regard, it is generally a good idea to occasionally check the batteries with a meter or to replace the batteries even if not used to make sure that they are fresh. Carrying along extra sets of batteries and spare light bulbs is also a good idea. The bulbs can be kept in with your extra parts for your carbide or electric headlamp or in your first aid kit. If you are a photographer, remember that most electronic flash units use AA-cells, so if you need them, do not forget about these "extras."

Waterproof flashlights are occasionally warranted but they tend to be expensive. However, a relatively inexpensive waterproof flashlight is Eveready's Jr. Skipper. This light uses two C-cells and even has room inside the case to carry an extra light bulb. There is also a D-cell size Skipper. Mallory type AA flashlights can be made waterproof by packing them with petroleum jelly. Although this procedure is messy, it seems to create a relatively good and inexpensive waterproof flashlight. If a very waterproof compact flashlight is needed, consult your local scuba diving shop. One good, reliable waterproof mini-flashlight is called the Tekna-Lite and comes in various sizes.

Another suggestion regarding caving flashlights is to attach a wrist or neck lanyard or retaining line to them.

When a neck lanyard is used, be sure that its breaking strength is low enough to break before strangling you if the cord catches a projection while you are rappeling. This cord can prevent the loss of your flashlight and provide a convenient way of finding the flashlight in the dark in a fully loaded pack. Merely attach the lanyard to your pack's strap and, when you need the flashlight, find the cord and pull.

The recent development of disposable flashlights needs to be mentioned. For the most part these look like the Mallory type flashlights except that when the batteries are dead, you throw the entire flashlight away (outside of the cave in the proper place!). Although these lights tend to be inexpensive, there are several drawbacks to their use in caving. First, it is difficult to tell the state of their batteries when you purchase them. Shoppers occasionally "play" with them in the store by turning them on and off. This, of course, wears down the batteries. Secondly, the batteries cannot be reversed to prevent accidental discharge in your pack or pocket. Finally, many cavers have found that these lights have a tendency to corrode internally because of their exposure to damp cave environments. This is particularly serious with regard to these lights since you cannot open them to examine their interiors as you can with standard flashlights.

Candles

Until recently the most common third source of light carried by most cavers was candles. The common plumber or household candles were used and these can generally be found in many stores and most supermarkets. The wicks of these candles should be trimmed so that they can be easily lit. One drawback of standard candles is that they tend to drip wax in the cave which seems to be at odds with the NSS conservation message "...leave nothing but footprints." A simple solution to this problem is to bring along a piece of aluminum foil to catch drips. Remember that if you are using a candle as an emergency light source, you must be sure to take along matches or a lighter. Do not rely on your carbide lamp to light your candle for then these two light sources are not independent. An open candle flame is not a useful source of light while climbing and crawling through a cave. Its use is best reserved for those times you intend to remain in one location for a short while.

Matches and Lighters

Matches carried during caving should be stored in a waterproof container and kept with the candles. Matches will also stay dry if carried in a carbide container, but to maintain complete independence of light sources, one should consider use of a container separate from that used to fuel the carbide lamp. In addition to the matches in a waterproof container, some sort of rough surface to use for striking the matches is generally handy. Occasionally cavers are confronted with the situation in which they have dry matches, but no dry place on which to strike them. A small piece of sandpaper or emery cloth kept in the waterproof container with the matches works well.

With the advent of the disposable lighter, many cavers have opted for carrying them in lieu of matches. To be sure, this modern day convenience makes lighting lamps and candles a simple matter of a "flick" but there are certain disadvantages inherent with lighters. For one thing, most disposable lighters burn butane which is turned on by pressing a lever and ignited by a spark from a piece of flint. Unfortunately for cavers, this lever may be accidentally turned on so that all the butane escapes. This problem with disposable lighters may be circumvented by wrapping an elastic band around the lighter under its lever or by using a nondisposable lighter which burns lighter fluid.

A second potential disadvantage of most standard lighters is that the ignition is from a spark created from a flint. When the flint gets wet, occasionally it does not spark. This problem may be avoided by using a piezoelectric lighter which utilizes a piezoelectric crystal to provide the initial spark for ignition. These crystals seem to work even when wet from being submerged all day long. Unfortunately, these lighters have recently become very expensive.

A third danger of some disposable makes is that they may melt or explode if burned continuously for an extended period of time or if the case is ruptured by being hit or dropped. Still, lighters tend to be easier to use than matches and have the added advantage of being able to be used as a candle-type device for a short period of time. Both these features make them an attractive alternative to matches.

Chemical Lights

The most recent innovation in lighting technology to hit the caving community has been the advent of chemical lights, generally known as Cyalume® or lightsticks. These chemical lights consist of a plastic tube, six inches in length, containing a glass ampule of activating chemical floating in a green luminescent liquid. When the plastic tube is bent sufficiently to break the inner glass tube, the two solutions mix, and instantly produce a bright yellow-green light when the light stick is shaken.

The light output of a chemical light stick during its first hour of operation is equivalent to an AA-cell flashlight but the light is diffused in all directions. By carrying a piece of aluminum foil, a reflector may be constructed to direct and concentrate the light. By drilling two pairs of holes in your carbide lamp reflector and using twist-ties, a chemical light stick may even use the standard carbide lamp reflector.

There are several advantages and disadvantages to using chemical light sticks as a backup light source. One advantage is that although the intensity of the light gradually diminishes over a period of several hours, the human eye is particularly sensitive to its yellow-green color. Also, whereas a candle or flashlight of similar size will no longer be useful after about three hours, the chemical light will continue to glow for twenty-four hours or more. This can be an important source of morale for a caver lost in a cave. Light sticks also work even when submerged and, unlike open flame light sources, do not burn oxygen, an important consideration if caught in a bad air section of a cave or when involved in tight crawling or digging situations. Finally, unlike most light sources which may be damaged by dropping or being bashed around, if a light stick is "damaged" all it will do is to start working!

This final advantage of light sticks is also a disadvantage in that the stick may be accidentally "turned on." This may be prevented by storing the light in a cigar tube or a piece of lightweight pipe (aluminum, copper, or PVC). Some cavers have gone so far as placing the light stick in a piece of pipe and then sewing the pipe right into their coveralls. Thus this light source will always be with them.

Another disadvantage of these lights is that they are sensitive to storage in air, moisture, light and heat. Because of this, they should always be left in their foil wrapper until ready for use. Unfortunately, this means that you cannot tell whether or not the stick has been damaged until you are about to use it. Light sticks should not be subjected to heat as this tends to reduce their efficiency (i.e. do not store them in the trunk of your car). These sticks also tend to deteriorate with time. They have a "shelf life" of about two years under normal temperatures and are best stored in a refrigerator. Finally, note that each light stick may only be used once.

Mantle Lanterns

A good bright light, but of limited use in caves, is the Coleman Lantern or other mantle-type lanterns. These lanterns use Coleman fuel, kerosene, or special tanks of butane for fuel. They are carried by a wire handle at one's side.

In large walking passages, one of these lanterns will be enough for several people and the entire passage will be lit except for a shadow directly above the lantern. But the disadvantages are many. A hand is required to carry the lantern, making easy climbs difficult, and they must be carried upright which becomes a problem in crawlways. The glass globe and mantle are easily broken. Extra mantles can be carried and replaced. However, it would be difficult to carry extra globes, but the glass can be taken out where there is no wind. Lanterns are seldom used by cavers but at times can be handy.

CAVING HELMETS

Jim Pisarowicz
NSS 16872

Have you ever wondered about your caving helmet? Sure, you know that it protects your head when you stand up and the room isn't as tall as you are and it provides a good platform to mount your lamp—but would it actually save your life in a fall? And what would happen if a falling rock hit you on the head? Maybe you should think some more about your caving helmet because, after all, you entrust the safekeeping of your most vital body system to your helmet.

Unfortunately, there isn't any single federal specification that is complete enough for caving helmets. Such is not surprising for Robert Berger of the American Society of Testing Materials, National Bureau of Standards in Washington, D.C. has noted: "... few standards exist for any type of helmet." Should we as cavers then expect some sort of safety standard for our helmets? Of course, we should; but those that exist are inadequate at best. In this regard, the federal z-89 standard covers the cushioning of your head from top impact (i.e. falling rock), but does not mention side impact (such as a tumbling fall down breakdown or swinging fall as when on belay). On the other hand, the federal z-90 standard covers the cushioning of side impact, but does not mention top impact. Just to get things straight, let's look at these two standards.

American National Standards Institute
ANSI z-89.1

In order to meet this standard, a helmet must have a suspension or lining in the top that reduces the transmitted force of a steel ball weighing eight pounds dropping five feet onto the top of the helmet to not over 850 pounds.

American National Standards Institute
ANSI z-90.1

The chin strap must have a strength of at least 300 pounds. When a headform "wearing" a helmet is dropped six feet onto a solid floor, striking on the side of the helmet, the maximum deceleration of the headform should not exceed 400 g's. If the head weighs 11 pounds, that amounts to 4400 pounds of force.

You may wonder why the maximum allowable force is 4400 pounds sideways and only 850 pounds from the top. This is because in side blows the brain is encapsulated in the skull and hence protected against deformation. But in top blows, the hazard is fracture of the neck vertebrae, a different problem. At intermediate angles, the problem is complex and is not addressed in either standard.

To complicate things even more, there are figures available which seem to indicate that if you could remove your head, hold it out at arm's length and drop it on the ground, there would be no helmet on the market that would protect it adequately. This does not mean that helmets are worthless when it comes to protecting your head from rock fall or just plain falling down in a cave, but it does mean that no matter what you wear on your head, you'd better use the contents as much as possible to keep from getting into trouble in the first place. This philosophy is well summarized in the following statement from the Snell Foundation (a helmet testing organization established by race car drivers): "The protection given by any protective headgear is necessarily less than complete. The best helmet is but one link in a long chain of safety including safety education."

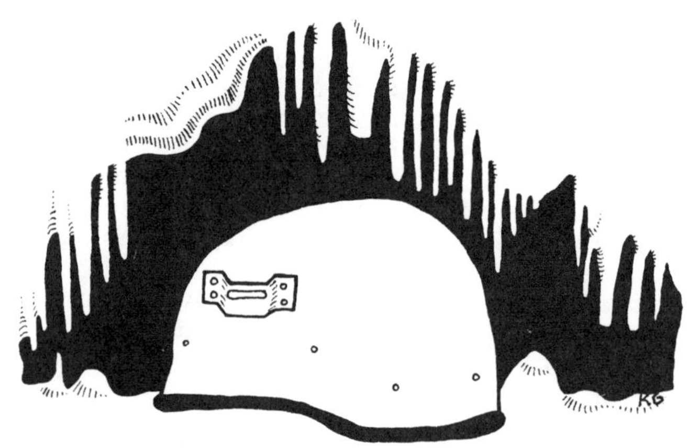

Granted that the preceding statement is true, what sorts of things should you look for in a good caving helmet? John Armitage (1966) noted some characteristics of good climbing helmets. Although cavers and climbers are often worlds apart in the equipment they use and how it is used, Armitage's comments on helmets seem reasonable:

1. The helmet must be on your head when you need it. The chin strap must be designed to hold the helmet on your head, both in a tumbling fall and in normal climbing (i.e. caving).
2. The helmet should not be heavy or bulky or restrictive of hearing.
3. The shell must be rigid enough to spread the load of an impacting object to protect against skull fractures.
4. The shell must resist penetration by pointed objects.
5. The helmet must have an energy-absorbing lining around the head band area to cushion side impact in a tumbling fall.
6. The cost should not be too high.

To Armitage's points, the Mountain Safety Research Group added:

7. The helmet must have an energy-absorbing suspension to reduce the peak force of a top impact (falling rock).

8. The side-to-side rigidity must be reasonably good.

Okay, granted these points, what about helmets commonly seen being worn by cavers?

Helmets

Most cavers wear some sort of modified construction-type helmet. The reason for this is simple—these helmets are cheap and do provide some protection (i.e. when banging your head on the ceiling). Unfortunately, most cavers will rig these helmets with inadequate elastic chin straps. If one starts to fall down a slope, the helmet is likely to be lost immediately. The head can take a terrific beating as the caver rolls and bounces down the slope. Also, these helmets often only meet the z-89.1 standard and so it is questionable whether the helmet would protect the caver even if it stayed on the head during a fall as described above.

Pick up one of these helmets and squeeze the sides together. It is possible to move the sides inward at least an inch or so without all that much effort. This is also true for other "caving" helmets that are sold. Try the above procedure on one of the Speleoshoppe's "Deluxe Caving Helmets" (circa 1979 or before). Remember that just because it's sold as a "caving helmet," does not mean that it is safe for all kinds of caving. The Speleoshoppe's helmets do have adequate suspension systems which should keep the helmet on in a tumbling fall.

On the positive side, it can be said that most of these helmets are reasonably cheap, lightweight, fairly cool and do protect the head from falling objects, bumping your head, etc. But, if you intend to do vertical caving, or are planning on doing lots of caving, perhaps a better helmet is in your future.

Just because you go out and spend $40, $50, or more for a caving helmet does not mean that you should not shop carefully. If you are going to spend this much money, you will probably be looking at so-called "climbing helmets" (Bell, Joe Brown, MSR, Ultimate, etc.), and for the most part these will provide your head with much more protection than the modified construction type helmets.

First, these helmets tend to be expensive. There is a definite difference between $5 and $35 and if we were all required to purchase these expensive helmets for caving, many of us probably would not have started to cave. Second, many of these climbing helmets are hot to wear, almost unpleasantly so even in alpine caving areas. Some cavers have tried to remedy this problem by drilling holes in their Ultimates, Bells or Joe Browns to provide ventilation for their heads. The MSR helmets come with holes already designed into the helmet. In the case of the former three mentioned above, it should be noted that by drilling holes you may compromise the added protection provided by these helmets. They were not designed to have holes drilled in them and it is unknown how these holes affect their primary function of protecting your head. Also, holes in the helmet shell (and this goes for the MSR helmet as well) provide a place for a falling rock to "catch" thus transmitting its falling force onto a small portion of the helmet. Without these holes, a rock would probably merely glance off the helmet with its force being dissipated accordingly. Thirdly, you should carefully inspect any climbing helmet for other desirable caving and/or climbing qualities. For instance, although most climbing helmets have excellent strap systems for holding the helmet on your head, it is sometimes difficult to get these helmets off when confined in tight or awkward places. Also, since most of these helmets were not designed with caving in mind, adding a lamp to the front of them often causes them to tip forward, especially with the weight of a carbide lamp. This, of course, means that even though you may have spent a considerable amount of money on your helmet, modifications may still be required to its suspension system.

None of these helmets come with lamp brackets so these must be added. Remember to be careful when installing your bracket so that you do not end up with screws, bolts, or any other rigid projection inside the shell of your helmet which is longer than half the thickness of the foam.

A very good helmet accessory, especially for carbide cavers, is a stout rubber band, such as can be cut from an old innertube. When pulled across the bottom of one's lamp, it helps keep it from being jarred off at bad moments. Other objects can also be temporarily carried on the head by slipping under the band, such as a pocket light, lighter, notebook, pencil, etc., especially when negotiating deep water.

To be sure, climbing helmets will protect your head better than the construction-type helmet. These manufacturers are more concerned about their products and Bell and MSR tell their customers that if they should have a bad fall, the helmet should be returned to them. These manufacturers will then test the helmet and replace it if it is found to be defective.

The helmet question is still up to the individual caver. Hopefully, you can assess the amount and kind of caving you do and how that relates to this information about caving helmets. So when looking for a helmet, be informed and be observant, for after all, it's your head.

Reference

Armitage, J. (1966)—A Report on helmets for climbing: Summit **12**(3)(17-22).

CLOTHING FOR THE CAVER

Mary Looney
NSS 9805

Basic Concepts

Although cavers' clothing varies almost as much as cavers, a few basic considerations need to be applied. First: caving clothes must be rugged. They will be subjected to hard wear and intimate contact with rocky surfaces and gritty soils. Second: caving clothes must be loose enough to permit all sorts of contortions while crawling, slithering through holes, and other typical caving maneuvers, and at the same time be fitted well enough to allow the caver to use ascending and descending devices on ropes. Third: caving clothes should be warm enough for protection in cool to cold caves and absorbent enough to soak up perspiration in 100% humidity.

Outer Layer

For the outer layer of clothing, many cavers prefer coveralls. The one-piece design covers all of you, thus eliminating the gap which will often appear between pants and shirt when crawling through tight places. Nothing is more disconcerting than to try to slip down through a tight hole in the floor of a cave only to find your shirt, jacket, or whatever jerked upward imprisoning your arms and covering your face. There are no loose shirt tails to present a safety hazard on ropes. (A shirt tail threaded through carabiners or a rack presents a multitude of problems—none welcome when a rocky cave floor is from 30 to 200 feet below you.) Coveralls are made of rugged materials, usually containing a fairly high percentage of synthetic fiber. This gives the fabric a greater resistance to abrasion and tearing than that of pure cotton fabrics. They are reasonably priced and easily obtainable: Sears, Montgomery Ward and JC Penney all sell coveralls and they are also available in many other department and discount stores.

Most coveralls come with several pockets and a double front zipper which can be undone from either the bottom or the top. Males find this handy, but I, personally, never use this feature. Coveralls are usually sized to wear over other clothes and are made with a slit on the side to allow access to underneath pockets. The most practical thing to do with this slit is to sew it securely together to prevent the opening catching on projections in crawlways. Pockets in caving clothes are not very useful. Hip pockets catch on rock projections and tear loose.

Side pockets could theoretically carry a number of small items, but in actual practice these tend to slide out.

Fig. 8. Two cavers about to enter a cave wearing coveralls and boots. Notice the sewed-on knee pads at the knees of the caver on the right.

Large items are impossible to crawl on and can present a real obstacle in tight climbs. The only useful pockets in caving clothes are breast pockets, and only a few small items should be carried in them. It is far better to carry your belongings in a pack which can be pushed or dragged along with you when crawling. So, my first modification on a new pair of coveralls is to stitch up the side slits and then stitch down the tops of the hip pockets. There are several other modifications to the standard coverall which can be added to protect knees and elbows which will be discussed later on. One I personally like is to hem the bottom of the legs and run elastic through the hems. This makes it possible to blouse the bottoms above the tops of your boots, thus avoiding a heavy coating of mud on the bottom of the pants legs.

An advantage of wearing a jacket and pants is freedom of movement at the waist. Also a jacket is easier to shed if you get too warm.

Under the Outer Layer

What goes under this outer layer? The primary consideration here is how cold and/or wet the cave is. For the ordinary cave with a temperature of from 50 to 56°, most people will find a pair of old pants and a lightweight shirt over regular underwear is all that is necessary. If you are exploring new territory, "pushing" in caving language, you will be exerting yourself enough that you will generate a lot of body heat. If you are going to be mapping, collecting cave life, or taking a lot of pictures, your progress is going to be a lot slower, and less arduous; consequently, you might need a heavier shirt or a light sweater. If you are going to be in a very cold cave, you might need to add long underwear. If you are going to be in a very wet cave, one where you are going to be getting in and out of rubber rafts, wading in water more than knee deep, or crawling in water, you need wool—wool underwear or wool pants and shirts, or both. Surplus GI or any old rugged wool clothes are fine for this. Wool, unlike most other materials, does not mat when wet and still retains body heat. Knitted orlon is fair for this but cotton is terrible. A soaking wet pair of jeans is miserable. If the water is below 60°, a wetsuit would be in order.

For your first few caving trips and any subsequent trips out of your home caving territory, check with the leaders of the trip as to expected temperature and water conditions. You will learn to suit your clothes to your individual needs. If you are cold-natured, wear an extra layer. You can always take it off and stash it in a plastic bag if you are too warm, but do this before the garment becomes wet with sweat. A wet garment isn't very useful or comfortable. Nothing is more miserable, not to mention potentially dangerous, than to be cold to the point of continuous shivering deep in a cave.

For female cavers, one of the neatest tricks I know is to wear panty-hose under your old knit slacks. Most of the mud comes off with the hose. I like old knit banlon or orlon tops and polyester double-knit slacks better than woven ones and I find many men do too. They are soft, they "give" when necessary, give a margin of warmth and they soak up excess sweat. Other people swear by jeans and chambray shirts.

Footwear

Now you need to consider your feet. Few cavers will argue with the statement that you need boots. Furthermore, although you may settle for cheap boots or GI surplus, you will eventually find that you want the best boots you can afford to buy. The height of boots is an individual preference. Some cavers wear the low (just above the ankle) ones and seem to find them satisfactory. To me they have several drawbacks, the chief one being that it is easier to go in over the tops in soft mud or water. I also like the shin protection that a slightly higher-topped boot affords. Really high boots, those coming just below the knee, are seldom seen anymore and are too heavy and stiff for practical use.

Good, reasonably light, lined hiking boots make good caving boots. They need to be lined and need a solid tongue which keeps out water when the boot is immersed ankle deep. Above all, boots should have ribbed lug soles. Good footing is important in caves, and the Vibram® sole is about the best modern design for stability. They will pick up masses of mud in a really muddy cave, but so will almost anything else.

The "Vietnam" or jungle boot was popular for a long time and some cavers are still using them. They were never intended to be waterproof since their design allows water to drain out. If they are worn with wool socks or wet suit booties, some people find them adequate. If you are using wet suit booties, get your boots at least a half size larger than normal. Good high-topped work shoes can also be used although they usually do not have the type of sole which offers safe footing on slick mud. Leather soles are completely impractical. Even so-called "cheap" boots today cost close to $25 a pair. Good ones go up into the $70 to $120 range and the $5 GI surplus boots are no more. Your boots are going to be one of your largest expenditures. Get the best you can, but be sure they are comfortable and give them good care.

Keep your boots clean: clean the mud and grit out of the inside after every cave trip, wash the outsides and dry, out of direct sun and heat. Then condition them with either silicone spray, neats-foot oil, mink oil or Sno-Seal. If this is done often your boots will remain soft and comfortable throughout their life. A heavy application of a good polish further protects the outside from rubbing and wear.

Under your boots the same rules apply as for hiking. Wear a lightweight, slick pair of inner socks and a soft fluffy pair of outer socks. Wool is ideal while the heavier, thick orlon socks are acceptable. Wool (and to some degree orlon) will absorb perspiration and will remain warm even if wet. Cotton sweat socks are a very poor third choice. The slick inner sock plus the slick lining of your boots with the soft cushioned sock in between protects your feet from rubbing and blisters. Always start a trip in clean socks if you can. Stiff, muddy, gritty socks at the beginning of a trip make for uncomfortable feet. Thin wet suit booties are another good alternative in all but dry caves. They do not mat down when wet so retain much of the body's heat. Cost is a drawback, but they can be easily homemade. Wearing nylon socks over the booties reduces abrasion from boot contact and dramatically increases their life.

A few cavers wear tennis shoes. I once knew a very good caver who bought good tennis shoes and had lug soles put on them. Tennis shoes are cold, they offer little protection to your feet and they wear out rapidly. Generally speaking, the only use for tennis shoes in caving is in a cave where almost all of the going is either in very deep water or in boats. If you are going to be totally submerged in water, your boots will fill with water and your feet will be soaking wet anyhow. Even here, boots are needed to protect your feet from rocks under water. Low-cut tennis shoes are of no use even in water and you are almost sure to lose them several times or permanently.

Gloves

Gloves are a necessity in a cave since they protect your hands from sharp rocks and rope burn, enable you to have hands clean enough to change your carbide or batteries and keep your hands a little warmer. Supposedly, a good pair of fabric-lined leather gloves would be ideal for caving. The only trouble here is that such gloves are costly and no matter how careful you are, they don't last long. Most cavers settle for less expensive woven cotton gloves, some with plastic coating, or some with plastic dots for better grip. A good, medium-priced glove is that made of heavy plastic impregnated cloth such as the Edmont "Snorkels." If you will be using a camera and need reasonably clean hands, a lightweight pair of gloves covered with a heavier pair helps. Be sure gloves fit, especially for use with rappel and climbing devices. Wash them as often as you can—ideally after each use. A spare pair in the bottom of your pack is good insurance. Gloves are all too easy to lose in caves.

Padding

Unfortunately, most cave trips include some crawling. Although babies seem to be able to do it without much pain, the adult knee just isn't suited to long, rocky crawls without some kind of protection. There are several ways of providing this protection, none of which are completely satisfactory, although some are better than others. Many cavers carefully sew long, outside pockets to their coveralls on both legs and arms and insert foam in them. Unfortunately, this makes both arms and legs of coveralls somewhat stiff and uncomfortable. Both sleeves and pants legs do twist at times so that you end up with the protection on top and your bones on the rocks. The National Parks supply rubber knee pads worn by cement finishers to the cavers taking their wild cave trips. Since you can only walk in them with difficulty, they must be carried and strapped on before starting to crawl. They were never intended for this use and frequently come off. Rubber knee pads with elastic straps, such as Rockmasters, are much better and can be worn while walking.

My personal choice for knee pads are the short (eight-inch or so) athletic pads. I wear them just above my boots and pull them up when I start to crawl. If you are interspersing crawling with walking and climbing, they can remain in place without too much discomfort. I wouldn't advise hiking three miles with them over your knees—they might blister the back of your knees. Small elbow pads can be worn around your wrists and pushed up when needed or remain in place for fairly long periods. Since they don't usually cover the joint itself but the area immediately below your elbow, they are fairly comfortable. Most people find that by varying their crawling techniques they can get along without elbow pads fairly well.

Care

I have frequently mentioned washing your caving clothes. There are those who consider this unnecessary. I have never been able to go along with the minimum wash theory, but it is a matter of personal preference. Cave grit is all pervading. Once cave clothes have been worn, not only the outside but also the inside is liberally crusted with gritty cave mud. I don't care for the sensation. In extreme circumstances it is possible to dry coveralls and wear over clean clothes. Personally, I prefer to wash my coveralls after each trip—they last longer that way too.

If you are using a washer to wash cave clothes, prewash them thoroughly with a hose. The amount of mud in a really groady pair of coveralls can do drastic things to the pump in an automatic washer. Hang your clothes on a line (or a bush) and hose them down. Dry and shake and then launder. Borax will remove the musty cave smell from cave clothes. Use along with regular detergent.

The obvious rules about washing woolen socks and undergarments apply. Use mild soap and warm water, and either dry in the air or on the air setting of a dryer. If you are using commercial laundromats, bring your wool stuff home for drying. An exception to this is GI surplus clothing. Drying in commercial dryers doesn't seem to hurt it. Knee and elbow pads with elastic in them should be washed in warm water and dried carefully. Hot dryer temperatures will destroy the elastic. Use a low heat setting or air dry.

Care of boots has already been covered. Even on a prolonged caving trip, the outside of your boots can have the excess mud knocked off and the inside can be wiped out. If boots are wet, dry as much as possible between trips. An old hikers trick is to warm a bucket of clean sand and pour in your boots. Leave overnight and then dump out the sand and carefully wipe out the inside. The toes of your boots will wear quickly. Many cavers attempt to reinforce the toe with layers of epoxy-type substances.

Canvas Grip, available from some of the vendors listed in Appendix C, is an adhesive used to glue cloth and canvas products together. As such, it is a boon to cavers who may not have the facilities or assistance to constantly mend their caving clothes. It really holds and it's easy to use.

When you have been caving a few years, you may agree or disagree with my ideas, but this is intended as a guide for those of you who are just getting started. Once you are experienced, you will have your own set of caving clothes and your own ideas.

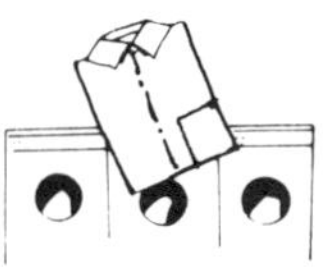

CAVE PACKS

Alan Williams
NSS 9700F

Selecting A Cave Pack

Any caver, before entering a cave, must be carrying a certain minimum amount of gear to ensure his safety: three sources of light, hard hat, spare parts, water, food, etc. (See chapter on General Equipment.) In addition, the equipment list can quickly expand to include vertical gear, survey equipment, camera gear and many other items depending upon the nature of the cave being visited and the interests of the individual caver.

Most cavers solve their transport problems by stuffing all the gear they can't wear into a CAVE PACK. Cave packs are found in an almost endless variety of shapes, sizes, weights and modes of attachment to the human body. However, a few grand generalizations can be made about their desirable characteristics. A cave pack should:

1. Be of rugged construction.
2. Be as compact as possible.
3. Allow for comfortable carrying.
4. Have a trouble-free method for opening and closing.

Some specific descriptions of the kinds of cave packs in general use by NSS cavers follow.

Military Surplus Packs. A majority of cavers have found the answer to their cave pack needs in the large variety of "Army" sidepacks, field packs and bags available in surplus stores throughout the country. The selection is not quite as varied as it once was, and certain desirable styles are becoming scarce, but a caver can find a suitable pack if he looks hard enough.

Army packs are inevitably made of durable heavy canvas, have secure closure devices and usually come with their own array of carrying straps. The most common type in current use is the "gas mask bag" in all its many varieties. These packs are usually not larger than a foot in any dimension. They are designed to be slung over the shoulder by a single strap (the mode generally preferred by cavers). A typical gas mask bag is capable of holding the gear for most caving trips, providing you don't bring along all kinds of camera, surveying and vertical equipment. A selection of gas mask bags is shown in Fig. 9.

Fig. 9. A variety of Cave Packs: 1) Field Phone bag; 2) German Gas Mask Bag (note button closure); 3) Small Waterproof Pouch; 4, 5 & 6) various styles of Gas Mask Bags; 7) Polyethylene Pig; 8) Field Pack.

Another surplus pack in general use is the so-called "field pack." Originally designed to be carried on the shoulders like a knapsack or suspended on the hips by a webbing belt, these packs have approximately twice the capacity of an average gas mask bag, yet are still relatively compact. They usually are fitted out with an assortment of small straps and buckles intended for fastening oversize items to the outside of the pack. Field packs have only short, 'knapsack" type straps for carrying and must be fitted with a longer shoulder strap if this is desired. The larger capacity of these packs is useful when camera gear, etc. is being carried, eliminating the necessity of carrying two gas mask size packs.

A surplus pack, indeed, any type of cave pack which is larger than a field pack verges on the impractical (immovable when you stuff it full of gear). Oversize packs, up to duffle-bag backpack size occasionally are required for elaborate expeditions but generally the smaller the better for convenience and ease of carrying.

There are two common types of closures on surplus packs: the "buckle-and-strap" and the "eyelet-snap", illustrated in Fig. 10. Both closures are acceptable, but the eyelet-snap type is much more subject to fouling with mud and grit. Vaseline packed into the snap before a trip will reduce this clogging. Almost any cave pack with snaps, after a few cave trips, will have one or more of these snaps rendered unworkable. Diligent post-trip cleaning can help alleviate this problem. When the eyelet-snap no longer functions, a cord, or even a shock cord, can be fastened in the eyelet and hooked to another part of the bag to close it. The buckle-and-strap closure is virtually foolproof, although it requires more manipulation to open and close than a functional snap type.

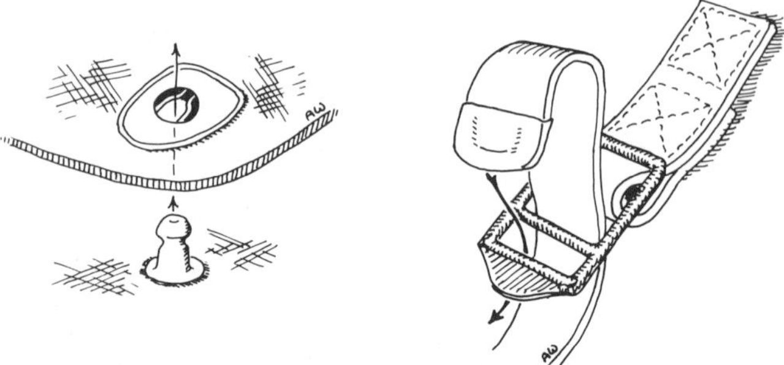

Fig. 10. Eyelet-snap and buckle-and-strap closures.

Zippers are occasionally found on surplus packs. They are even more subject to fouling than snaps and should be avoided. Less common are button closures (usually on foreign-made packs). Buttons are simple and trouble-free as long as the button holes are tight and the buttons don't tear off.

Ammunition Boxes. Many cavers use these military surplus metal boxes as protective containers for their camera gear. Two sizes are readily available: .30 cal. and .50 cal., the .30 cal. box being the smaller of the two. The use of ammo boxes as cave packs is a questionable practice with regard to the well-being of both the caver and the cave. The metal box is hard and unyielding, with eight sharp corners to chip any flowstone they might touch. The box is heavy and ungainly to carry. Unless somehow tightly fastened to the body, it will be hitting shins, knees and hips continually. An ammo box in good condition is watertight and thus may be useful for caving trips involving lots of crawling in stream passages.

Both advantages of ammo boxes—protection and water-tightness—can be achieved using soft cave packs and appropriate methods of wrapping and cushioning vulnerable items. For the well-being of both you and the cave, avoid ammo boxes if at all possible.

Miscellaneous Surplus. Many other surplus items are available which have application in cave packing. These include:

1. Belt pouches of various sizes.
2. Waterproof bags.
3. Sheaths.
4. Leather pouches.

If every surplus pack disappeared tomorrow, a caver's life would be more difficult and much more expensive. However, alternative packs do exist and are in general, though minority, use.

Polyethylene Pigs. This ingenious and inexpensive pack is made from two identical one-gallon polyethylene jugs, usually bleach or anti-freeze bottles. The bottom one-quarter of each jug is cut away, allowing the two to be pushed together, one inside the other, as shown in Figs. 9 and 11. A carrying strap is attached at both jug handles. Often a second short strap or shock cord is attached which can be cinched tight to further ensure the pack won't fall open.

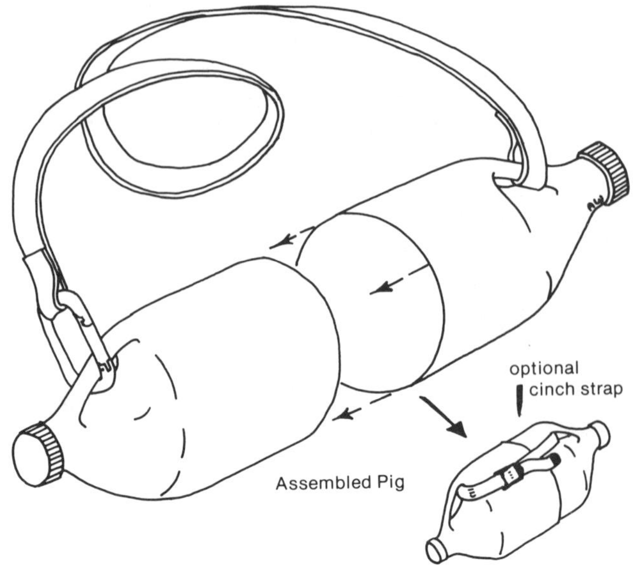

Fig. 11. Polyethylene Bottle Pig.

Your Own Body. Some cavers find they can dispense with a separate cave pack altogether. They do this by adapting their clothing, usually coveralls, into a cave pack. By sewing additional pockets in strategic places, along the inside of the legs and arms, for example, most gear can be stowed in an out-of-the-way place. This method of packing is effective on "routine" trips, where the caver knows exactly what will be needed to safely visit the cave and no extraneous gear will be required. Of course, one should never skimp on the recommended essential gear in order to avoid carrying a separate pack!

Day Packs. Manufactured for hiking outdoors, these packs are vastly inferior to surplus packs for caving. Usually they are (1) a bit too big and bulky, (2) made of too-light material, (3) too difficult to open and close securely, and (4) too expensive. However, they are acceptable for a few trips until something better can be obtained.

Hip Packs. These packs are made for skiers and bicyclists. They are put on like a belt with the pack fitting snugly across the back at hip level. These packs are compact, but suffer from the disadvantage of any pack which is tightly attached to the body: there are inevitably situations where the pack must be removed to negotiate tight or awkward places.

Custom-designed Packs. While the possibility of dreaming up a completely original pack style is slim, there are many individual touches one can apply to improve an existing pack or to assemble a new one. These touches range from simply tying on a length of webbing as a shoulder strap to reinforcing pack corners with epoxy or leather patches to experimenting with Velcro closures. An interesting home-made pack recently seen consisted of an inner-tube-like circle of canvas three feet in diameter. Pack items are placed into compartments in the tube. The pack is carried like a bandolier in most situations, but can be unslung quickly and dragged if necessary.

Packing the Cave Pack

Once the desired cave pack is obtained, there are a number of hints on how to efficiently fit all that essential gear inside it. One of the most useful and widely used pack items is the plastic baby bottle, either sans rubber nipple or with the nipple trimmed to form a gasket. Baby bottles come in four and eight ounce sizes with the eight ounce being standard. They are light, compact, watertight and extremely rugged. An eight ounce bottle will hold six to eight charges of carbide, i.e. up to 16 hours of light. Cave foods such as gorp, granola or M&Ms fit conviently inside. Spare parts, flashbulbs, water—all can be carried in baby bottles. A baby bottle is made more cave-worthy by cementing together the two pieces of the screw cap. **Mark the bottle used for carbide** so as not to have an unexpected mouthful of carbide for lunch.

Plastic food storage bags have also found their way into universal usage. Obviously, they are not as rugged as baby bottles, but doubled bags can securely wrap just about everything that goes into a cave pack. Carefully wrapped items will be waterproof inside plastic bags; but for long periods of immersion in water passages, baby bottles are more reliable protection. The one gallon size bags are the most versatile and many cavers prefer the "ziploc" style of closure. However, do not get mud in the ziploc threads if the bag is to be reclosed.

Other containers for packing include snap-lid film canisters for spare parts, pieces of foam rubber for wrapping cameras, ruberized bags for camera or surveying gear and any sort of handy box or bag a resourceful caver can come across.

Carrying the Cave Pack

No arrangement for carrying a cave pack will be trouble-free in every situation. However, some recommendations can be made to minimize the struggle. By far the most favored method of carrying a pack is to sling it at hip level by means of a single strap passing over the shoulder. This loose attachment to the body allows for immediate removal when necessary to negotiate tight spots. Little or no hesitation in "caving rhythm" occurs since this pack can be swung easily out of the way or removed entirely without interrupting forward motion. The pack is most conveniently slung at hip level. Slung lower, the pack continually beats against the thighs; slung higher, the shoulder strap becomes too short to pass easily over a helmeted head. In addition to the shoulder strap, many cavers like a waist strap on their pack. A waist strap will hold the pack next to the body thus preventing it from swinging loose. A pack held in place with both a shoulder and waist strap will not have to be removed as often as those packs with only a shoulder strap. Also a pack that does not swing around can be more efficient to carry.

Cave packs carried like a knapsack on the shoulders present frequent inconvenience in caving. While this pack is more comfortable to carry when walking upright, it is necessary to stop to remove it or put it on—a situation which will occur before and after every crawlway.

A good indication of the practicality of a given cave pack is to note the amount of time it is carried in the hand. A pack which must be constantly taken off, or which is difficult to put on, will most often be carried by hand. This is an undesirable situation, since both hands should be free for caving. A convenient pack will have to be removed only for the tightest crawls and will seldom be hand carried.

Another good rule to follow is: take your pack with you wherever you go in the cave. The quote, "I'll leave my pack here while I check this lead for a few minutes" is a familiar one. The result, 50% of the time, is that

20 minutes into the "little lead", the caver must madly dash back to his pack to change carbide. Either that or he yells back for his friends to "Come on through, and bring my pack with you!" Pulling this trick too often results in disgruntled companions.

Finally, a point of caving etiquette regarding cave packs is to resist the temptation to pass your pack across every obstacle to someone on the other side. Occasionally, it is more efficient to hand all the packs through at one time; but many cavers overuse this technique—making their fellow cavers pause and help them continually. It is good for a caver's soul to wrestle his own gear through the cave, with minimum help.

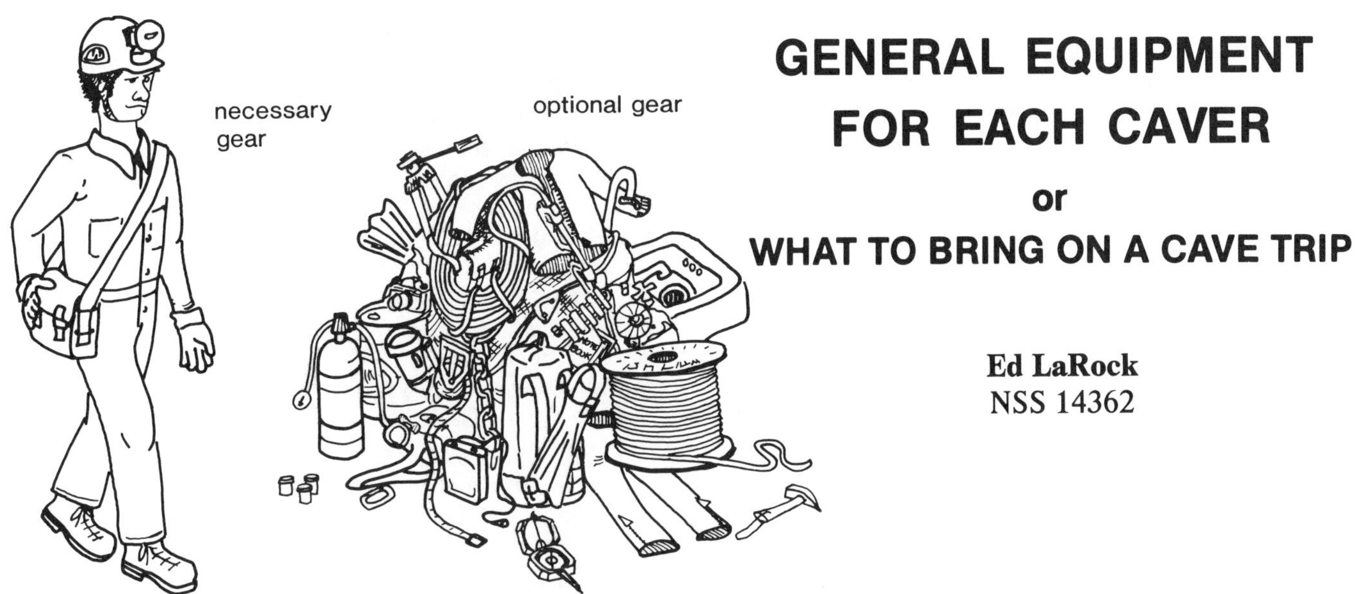

GENERAL EQUIPMENT FOR EACH CAVER

or

WHAT TO BRING ON A CAVE TRIP

Ed LaRock
NSS 14362

This section is designed to bring together other parts of the manual into one checklist or guide to what items to bring on a cave trip. As a result some items, such as lamps or cave packs, which have been detailed elsewhere, will need no explanation when mentioned here. Items to bring on a cave trip can be broken down into the "basic necessities" which **each caver should carry on every cave trip** and "optional items" that depend largely on the type of cave trip planned, some of which may be distributed among the cave party.

The basic necessities should be taken on even the "easiest two-hour" cave trip since unexpected events may lengthen your trip underground. The basics should be carried in a handy, easily reached place as they may be in frequent use.

The Basics

I. Primary Light Source and Helmet—should be helmet-mounted to leave hands free and to always illuminate your line of vision. Helmet should have a good chin strap.

A) Carbide Lamp

1. Spare carbide and water for lamp—at least twice the amount you plan to use.
2. Container for spent carbide—never dump your spent carbide in the cave.
3. Spare parts such as an extra lamp bottom, tip, felt, gasket, wing nut and flints, along with a tip cleaner and even some electrician's tape for emergency bracket repair.

OR

B) Electric Headlamp

1. Spare batteries—again twice the amount you'll need.
2. Spare bulbs and any other spare electrical parts.
3. Electrician's tape for cord repair and emergency mounting.
4. Pocket knife for making repairs.

II. Extra Light Sources—at least two independent sources which can be used to exit the cave.

A) Most commonly a flashlight with wrist strap and some chemical lightsticks with aluminum foil for a makeshift reflector—many cavers carry a spare carbide lamp charged and ready to go in addition to a flashlight and chemical lightsticks.

1. Extra parts for your extra light sources.

B) Waterproof matches or a cigarette lighter are also very useful to carry.

C) Candles, mostly to be used during rest stops or while repairing items.

III. General items that everyone should have.

A) Small pair of pliers needed for lamp repairs, tightening rappel racks, etc.

B) Pocket knife to sharpen pencils, cut webbing, make repairs on lamps, open cans and so on.

C) Short lengths of string and wire can be very useful.

IV. Food and Emergency Gear

A) Food and drinking water.

1. Requirements will depend on length of trip and the individual.
2. Each person should at least carry some small emergency food item on any trip, i.e. candy bar, food sticks.

B) Space blanket (which may degrade with time if wet) or a large, heavy duty plastic bag—these are excellent emergency insulators that have prevented many cases of hypothermia and should always be carried.

C) A small pocket-sized first aid kit, a short length

of cord or webbing for use as pack strap repair, emergency lamp mounting, arm sling, handlines, or rigging points, and even a small whistle for signalling. These final three items may be considered optional but take up little space or weight and could be lifesavers.

V. Pencil and paper for leaving and/or taking notes.

VI. List of rescue phone numbers (could be left in the vehicle or at the entrance) and some coins for emergency phone calls.

Optional Gear

Optional caving gear will often depend on the type and length of cave trip planned such as a mapping trip and/or vertical cave trip.

I. General—useful items for someone on the trip to be carrying.

A) Some removable flagging tape for marking the way in a new or complex cave and for survey stations when mapping. Also can be used to mark off areas of delicate speleothems and trails.
B) A map of the cave (if available) in a plastic bag.
C) Compass.
D) Watch.

II. Survey or Mapping Gear—should be packed in a separate sack or baggie in a cave pack.

A) Compass with/and inclinometer.
B) Waterproof notebook—also useful for leaving notes for other parties, that is, if you also have pencils.
C) Measuring tape, 25- to 100-foot length.

III. Photography Gear

IV. Vertical Cave Trip—each person should carry his own complete set, possibly in a separate sack or pack for convenience.

A) Ascending/climbing gear.
B) Descending/rappelling gear, including gloves.
C) Seat and chest harness(es).
D) Rope—carrying shared by the cave party members.

V. Extra long trips or expedition—this belongs in a separate category beyond basic caving. However, extra food, lighting supplies, wet suits or exposure suits for wet caves, sleeping gear, and larger and specially designed packs should all be considered for long, strenuous trips underground.

Finally, items brought on a cave trip will have to be transported in some way, but more importantly they should be individually dirt resistant, waterproof and durable. Several hints on containers and "cave-proofing" will be summarized here.

All contents of the cave pack(s) can be placed and sealed inside a plastic trash bag for transport through wet caves or near sumps. This will also cause the pack to be bouyant.

Plastic containers, baby bottles, film canisters and double ziplock baggies are rugged and usually waterproof for carrying most anything.

Water containers with "flip-tops" are handy for filling carbide lamps.

Drinking water should be carried in a separate container since a caver may want to refill his lamp waterbottle with water from the cave.

It is wise to use a piece of plastic bag or wrap as a container. Seal to prevent leakage or contamination.

Collapsible plastic containers take up less space as the contents are used up and/or can be compressed and stowed away until needed.

In conclusion, the chance of a mishap or inconvenience while in a cave can be greatly reduced if every caver in the party is carrying his or her own basic cave necessities. Provisions for optional gear should be worked out with the trip leader before the trip.

MOVING THROUGH A CAVE

Roger W. Brucker
NSS 1999HF

Introduction

Caving can be very strenuous, especially if you are not in good physical shape. Even those who run or swim, for example, may complain of sore muscles after a tough cave trip. Caving uses muscles you never knew you had; their pain will inform you of their presence! The best cure for sore caving muscles is to go caving again right away. After months and years of caving you will wonder how you could have hurt so much.

This section is not about pain, however. It is about how to obtain the most pleasure from caving. Happiness comes from learning how to move through a cave so that you enjoy it to the fullest, see everything and waste the least amount of energy. We will look at the relationship between mental attitude and physical condition. We will see how to harness your eyes to the task of moving with the least effort. We will learn some tricks of experienced cavers. And we will talk about the relationship of movement skills to getting back out of the cave safely.

Mental and Physical Aspects

There are many good books about physical fitness. Their message boils down to the fact that you will feel better and be healthier if you are fit. You also will enjoy cave exploring more because you will have more endurance, you will be able to go places that require hard physical effort and you will be putting your body and mind on the adventure line. Doing something "neat" out on the far edge of adventure can make life more satisfying. You may gain exciting new insights on the world around you and you may meet new friends with attractive qualities far beyond the everyday. For some, caving is indeed living.

The thought of going caving may produce fears. These are natural and healthy. In fact, the person who claims to be fearless in the presence of the unknown is either dishonest or insensitive. This fearfulness or apprehension is useful if it causes you to check your equipment one more time, to take a last look at the map before you enter the cave, or to check the rigging on a drop after the "expert" has told you the knots are O.K. When you hear expert cavers tell morbid jokes before going into the cave, you will know they too are feeling the same excitement or fear that you are. Jim Dyer, one of the best cavers ever, used to un-nerve new explorers in the Flint Ridge Cave System with the dry comment, "Now when we get to the Bottomless Pit, I want you to tie up the legs of your jeans. It's a very scary crossing on a slippery ledge, and we want to be considerate of anyone who happens to be below." Jim was as brave as any caver, but he knew fear also.

Your brain is the most important part of your body in moving through a cave. Your eyes are the second most important. Try to cultivate a habit of looking at the spaces you will move into and analyzing how your body will fit them. Imagine yourself and what you will be doing next. Will I have to duck to get under that low ledge? Can I keep my head a little higher if I go under where that notch is? If I lead with my left foot, where will my right foot hit? Such questions may seem forced and silly, but they soon become automatic. By themselves, questions are not very useful, except that they force you to make some future guesses about your body's fit and movement through inner space.

These guesses are then quickly proven right or wrong as you move. You are cultivating the habit of making predictions and obtaining instant feedback. Using this technique, you will rapidly learn how to move easily and naturally through the toughest cave. Your guesses will get better. As an example, when you whack your head on the ceiling, you may see that the headlamp on your hardhat fails to illuminate a blind area immediately above it. You adjust to this by checking out low ceiling ahead of your light's blind spot.

Some cavers who have tried this prediction and feedback method have reported astonishment at how rapidly they learned to move. A few have reported dreams of flying through a cave with ease, their bodies gliding through the smallest and most convoluted passages.

Physiologists might explain this mind-body mastery on the basis of kinesthetic theory. Natural athletes seem endowed with such awareness at an early age. But no matter how clumsy you are, you can improve your caving movements. Good cavers can become excellent—measured by endurance—by learning the method of imagining your own body moving ahead of where you really are.

The third mental aspect of good caving is to develop an attitude: "I will conserve energy at every opportunity." This sounds like a recipe for becoming lazy, but it is very practical advice for enjoying caving to the fullest. What this means is you should rest every muscle you can every chance you get. The practice will help you ward off fatigue and will keep you alert and happy long after others on the cave trip are bombed out. Don't rest too long because you will become chilled and your muscles will stiffen.

You can conserve energy by not using more than you need, or by replacing it with food. Good cavers do both. Let's talk about food first, since that is the easiest, and most misunderstood, way to conserve energy. Energy is calories. Most cavers carry candy bars, whose sugar is a handy source of quick energy. In as little as 15 minutes after eating a candy bar, you may feel less tired and more alert. On the other hand, energy from candy bars seems short-lived, and many cavers report that they feel more tired than ever after the candy "lift" wears off. A few cavers report upset stomach from "candy overload." What you eat and how it affects you is a highly individual matter, of course, and you should experiment with what you eat until you know your own needs.

One eating strategy that has worked for many years in the Mammoth Cave System, where cavers go for 20 hours or more, is to eat a variety of foods in the cave for longer-lasting energy. A typical meal may consist of canned boned chicken or turkey or beef stew, canned fruit and a candy bar. Such meals are eaten 45 minutes or so before the cavers grow hungry, so there is no lag while energy levels work back up from low levels. Eat a large meal containing fats before entering the cave. Fats are slowly metabolized and provide energy for a long period of time.

A mental attitude of conserving energy can be cultivated just as easily as the predictive-feedback method of learning how to move. You ask yourself, "How can I do this with less effort?" Then you try acting on your answer. If you are resting, for example, your answer may be that sitting up takes more energy than lying down, so try lying down. Elevate the legs above the level of the torso while lying down; to some, this seems to relax the leg muscles. Practice regularly, you will work out your own little tricks for reducing exertion and prolonging your strength. Also try asking other cavers for pet methods of being lazy in a cave.

Tricks of Moving Easily

Here are some tricks of moving easily through caves that have proven useful for over 25 years. No doubt the list could be expanded by any caver. The discovery of practical ideas like these can increase your sense of joy from caving.

Keep your head up. Keep your head as high as possible, whether you move through vast galleries or chest-compressor crawlways. It will improve your posture, and will make it easier to move along briskly. In a passage four feet high, for example, you may have a choice. You could crouch. You might even squirm on your belly. Choose the crouch, keeping your head as high and close to the ceiling as you possibly can. Will you hit your head? Sure! But that is why you sport that expensive hardhat. By clonking your hardhat on the ceiling a few times, you will improve your aim. That is, you will learn just how high you can carry your head without colliding too often with the ceiling. If you never collide, you are moving with your head too low. Also, with impressive scars and scuffs in your hardhat, people will believe you are an old-time hard-core caver rather than a greenhorn. However, when in low passages where speleothems line the ceiling, stay below them.

In many crawlways there will be a channel or groove in the ceiling. If you track along with your head up in that groove, you will spend less energy. In chest-compressors and belly crawls you may see experienced cavers remove their hardhats. The extra inch or so of headroom this provides may make a big difference in the ease of moving. Moving small loose pebbles out of one's way in chest-compressors is easy to do, saves much wear and tear on the body, but is often neglected.

Stay level. When you walk along a trunk passage or come to a room in a cave, there may be many routes ahead. You could climb to the bottom, go to the top, and

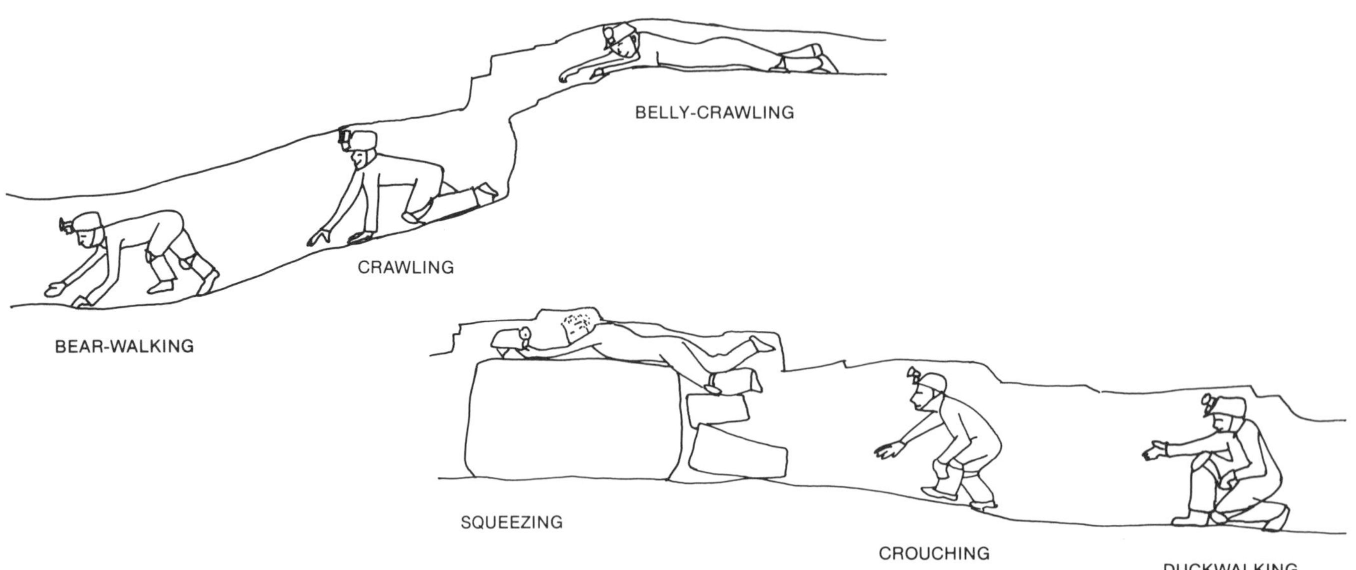

Fig. 12. Various methods for moving through a passage. (From *The Longest Cave* by Roger W. Brucker and Richard A. Watson, Cave Research Foundation, 1976, Copyrighted. Used by permission.)

so on. The energy-saving trick is to eyeball a level line from you to the place you want to go. It may take you over breakdown blocks and swing you wide of a direct bee-line. But the level route will require less energy to traverse. Pick out intermediate landmarks to head for to keep you straight on your course. The same applies to walking in a passage. If you encounter a rock, either step over it or walk around it, but do not use it as a stepping stone. This requires elevating the body and is a needless loss of energy.

Balance yourself. There are many different tricks to trim and balance yourself while moving and resting; all will give you an extra measure of energy. For example, you are crouching along through a low passage with your arms moving naturally along your sides. Bent over, you are unbalanced. To trim yourself, swing your pack over your buttocks and hold the straps in your hands locked together behind you. The redistribution of weight to your hips unloads your trunk and shoulders, and you feel you can almost fly through the passage with much less effort than you have been expending.

A related trick is to fit your pack with a waist strap in addition to a shoulder strap. Two straps distribute the weight for better balance. Be sure, however, that you can still move your pack around as a handy counterweight when you need to. Run some experiments climbing a steep, slippery slope and you will soon see that the pack, when moved around or held out from the body, can help or hinder your progress. In general, don't take your pack off except in the tightest passages.

Some cavers add counterweights to the back of their hardhats to balance the overhung weight of the lamp on the front. A way to balance yourself at rest is to remove your pack. If you are carrying a load, such as coiled ropes, try to distribute the load evenly on your body, or carry a load in each hand. With just a little thought, balancing will become automatic to you in nearly every caving situation.

Climb easier with layback methods. An experienced rock climber seems to flow up a cliff in one continuous liquid movement. If you watch each move closely, you will see a number of moves in which one muscle is pitted in opposition to another. For example, the climber may jam a fist back into a smooth-walled crack in the face. He then pulls outward with his arm and lifts with his shoulder as he pushes against the face with his feet. He literally walks upward. He is held on the face by the opposition of forces—pulling with the arm and pushing with the legs. He uses muscle power to overcome gravity. To be sure, a climber would soon tire from such exertion. Layback climbing, which uses this method, is for getting past places where there seem to be no handholds, or where overhangs project to block more direct moves.

There are many places in caves, and not just on pitches, where layback methods will conserve energy and make otherwise difficult maneuvers rather easy. One such instance is ascending a standing line on knots or mechanical ascenders to the place where the line bends over the protected edge of a drop. Getting over that lip is the problem. You could use brute-force. But the easier way is to grasp the standing line **above** the lip, pull with your arms, and push out with your feet in opposition. Your body will neatly swing out and upward, passing the lip in a smooth movement. The others will thrash and dangle, rip clothing, lose equipment from pockets, sweat and swear—while you just smile.

Don't save layback methods just for spectacular moves. Their real utility comes in the dozens of ways you steady yourself here and brace yourself there—where there are no apparent handholds. Variations include crossing ledges by pressing the ceiling with your fingers in opposition to your leg muscles on the ledge. Chimneying uses muscles in opposition, pressing outward on two sides to maintain your headway or position in slippery canyons. While the chimney moves seem natural, the layback moves do not, even though they operate the same way. Practice will make them second nature.

Catalog comfort tricks. A variety of ideas will make movement in a cave easier, even though the ideas don't seem to relate to moving along. For example, try to stay dry, but if you must wade eventually, don't spend energy avoiding wading. If you are going to spend a long time moving in water, take a salt tablet. Caving dehydrates the body and caving in water will chill the body. Dehydration plus chill causes cramps in some cavers, perhaps caused by insufficient electrolytes in the body. If you swallow a salt tablet, chances of cramping are reduced, and you will be able to move with ease.

Another trick related to chilling and the slow-down of movement that occurs is the use of the Palmer Furnace, as perfected by Arthur N. Palmer. When you are cold, you sit down. Remove your carbide lamp from your hardhat. Pull out your shirt from your body and hold the lamp at the bottom edge, so the heated air rises through the "chimney" created between your body and the stretched-out shirt. After a few minutes you will have a toasty, warm belly and a better attitude. Variations can involve crouching on all fours over the lamp, or having a friend hold the lamp under the back of your shirt. When you warm up, get moving again to restore energy.

Sit on your gloves when you pause to rest on a damp floor. That's another way to ward off chills, which rob energy. If you take off your gloves in a dry cave, lay them on your legs to keep them warm. Good knee pads also save energy. Mix up the way you move through long, monotonous passages; crawl on one side, then the other, then crouch, then roll. After you have caved for a while, you will have your own catalog of tricks for staying comfortable.

Look Where You Go

As we have seen, movement through a cave depends on seeing the cave—really seeing it. Some cavers will tell you

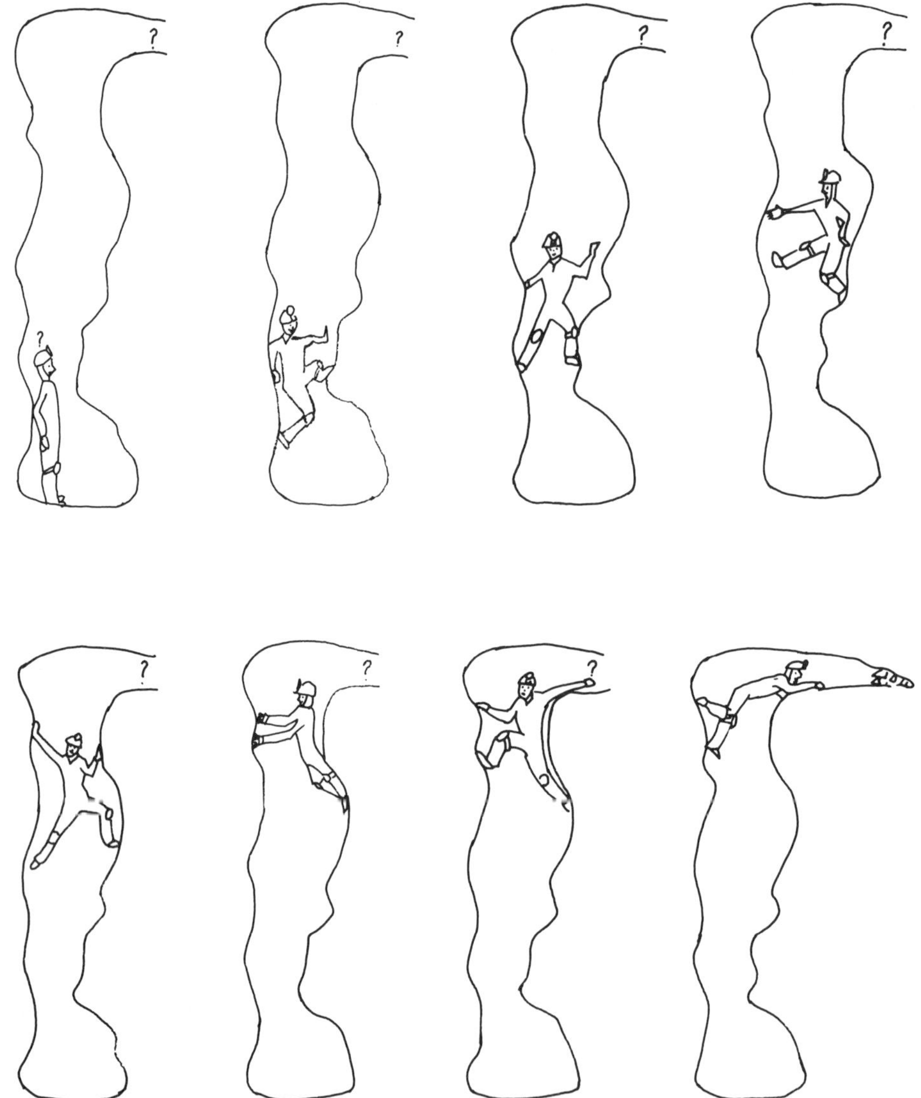

Fig. 13. Chimneying. (From *The Longest Cave* by Roger W. Brucker and Richard A. Watson, Cave Research Foundation, 1976. Copyrighted. Used by permission.)

that they only see a cave when they are surveying a passageway. The slower pace gives them time to find and observe things that they would miss by going along at a brisk pace. You may be in a party with other people, and thus may not be able to set the pace you want. That should not prevent you from sharpening your powers of observation.

Watch the caver in front of you. His lamp illuminates the route a good distance ahead. If he has trouble, learn from his experience.

Turn around frequently and look behind you. Passages often look entirely different heading the other way. When you come to a change in the character of the passage, see if you can spot the reason. Has the bedrock changed? In Mammoth Cave one time, Will White and George Deike were struck by a passage that changed abruptly from an oval tube to a rectangular cross section. By leveling, they also discovered that the slope had changed, too. They concluded they had found the place where a vadose water passage above the water table had turned into a phreatic water passage below the old water table. You, too, can find and solve puzzling mysteries in caves if you keep your eyes open.

One place to be especially wary is where passages join. Examine all junctions from different viewpoints. One practical reason to do this is that junctions are confusing, and if you have to lead the party out, you will want to be clear about which way to go. Prominent landmarks deserve a second look for the same reason. Watch that you don't make the mistake of one caver. He loudly named a rock in the middle of the passage Dog Rock, because you had to lift your leg to crawl over it. He didn't realize that other rocks in that passage and many others resembled it. When it came his turn to lead out, he blithely led the group down a passage he had never been in. He knew he was on the right route when he shouted "There's DOG ROCK!" Only it wasn't, as he found out an hour later when he gave up in disgust at being lost. Make sure landmarks are unique before you name them.

All this emphasis on leading out and not getting lost is not just related to safety. Many cavers never really look at a cave until they experience the hopeless feeling of being lost. Then, by god, they pay attention! The Cave Research Foundation has found that good cavers are ready to become good party leaders only after they have experienced the "Ahaa! I am lost!" feeling. Then, and only then, do they observe the cave clearly enough to travel through it responsibly.

The Marked Route

In the bad old days of long ago, cavers used to smoke direction arrows on the walls of passages, with the head usually pointing back toward the entrance. Marking walls is a form of vandalism that detracts from the natural appearance of the cave. But directional markers are sometimes placed in new discoveries until the cavers learn the routes.

In the Mammoth Cave System about a mile of virgin cave is discovered every month. Often, four or five different survey teams will move into it to chart and explore it. They will mark confusing junctions by building small cairns, with an adjacent rock pointing the way back toward known cave. Or a sharp-pointed rock may be propped up for the same purpose. Directional notes are written on paper and left. In a few very confusing junctions, the notes have been replaced with rectangles of cement board with permanent felt marker direction messages on them.

In some caves explorers leave route markers in the form of flags or bits of plastic survey marking tape. The general rule is to underdo it.

Getting Back Out

We have looked at ways of making movement in caves easy, and at ways of seeing the cave and remaining oriented. But what about those situations that can restrict or eliminate movement in caves? (Death is nature's way of telling you to slow down.)

Elsewhere safety is discussed at length. Yet, no consideration of moving through caves would be complete without commenting on dangerous situations.

Floyd Collins considered himself an expert caver. Yet, in 1925 he got himself trapped in a cave. He died there, despite earnest rescue efforts. Never mind that he violated every rule of caving, the point is he got into a situation where nobody could help him. There was no room to crawl past his body, which completely filled the solid rock tube in which he was encased. The rescuers found themselves in crawlways the size of wastebaskets —with no room to move. The moral, of course, is don't move into anything you can't get out of, and especially into places where nobody can rescue you.

If you come to a pit and you can see a passage leading off down at the bottom, don't plunge in. Ask yourself, "How will I get out?" and "What if we all get down and the rope breaks?" When you have figured out the worst that can happen, you may be ready to brave the unknown with common sense and a healthy respect for the risks.

If all this sounds like fear to you, you may recognize that we have nearly returned to our starting point. Some cavers psyche themselves up by studying maps, others by cleaning and packing their equipment. To paraphrase a famous explorer, "The caver who meets the unexpected is unprepared." If you try out these ideas about moving in caves, if you keep your eyes open, and if you think about what you are experiencing in a cave, you'll love to come back again and again.

CAVING SAFETY

Ray Cole
NSS 12460

Introduction

Your chances of serious injury or even death while caving can be reduced by being aware of the dangers involved, by having adequate knowledge of equipment and techniques, and by cultivating good caving sense. Unfortunately for many, the needed knowledge comes only after years of caving experience and association with other cavers.

Caving accidents are statistically most attributable to poor judgement, little or no caving experience, and falls. Important reading for all cavers should be the annual reports on *American Caving Accidents*, edited and published by the NSS. Since the same types of accidents keep repeating themselves, needless deaths and injuries might be prevented if every caver read just one of these yearly reports.

Dangers in Caving

The most common caving accidents include: drowning, falling, being struck by falling objects and hypothermia.

Drowning. Unfortunately, accidents related to caves flooding often result in fatalities. Many of the deaths could be avoided and are the result of inexperienced cavers **ignoring the signs of rising water** and entering caves that are known to flood. Some caves flood so quickly that they are safe to enter only in the coldest winter weather when surface water is frozen. However, caves often flood due to rapid melting of snow when a sudden weather change occurs. This is especially true when rain falls on frozen and/or snow-covered ground and natural water absorption is prevented. As a result of this, large quantities of run-off can flow directly into low-lying cave entrances. The experienced caver looks for the telltale signs of a cave that floods. Some of these are: low-lying caves that drain large surface areas with either dry or active streams present; organic material lodged in crevices in the walls and ceiling of the cave. If you are ever trapped in a flood cave, head for the highest section possible. Several cavers have drowned while trying to leave a flooding cave instead of retreating to safety.

Flooding is not the only cause of drownings in caves. Cavers have always been challenged by sumps (where the ceiling dips below the water level) and the alluring quest for what lies beyond. Whether using scuba equipment or free diving, going through a sump is risky business. The dangers associated with this include bad air when resurfacing, disorientation, no visibility due to disturbed sediment and underwater mazes. If you need to go through a sump, it is recommended that you contact members of the Cave Diving Section of the NSS for proper advice and training.

Falling. To reduce the risk of falling, one should avoid jumping and uncontrolled sliding down slopes, wear proper footwear, check and discard any faulty or worn vertical equipment, obtain proper training in the use of vertical equipment, use a proper belay when exposure dictates, always use a belay on a cable ladder, and use common sense.

Falling Objects. Accidents caused by falling objects are best avoided by **always wearing** a helmet, staying clear of the base of drops and climbs, and securing all items of equipment so that they will not drop on cavers below.

Hypothermia. The temperature of the body core is about 98° F. If this temperature drops more than a few degrees, the body can no longer function properly. Even if placed in a warmer environment, the body core temperature may continue to drop, resulting in certain death unless the condition can be reversed. This condition, called hypothermia, or exposure as it has often been referred to in the past, can kill the unprepared and unexpecting. A factor in many caves that accelerates the loss of body heat is the presence of water. A person immersed in 54° F. water has about 2½ hours to live but loses the ability and will to function normally much sooner. The most common situation where hypothermia occurs is climbing in waterfalls, where, for reason of fatigue or equipment failure, the caver is no longer able to climb or descend. Without assistance from his caving companions, death is the usual disastrous result. The situation is best avoided by rigging drops out of waterfalls when possible, and by using wet suits when lengthy exposure to water is required or anticipated.

Other Hazards. Not all caving problems involve injuries. A few people do get lost in caves, become stuck, or are unable to climb up a ledge or rope to get out of the cave. Exhaustion and a lack of light (or light failure) may cause someone to become lost who might otherwise have found his own way out of the cave.

Serious cavers seldom become lost in caves since they keep careful track of their whereabouts and are careful to note important landmarks in the cave. An easy place to get confused is at the intersection of two passages, one smaller than the other. It can be harder than one might think to find the smaller passage. By leaving a highly visible arrow made from reflective tape, the location is easily found again. The reflective marker can be picked up on the way out and used again.

Everybody gets stuck occasionally when caving and it doesn't take a new caver long to learn to remain calm and in control when it happens. In some cases extra clothing can be removed so that a little extra clearance can be obtained.

Potential hazards in the cave other than the cave itself may involve the equipment carried by cavers. The flame of a carbide lamp, the most common piece of equipment, can cause serious burns. Another common situation occurs when the base of the carbide lamp has not been screwed on tightly or a poor gasket is used and gas escaping around the bottom suddenly bursts into flames. A burned hand may result when the startled caver reaches for the lamp without first extinguishing the flame.

Electric lamps are not without their problems. A shorted headpiece with a high current capacity battery could produce a dangerously hot cord. All such cords should have an in-line fuse. Leaking acid electrolyte from lead acid batteries can dangerously weaken nylon ropes and slings used for vertical caving.

Caving Emergencies

What do you do when something goes wrong during your caving trip? Most situations of injury or a disabled person are dealt with by members of the group involved. If the group is not able to handle the situation, it will be necessary to bring in outside help. Suddenly, you realize just how alien the cave environment can be. Caves are often located in remote areas away from roads, population centers, and the local rescue squads that the modern city dweller too often takes for granted. To further complicate matters, help could be needed in an area that is many hours into the cave, beyond crawls and down drops, making the removal of an injured person a difficult technical problem.

When needing assistance you can either wait until someone comes looking for you, or you can send two people for help. If you send for help, you must have one person stay with the injured person. The two cavers going for help should leave any extra supplies, including clothing. For this reason a **caving party of four** should be considered as a **minimum group** and, of course, you should never cave alone.

The primary objective is not to rush the victim out of the cave, but to keep him alive (to stabilize the victim). First aid should be administered. All cavers should have first aid training. Extra clothes should be placed under the injured person to prevent heat loss due to conduction. Keeping an injured person warm is vital since he will probably be in shock. Large plastic trash bags make nice bivouac shelters, especially with the warm glow of a carbide lamp inside. Don't burn yourself or the victim and leave a vent hole for a little air circulation. A "people sandwich" is a good way to keep warm. To achieve this effect place a person on either side of the injured party.

When members of the party seeking help reach the surface, they usually will rely on the telephone to communicate their need. Many parts of the country have special telephone numbers for the purpose of coordinating cave rescues. If the number is not known for your caving area, call the local sheriff. Whoever is called must be told that it is a caving emergency and you must state the nature of the emergency. Make sure they have the telephone number of the phone you are calling from. Have someone available at that phone until the rescue has been completed. In addition to local rescue personnel, the local law enforcement authorities in caving areas may have information on area cavers as well as the regional cave rescue coordination number to call for additional assistance.

If you are using a pay phone and have limited change, tell the operator that it is an emergency and he or she will stay on the line with you, allowing as many calls as necessary. It is vital that the persons calling for assistance remain where they can be found by the rescuers, and that they be available to lead teams and equipment to the victim. Hopefully, the people with the necessary skills and equipment will soon be on the scene to successfully complete the rescue operation.

An opportune time to rally your fellow cavers and/or grotto members to do the things that should have been done to prevent an accident is soon after an accident has occurred. The first of these is a training program for new cavers. This is a good chance for the old timers to brush up on the basics, as well as to assist the new cavers. A good outline for this course might be this manual. Don't forget, caver training must include training trips to caves.

You should find out where first aid training is available in your area and encourage members of your group to enroll and learn essential life-saving skills. First aid courses are available through the American Red Cross and Emergency Medical Technician programs.

Learn the telephone numbers for cave rescue coordination in the areas in which you go caving. Publish these numbers in your newsletter frequently. Print them on small cards that can be carried easily and distribute them to local cavers. Groups wishing to participate in cave rescue should contact the National Cave Rescue Commission of the NSS.

Preparation

The best way to promote safety is to start before the caving trip. Consider these points: get yourself in shape;

caving is a strenuous activity. Learn all you can about the cave you will visit and pick caving companions carefully. When selecting your caving companions, consider what the others would do if something happened to you. A minimum of four cavers in a party is best. Now consider the basic items of equipment used for caving.

Equipment

What to take along on a trip depends on the nature of the cave, expected length of trip, special personal requirements and experience. Experienced cavers just take along what they will need plus adequate equipment for emergencies. Today, the trend in caving is to pack light so you can go fast and far. Thus, it becomes even more important to consider each item of equipment for safety.

The helmet should have a lamp bracket, cord loop on the rear for electric lights, and a quick release chin strap.

Cavers should have boots with good support that come at least up to the ankle. While lug soles are good for walking on rock with small scree, they will pick up large quantities of sticky cave mud. They should not have metal hooks which will catch on cable ladders. Tennis shoes do not give adequate support or provide much protection.

For the primary light source, carbide or electric lamps are most commonly used. It is essential that this light source fit on the helmet to allow two hands free for caving. At least two backup sources of light such as an extra carbide lamp, flashlights or chemical lights should always be carried. If a flashlight is used as one backup, you should have spare batteries and bulbs. Ordinary carbon-zinc batteries should not be used for caving since they have a short shelf life and may have very limited capacity when used. The alkaline variety hold their charge much longer and provide added capacity for an extra margin of safety.

Include fuel and parts for all light sources. For carbide cavers this means an adequate supply of carbide in a strong, waterproof container, water, container for spent carbide, extra tips and felts. A spare base containing carbide is useful for a quick change. Tiny pliers are helpful to replace tips and a tip cleaner or reamer is necessary. Electric cavers need extra bulbs, small knife, screwdriver and any special items required to service their equipment.

It is a good idea to include with your first aid equipment items that are necessary for survival in the cave if unexpected events lengthen your stay. Survival items include: large plastic bags or space blanket, high energy food, waterproof matches, candles and whistle. Another use of a first aid kit is to treat those minor ailments and injuries that, while not life threatening, often occur. While not essential, these include: aspirin, band-aids and an elastic bandage for sprains. Another category of first-aid equipment is necessary for dealing with life threatening bodily injury. Here the contents depend somewhat on the expertise of the caver, but every kit should contain these minimum items: change for at least two telephone calls, sterile dressings, razor blade and/or scissors, adhesive tape and butterfly closures.

While being far from an adequate amount of medical supplies for treating injuries, this is about all the average caver is willing to pack with him. If much more is added and the kit isn't used often, it will soon be left out of the cave pack. The remaining essential items needed for treating serious injuries would have to be improvised. For example, bandages and cravats can be made by cutting strips out of clothing. Likewise, a makeshift splint can be improvised by rolling heavy items of clothing. Far more important than any supplies on hand is knowing the right thing to do.

Package the first-aid items in a waterproof container. Individually packaged items are more likely to survive the rigors of caving. After each trip replace items that have become damaged.

If you require special medication, be sure to have it with you and inform the other members of your group of this fact.

Food for a short caving trip need not provide all the nutrient and vitamin content found in your daily diet. The cave food should be high in carbohydrates and sugar to supply the large energy requirements the body needs while caving. An extra ration of high energy food is good to have just in case your stay in the cave is longer than expected.

The Trip

After having found out about the cave to be visited, you will probably put together your equipment in advance to make sure you'll have everything you need. You can make a checklist to be sure.

Explain your caving plans to another caver or your family. Make sure that these people know who to call if the need arises. In the unlikely event you do not return by the allotted time, they will make arrangements to get help to you. You must realize that they can only do this if your plans have been explicit. As a caver you must be cautious about **meeting your schedule** if you are going to expect help when needed. Have at least one waterproof watch in the party.

After all the training, planning and packing, it is quite a relief to finally get into the cave. Once in the cave the most difficult decision most cavers face is when to start out. Generally, if any member of the party indicates it's time to start out, then you should do so. Caving should not be made a do or die activity. Know your group's ability and learn not to push their physical endurance.

SAFE CAVING

CAVE CONSERVATION

Tom Strong
NSS 9110F

The Importance of Cave Conservation

When entering a cave for the first time, a person quickly realizes that a cave is a unique environment. The effects of time and water are evident in ways that cannot be seen on the surface. The original dissolution of the limestone and the reverse process of calcite deposition lead to strange and beautiful formations (speleothems), some massive, some incredibly delicate. The absence of light has allowed the evolution of life forms adapted to live in an environment of total darkness.

The uniqueness of the caving experience often leads to a fascination and a desire to return to caves and to learn more about them. It is likely that a person's first several trips will be to caves which are heavily visited. Caves of this type make all too obvious the effects of heavy traffic by persons who often have little appreciation of the caves' beauty. The floors could be littered with all imaginable types of trash and garbage, the walls covered with signatures and other graffiti, and streams and pools may be black with pollution. All of these things should make the need for cave conservation obvious to anyone with a sensitivity for and an appreciation of the natural environment.

Recognizing a need for conservation is only the first step in the process. It is also important to find out what can be done to prevent these abuses of caves and what steps may be taken to restore a cave which has been vandalized. The next few pages will attempt to provide some answers to these questions and to increase the conservation awareness of beginning and experienced cavers.

NSS Conservation Policy

The National Speleological Society is an organization dedicated to the exploration, study and conservation of caves. Of these three goals, conservation should take priority, because without conservation there may, someday, be nothing left worth exploring or studying. Caves must be considered a finite, essentially non-renewable resource, and at present their rate of destruction by vandalism is much greater than their rate of growth. It is clear that unless active steps are taken to reverse this trend, all readily accessible caves will be badly damaged.

The NSS position on cave conservation is summarized in the following policy statement adopted by the Board of Governors on December 28, 1960:

"The National Speleological Society believes: That caves have unique scientific, recreational, and scenic values; That these values are endangered by both carelessness and intentional vandalism; That these values, once gone, cannot be recovered; and that the responsibility for protecting caves must be assumed by those who study and enjoy them.

"Accordingly, the intention of the Society is to work for the preservation of caves with a realistic policy supported by effective programs for: the encouragement of self-discipline among cavers; education and research concerning the causes and prevention of cave damage; and special projects, including cooperation with other groups similarly dedicated to the conservation of natural areas. Specifically:

"All contents of a cave—formations, life and loose deposits—are significant for its enjoyment and interpretation. Therefore, caving parties should leave a cave as they find it. They should provide means for the removal of waste; limit marking to a few, small and removable signs as are needed for surveys; and, especially, exercise extreme care not to accidentally break or soil formations, disturb life forms, or unnecessarily increase the number of disfiguring paths through an area.

"Scientific collection is professional, selective, and minimal. The collection of mineral or biological material for display purposes, including previously broken or dead specimens, is never justified, as it encourages others to collect and destroys the interest of the cave.

"The Society encourages projects such as: establishing cave preserves; placing entrance gates where appropriate; opposing the sale of speleothems; supporting effective protective measures; cleaning and restoring over-used caves; cooperating with private cave owners by providing knowledge about their cave and assisting them in protecting their cave and property from damage during cave visits; and encouraging commercial cave owners to make use of their opportunity to aid the public in understanding caves and the importance of their conservation.

"Where there is reason to believe that publication of cave locations will lead to vandalism before adequate protection can be established, the Society will oppose such publication.

"It is the duty of every Society member to take personal responsibility for spreading a consciousness of cave conservation to each potential user of caves. Without this, the beauty and value of our caves will not long remain with us."

This statement gives an excellent summary of the conservation goals of the NSS, but it might be worthwhile to go into more detail in some areas.

Geological Values of Caves

Speleothems, the water-deposited crystalline rocks found in many caves, are among the most noticeable features of a cave and contribute greatly to the aesthetic value of a cave. These mineral deposits are also highly vulnerable to intentional vandalism. If you have read this far, you are probably not likely to deliberately deface a cave, but the point cannot be overemphasized: Speleothems belong inside caves, not drying out on someone's mantel or collecting dust in a mineral collection. There is nothing to be gained by removing speleothems, but the caves will be the losers and the experience of all subsequent visitors will be lessened.

The same may be said for defacing a cave with graffiti or litter. We have no right to destroy in a few minutes features that have developed over centuries. This rule applies not only to all deposits in caves but also to bare walls. Seemingly blank walls may on closer inspection reveal delicate crystalline features, fossils, or scallops and other solutional features. Bare walls are generally much more useful than speleothems in interpreting the geologic history and structure of caves.

Speleothems may also be susceptible to unintentional damage, as well as to deliberate vandalism. This type of damage is often caused by cavers who fail to use proper care in travelling through a cave. There are probably very few cavers who have not broken a stalactite by turning their heads at the wrong time. The floor of a cave may suffer greatly from careless or excessive traffic. The most obvious example might be muddy footprints across white flowstone. This mud has a tendency to get into small pores in the flowstone and cannot easily be washed off. Selenite needles and gypsum flowers may be destroyed by a single careless step. Calcite raft deposits, cave pearls and rimstone dams are among the other formations on cave floors which may be damaged.

Unintentional damage will never be totally eliminated, but it can be minimized by using extra care while moving through a cave. Taking the time to see exactly where you are stepping will not slow you down too much, and it may allow you to see and appreciate features which might have been overlooked otherwise. In decorated areas, particularly in virgin passages, it is best to travel single file so that the whole group will leave only one set of footprints. Indiscriminate wandering around should be avoided. Occasionally, conscientious cavers find it necessary to remove muddy boots before crossing white flowstone or other formations. Clean socks, or even bare feet, are much less likely to cause damage.

The physical fitness of a caver can also affect the amount of unintentional damage. A tired caver is more likely to be careless and clumsy and may not have the mental alertness to prevent damage. This factor should be considered when making long trips; extra time and care should be taken in delicate areas.

Cave photography is another potential source of unintentional vandalism. There is no justification for having someone walk out onto a fragile area merely to pose for a picture, and objects (e.g. lens caps or pocket knives) should not be placed on delicate speleothems for scale. The NSS Photo Salon has rejected work which displayed poor conservation practices. Another procedure to be avoided is that of unnecessary movement in speleothem areas in order to get a better angle for a camera or flash. Although this practice is not normally obvious from the results, it can easily result in needless damage. Photography should not be considered more important than preservation of the cave resources.

Vertical cavers also need to use extra care to minimize damage to a cave. Safety is the primary consideration when rigging pits or using artificial climbing aids, but conservation practices should not be ignored. Maybe a little more effort would be needed to rig a pit to avoid a wall covered with speleothems, but it shouldn't be necessary to ask whether it's worth it. While rappelling or climbing, special care should be taken to know where one's body and the rope are at all times to avoid inadvertent damage to fragile features, particularly at overhangs. If possible, it is desirable to use natural rigging points, but if an artificial anchor must be set, do it right the first time and leave it. The syndrome of every party placing its own bolts should be avoided. For safety's sake, as well as for conservation, any rigging left in a cave should not be susceptible to rusting or rotting. However, use judgment before rigging your rope on an old bolt. Another practice that should be minimized is the dropping of rocks down pits. While this action is a useful way to estimate the depth of a new pit, dropping rocks just to hear them hit the bottom serves no useful purpose and may cause damage to the cave. It may also have fatal effects on cave life.

Cave surveyors must also be careful not to damage a cave by their activities, particularly in the placement of survey stations. If a survey is done properly and completely, there will be no need to recover most of the stations, so they should require no marking whatsoever. As with vertical caving, it's easiest on the cave to do things right the first time. If it is necessary to leave a "permanent" station, it should be done with the idea of removing it when no longer needed. In dry caves, a small dot with the station number written inconspicuously is usually sufficient. While this marking may be difficult for later teams to recover, preservation of the cave must take priority over ease of surveying. In wet caves, flagging tape or reflective tape on popsicle sticks may be used to mark stations. In caves which flood regularly, a small drill hole is possible, but the station must be chosen carefully so there will be no obvious damage to the cave. The use of large numbers written with a carbide lamp is generally neither necessary nor acceptable from a conservation standpoint. Similarly, brass caps set in concrete, either inside caves or at entrances, are totally unnecessary and their use should be avoided.

Another question which comes up occasionally during exploration is whether to break speleothems to check out a new lead. I won't attempt to give an absolute answer but I will suggest a few thoughts to consider if you are faced with this decision. What is the possibility of an alternate route into the lead? What is the possibility that the lead will go into a major extension, based on a survey or on geological considerations? Will the lead go back into a previously known section of the cave? What value do you place on the formations in the way—are they "one-of-a-kind," or are they quite common? How many other leads do you know of that don't require any destruction? Finally, a decision not to push the lead can be changed at any time, but breaking a formation is permanent.

Many of these factors should be considered when digging to extend a cave or open a new cave. It should also be noted that opening a new passage may have a severe effect on the climatic conditions, turning a wet cave into a dry cave, or vice versa. Another question to ask is whether exploration justifies any means needed to accomplish it.

Biological Values of Caves

The unique environment of caves provides a habitat for many highly specialized life forms which are very susceptible to human disturbance. Bats are often among the most noticeable animals in caves. Bat populations, particularly in the large colonies of the southwest, have declined in recent years due to the extensive use of agricultural pesticides. Many species of bats are currently listed as threatened or endangered species, (and as such are protected by the Endangered Species Act of 1972) and many caves provide critical habitats. Bats need all the friends they can get, and cavers should avoid disturbing them unnecessarily. Bats are especially vulnerable to disturbance during hibernation or when in nursing colonies, and moratoriums have been declared on visits to several caves to give the bats extra protection during critical periods.

Less noticeable than bats, but even more a part of the cave, are troglobites, those animals which are fully adapted to life in total darkness. These creatures, having lost vision and pigmentation through evolution, would be unable to survive outside the cave environment. This high degree of specialization makes them very sensitive to any changes in their surroundings. Cave-adapted life forms also tend to be quite small due to the limited food supply and may easily go unnoticed by a party of cavers. Special care must be taken to avoid harming the cave life. The most obvious hazard is that terrestrial forms could be stepped on and crushed, but this danger can be reduced by watching where you put your feet. Cave animals are also vulnerable in other ways. Dumping garbage in a cave may provide an extra food source, but it is an unnatural source and is likely to upset the delicate ecological balance within a cave. Dumping carbide in caves must also be avoided, for more than aesthetic reasons. Spent carbide is actually calcium hydroxide, a strong base and a poison to the cave life. If you're able to carry fresh carbide into a cave, there is no excuse for not carrying the spent carbide out. Also do not dump your spent carbide outside of the cave for it can harm livestock and wild animals as well.

Caves can provide a valuable laboratory for scientists studying ecological systems. Cave ecosystems are often simple enough that all factors influencing them can be known and examined individually. There is a danger to cave animals from over-eager collectors and pseudo-scientists who collect as many individuals and species from a cave as possible without considering the consequences. Because a cave may be a totally isolated ecosystem, evolution may have produced species which are restricted to a single cave. In a case such as this, the removal of only a few individuals might endanger the continued survival of a species. Indiscriminate collecting could also upset the ecological balance of a cave and break the food chain. Biological collecting should generally be left to experienced professionals, or persons being directed by them, engaged in specific studies.

Archeological, Paleontological and Historical Values of Caves

Because of their constant climatic conditions, caves are excellent sites for the preservation of archeological and paleontological remains. Much of the data on the life style of early man has been obtained from caves around the world. A number of caves contain large collections of Pleistocene animal bones. Many caves in the western United States contain pack rat middens, some of which have been dated at up to 40,000 years old (personal communication, Dr. Paul Martin, Univ. of Ariz., 1975). These middens may provide a continuous record of the environment in the vicinity of the cave.

Archeological and paleontological material may be present in a cave without the average caver being aware of its existence. The material is frequently buried in sediments near cave entrances, and it may tolerate a limited amount of traffic over the surface. If artifacts or other remains are found in a cave, great care should be taken to avoid any disturbance. Under no circumstances should the average caver remove any of this material or attempt to dig out more artifacts. The context in which something is found is often more important to a scientist than the material itself, and digging by the untrained could destroy valuable relationships. Archeological or paleontological finds should be reported to appropriate state agencies or universities, but don't be disappointed if the scientists don't rush right out to dig up what you have found. Conservation of these resources is just as difficult as cave conservation, and new sites are frequently left intact until there is a specific reason for digging them.

Historical artifacts in caves also deserve protection. The most obvious examples might be the remains of the saltpeter operations in eastern and southeastern caves. In addition to various state laws, the Federal Antiquities Act protects historical material as well as archeological material. Historical remains are generally obvious to the typical caver, and damage can be prevented by leaving the material alone. Wooden material in a damp environment will rot and even a minor contact could result in its destruction. The distinction between historical material and vandalism is often nothing more than age, which necessitates some discretion when working on clean-up projects.

Positive Action for Cave Conservation

Active cave conservation requires more than just avoiding breaking anything when you move through a cave. Cleaning up or rehabilitating a cave that has been vandalized and trying to prevent vandalism before it occurs are positive steps toward conserving cave resources.

Cave clean-up projects can range from a single member in a group carrying a trash bag in a cave pack to several groups working together to clean out a badly vandalized cave. Water and wire brushes may be used to clean graffiti off of walls and formations. In particularly difficult situations, dilute acid solutions have been used to remove graffiti. A certain amount of discretion is necessary when working with acid to avoid causing more damage than is removed. The acid works by dissolving the calcite and may cause some disfigurement of the speleothems. If hydrochloric acid is used, a by-product of the reaction is calcium chloride which is poisonous to cave life and may promote cementation of cave sediments. Acids also give off poisonous vapors which could be hazardous in an enclosed area. Dr. Rane Curl (1977) suggests that sulfuric acid would be a better choice of acid. Its reaction with limestone produces gypsum, already common in caves, and it doesn't give off any noxious fumes. Dilute sulfuric acid by adding the acid slowly to the water.

Cave restoration projects go beyond simple clean-up operations as attempts are made to restore a cave to its original condition. In addition to removing trash, spent carbide and graffiti, efforts have been made to wash mud off of formations and to rebuild broken formations with epoxy. In some cases, trails have been laid out in order to direct traffic around fragile areas. Large-scale restoration projects often require the cooperation of several grottos or many individuals.

Direct efforts to prevent vandalism may include such things as confronting potential vandals inside caves and trying to convince them of the merits of cave conservation. This approach may be very difficult, but it can provide good results. Another method for controlling vandalism is to restrict access to a cave. This procedure is used by many state and federal agencies who require permits to visit caves. Grottos have frequently provided gating assistance and management recommendations to these agencies. Some grottos have gained the control of access to caves through lease agreements in order to limit access to qualified, conscientious cavers. A policy of secrecy has been fairly effective in preventing vandalism. If vandals don't know where a cave is or, more important, don't even know of a cave's existence, they can't destroy it. A corollary to secrecy is the opposition to cave lists. These lists usually contain very little, if any, scientific information. Effective use of secrecy as a conservation tool does require a fair amount of discretion. If used improperly, it may create bad feelings between individuals or groups and might result in an increase in traffic and damage to a cave.

Grottos can be instrumental in the formulation of state cave protection laws and the enactment of legislation protecting caves and the contents of caves. Such laws could also require public hearing on any construction projects that would endanger a cave.

One more approach, which may in the long run be most effective in cave preservation, is education, although it doesn't yield immediate or measurable results. If people can be made aware of the aesthetic and scientific values of the cave environment, they are less likely to cause damage to a cave. They may even spread the word to others. Education can be on an individual basis, such as the confrontation inside a cave as mentioned above. Grottos or other caving groups can give conservation presentations to outdoor-oriented groups, such as Boy Scout troops or high school outing clubs, who might be involved in caving. Occasionally these groups can be encouraged to participate in clean-up projects. Efforts should also be made to get other conservation organizations involved in cave preservation.

In summary, cave conservation is an on-going problem which requires continual effort. It requires a knowledge of the resources within caves, the threats to these resources and methods for countering these threats. Everyone with an interest in caves must be willing to share the task of their preservation.

Reference

Curl, R. (1977)—Letter to the editor: NSS News **35**:41.

LANDOWNER RELATIONS

Guy Turenne
NSS 11443

STOP and THINK—How would you act if you were on your own property?

As a caver, landowner relations are something you may not yet have dealt with. Even among active and experienced cavers, it is a facet of caving that is often given secondary consideration. The first thing a caver should learn is that, **without access, you do not go caving.** In the eastern part of the country, over 90% of the known caves are located on private property. In the western caving areas this figure is reversed, the majority of caves being on public property. However, public property does not imply free access. Each geographic area has its own special problems. Be it private landowner or public agency, it is **essential that a cordial relationship be maintained**, or else caves will be closed to your visitation.

In dealing with caves on public (state or federal) land, it is often necessary to obtain permission from the particular agency involved—the National Park Service, U.S. Forest Service, Bureau of Land Management, state or federal game and fisheries agencies, etc. Many times the area involved may be under various use restrictions. A good example of restricted use to a caver is a gated entrance. In this instance the gate may serve to protect endangered bats during certain critical times of the year. At other times access may be available, however, it may be required that you sign personal injury waivers. This type of information is available from the particular area's superintendent. In many instances federal agencies are now requiring that a permit be obtained in writing prior to the actual cave trip (sometimes months prior) and then that you check in with a ranger on the day of the cave trip itself.

Caves are closed by their owners for a variety of reasons. Common ones are visitors leaving trash in the area, leaving gates open, driving across fields or not getting permission. Some less common reasons are immoral or provocative behavior offensive to the landowner, such as cavers changing clothes in public view, rowdy partying and caving on Sunday.

Establishing good relations with the private landowner can be as simple as being courteous or as difficult as convincing a previously maltreated landowner to reopen his cave. It is always much easier to prevent the problem than to rectify it. At times it may seem that each landowner is different, but there are certain basics for dealing with all of them.

The first thing to remember is that the landowner

controls access to his land. You have no God-given right to cross his land, posted or otherwise, without permission. In most cases simply stating your purpose and requesting permission will suffice to gain entry. Occasionally, you may be required to convince the owner of your competence. A local grotto or NSS membership card may be useful in these situations. When talking to the landowner, remember to treat him as your equal. If you make him feel uncomfortable, you probably will not get into his cave.

The following are some general rules for dealing with the landowner and questions you should ask. All of these basic questions should be asked; do not take anything for granted.

1. Always get the **owner's permission** to enter the cave. After several visits, the owner may indicate it is no longer necessary to stop and ask. Even so, you should stop on occasion just to say hello. Do not abuse your privilege. Remember, in many states you can be arrested for trespassing if you do not have permission.
2. **Park your car** where the owner indicates. If he expresses no preference, park in an unobtrusive area. Remember you may have permission to cross the land, but your vehicle may not. The landowner may not like pulling your car out of a freshly plowed field.
3. **Do not leave litter** in your wake; livestock may investigate and wind up eating something they shouldn't. Especially do not leave spent carbide outside the cave. Try to leave the area cleaner than you found it.
4. **Leave gates as you find them**. They are open or closed for a reason. However, if you notice gates or fences that are broken, the landowner might like to hear about it.
5. Above all, **do not wear out your welcome** by visiting the cave too often. Hordes of people, even if careful, can cause damage which is cumulative.

If you are travelling to an unfamiliar area, try to contact a local caver or grotto concerning access to various caves. If there is any doubt about getting into a cave, try to call the landowner prior to driving several hours. It is difficult to be considerate to a landowner if you have driven several hours and then are told "no." It should be noted that many grottos and regions of the NSS maintain closed cave lists. Try to consult these lists before planning a trip. In many cases individuals are working to reopen a particular cave you may be interested in. Additions and deletions occur regularly. Try to be informed. If a cave is on the closed cave list, do not try to go in. Appendix A is a sample of a closed cave list (first two pages only) from the Virginia Region. The entire list is ten pages long and lists over 250 caves. As you can see, poor landowner relations are a big problem for cavers and this sample is from just a small section of the country. This list is updated every six months, and, unfortunately, keeps growing longer.

Once you have gained entry to the cave, it is wise to promote good will by showing concern for both the cave and the owner. Most owners like to talk about their cave. Sit down and take time to talk with them. If you are a good photographer, provide them with some pictures. If you are into mapping, provide the owner with a copy upon its completion.

Certain caves become very popular for a number of reasons; they are photogenic, technically difficult, etc. In this case some landowners get tired of seeing hordes of people every weekend. At this point it becomes advantageous to take an active interest in the owner's well being. A far-reaching example would be to donate some of your time some weekend to help fix a gate or a fence. In one instance a grotto purchased a new aluminum pasture gate and installed it free of charge. This goes a long way towards promoting good will. If you have a favorite landowner, you might consider inviting him to a grotto picnic or banquet. The better he knows you, the better off you are.

On a larger scale one group of cavers periodically has a get-together with the landowners from their area, featuring a cookout and a slide show of the various caves and what the group has been up to since the last cookout. On another occasion a group of cavers provided a landowner with an accurate survey that enabled the landowner to drill a successful well.

When visiting commercial caves, cavers should act and dress like the normal visitor. Hardhats and muddy coveralls are not normal on a commercial tour. Cave guides are not usually cavers at heart. Do not make fun of them or correct them in front of a group. The guide is probably following a pre-drafted talk furnished by the cave management. If there are gross misinterpretations of cave features, a casual talk with the management might be a good idea, but be prepared to back up your talk with facts. Do not brag about seeing better speleothems in nearby wild caves.

As you can see, maintaining good landowner relations can be as simple as picking up your trash or as involved as you care to make it. The more you do for the landowner, the more he will do for you. Common sense goes a long way in dealing with landowners.

FITNESS AND NUTRITION

Louise Hose

NSS 13138F

Fitness

The most important piece of equipment a caver can possess is a fit body. Fitness is defined as the ability to accomplish a task with a reasonable degree of efficiency without undue fatigue. Adequate fitness of all members of a caving party often makes the difference between a pleasurable experience and a miserable time. Cavers' fitness should be sufficient not only for their usual caving activities, but also for emergency situations where someone's survival may depend on the fitness level of the other cavers in the group.

Judging a person's fitness by their bulging muscles or ability to run a mile under six minutes is a popular misconception. Fitness is specific to the task to be performed. It does not describe a general state of health. Top professional athletes, highly fit for their vocations, have been given general physical fitness tests and have been judged to be unfit in their cardiovascular endurance or muscular strength not specifically required by their sport.

Knowledge of Fitness

Knowledge of what fitness is makes it easy for you to improve your level of fitness for caving. There are two simple ways to change from unfit to fit without much time commitment or special training. The first way is to reduce the intensity of activity. If you feel unfit to keep up on an eight-hour exploratory trip, perhaps beginner training trips or family-oriented trips would be more appropriate.

A second way to improve your fitness without training is to improve your efficiency. Moving through a cave or up a rope at a slow but steady pace is more efficient than moving quickly and taking frequent rest breaks. The human body is most efficient when, like all machines, it works at a constant rate. You should pace your speed and stop only infrequently. When rest stops are needed or desired, it's best if they are brief. After starting any strenuous physical activity, it takes a while for the circulorespiratory system to catch up to the demands of the body. If you stop for long, the heart slows down. This makes it more difficult to resume activity at the previous level. The same principles, of course apply equally to the hike to the cave and to in-cave activities.

The state of your fitness depends on a number of factors. These include the suitability of your body structure for the work to be performed, the effectiveness with which your organs and systems support the effort, and your view of the task while approaching it and carrying it to completion.

Anatomical Fitness

The first of these is termed anatomical fitness. This refers to the shape and size of your body. It becomes obvious in caving that a 48-inch chest and tight crawlways are not compatible. Tall cavers often have an advantage in many climbs. But tight chimneys may give the advantage to short cavers. Because of the great variety of activities involved in caving, it is impossible to describe the perfect body type as is often done in other sports.

Perhaps the one statement which can be made is that being overweight is rarely an advantage in caving. Not only is it difficult to move the extra bulk through squeezes, it also means more weight for the legs to carry and the arms to lift.

Physiological fitness is far more complex, yet more alterable, than anatomical fitness. It refers to the ability of the respiratory, circulatory, homeokinetic, muscular, metabolic, and temperature-regulating systems to support performance.

It is often assumed that caving requires a high level of circulorespiratory fitness by placing considerable demand on the heart and lungs as they provide oxygen to the muscles. However, in a set of preliminary tests conducted by the author on the heart beat rate (a test for detecting strain on the heart and lungs) of cavers as they negotiated various cave obstacles, this assumption was generally not supported, except during lengthy rope climbs. So, while circulorespiratory fitness may improve general fitness, it may not be essential to most activities while in the cave. Outside of the cave, however, the considerations are different. Similar tests indicated that hiking to caves and ridge walking often placed considerable strain on the heart and lungs. It is suggested that cavers maintain a high level of circulorespiratory fitness to be prepared for difficult hikes to caves, long rope climbs, and those rare times in a cave when it may be helpful.

Any activity which raises the heart rate to 120-130 beats or more per minute for 15-20 minutes will, if it is done several times a week, improve one's circulorespiratory fitness. Jogging, swimming, and rope jumping are some of the best activities. Tennis, squash, and bicycling are good if they are done vigorously enough. Aerobics classes, WMCAs, and health clubs can provide fun means of training. Common sense fitness books, such as ones by Dr. Kenneth Cooper (Cooper, 1970, 1977) can provide information that will help increase the efficiency of any training program.

Caving is primarily a body-lifting activity. Cavers lift their bodies, not another object, from place to place. The amount of strength needed, therefore, is related to your own weight. But this is one case where it is advantageous to have more than enough. A great amount of strength is not overkill. A strong person needs fewer muscle fibers to perform a given act. When those fibers tire, others can be called upon. This gives the muscle greater endurance by allowing part of it to rest during activity.

To develop muscular endurance, exercise and weight training can be helpful. Push-ups, pull-ups, sit-ups, running, and other exercise can develop strength. Notice, also, weight training is to develop strength, endurance, and flexibility. Weight lifting is practiced only to increase the amount of weight one can lift.

Weight training should use relatively light weights and the individual activity should be repeated 8-15 times. Weight training can be helpful to cavers when used properly. For example, leg presses can be beneficial in preparing for trips which will involve a lot of rope work.

One thing to remember with a fitness program is to retain flexibility. Exercising one set of muscles without exercising the opposing muscles can result in a great loss of flexibility. For example a person who does bench presses (exercising the extending muscles of the arms) should also include rowing lifts (using the flexing muscles in the arms) as a part of the weight training program.

In all activities which are extended over a period of several minutes or more, homeokinetic fitness becomes important. This form of fitness refers to the body's ability to establish and maintain a steady state of elevated levels of physical activity. Limiting factors include the maintenance of adequate blood sugar levels, the preservation of optimal pH, and the provision of an adequate oxygen supply. The proper function of the nervous system, in particular, depends upon preventing homeokinetic breakdown. In extreme cases, collapse and coma occur. Improving overall caving fitness seems to be the best means of improving homeokinetic fitness.

Metabolic fitness describes, among other things, the body's ability to produce energy. Caving, an endurance type of activity which requires considerable energy, demands a high level of metabolic fitness. Diet plays a major role in metabolic fitness. In fact, all of the systems which contribute to caving fitness can be affected by diet. Eating properly before and during a caving trip can make a difference.

The demands made by the cave's environment on the body's temperature regulating system are extreme. Although caves are generally cool, dehydration and heat exhaustion can occur. The body is cooled by the evaporation of sweat. The hotter the body becomes, the more it sweats. In high humidity environment, like caves, little evaporation takes place so the body tends to stay hot and sweat profusely. Consequently, there may be a great loss of water and salt. This may lead to heat exhaustion if the caver does not drink adequate fluid. Intense thirst, headaches, weakness, dizziness, and muscle cramps are all indications of this problem.

Overheating while caving is one burden on the temperature regulating system. The other is overcooling. Getting wet, and especially staying wet, can rapidly cause hypothermia. Sitting still or moving too slowly to generate body heat at the same rate that it is lost to the cave can also bring it on. Hypothermia is a condition which is induced by the lowering of the body core temperature. Intense shivering, muscle tension, numbness, and stumbling are symptoms of its early stages. Lethargy and disorientation are symptoms of a more advanced stage. Death can occur.

Improving fitness of the temperature regulating system is largely a matter of buffering yourself against the cave environment. Efficient movement, adequate food and water intake, appropriate clothing, and good overall physical fitness offer the most effective buffers.

High elevation alpine caving may present unique problems. Because of the decreased density of air, endurance activities become more difficult and performance decreases. It is best to remember this limitation and move more slowly while at higher elevation. If at all possible, it is best to spend a few days at the higher elevation before strenuous activity. The body will rapidly start to acclimate and function better.

Last, the most important factor in endurance of any sort is motivation. How willing a person is to endure the discomfort accompanying fatigue can seriously affect performance.

A lack of motivation may result from all night precaving car rides, recent illness, colds, allergies, toothaches, hangovers, or just a lack of interest. Though not incapacitating, a "low" feeling should always be taken seriously as it reduces your efficiency, endurance, and overall performance. For safety's sake, it's better to spend a day on the surface if your level of motivation is minimal.

An adequate level of fitness for the type of caving you plan to participate in is not difficult to achieve and is essential to the protection of the caver, the entire caving party, and to the cave itself. An overextended caver becomes careless. Carelessness can endanger all members of the caving party and increase the chances of damage to the cave. Adequate fitness can help prevent these problems.

Nutrition

Nutrition can be a controversial topic. Many people, experts included, have different and contradictory ideas on the subject. Yet, proper nutrition before and during a caving trip can make a great deal of difference in your comfort and performance.

One of the most important substances which the body needs during a cave trip is adequate water. Dehydration can be a serious problem, even in cool caves. Unfortunately, drinking just enough water to meet your feelings of thirst is not always adequate. Every caver needs to make a conscientious effort to assure that enough water is consumed during a cave trip.

Probably the best way to assure sufficient fluid intake is to drink fruit juices and water at regular, frequent intervals. While alcoholic beverages, like beer, may be temporarily thirst quenching, they actually tend to dehydrate the body and upset the body's fluid balance. Furthermore, by dilating the blood vessels, alcohol also increases the chance of suffering from hypothermia. Coffee is popular and provides fluids for the body, but it can create special problems. Coffee is a stimulant to bowel action and thus is not advisable prior to a trip into a cave.

What you should eat before a trip into a cave is probably as debatable as what an athlete should eat before competition. Basically, a balanced diet which provides all the necessary nutrients without an excess of calories is best.

For many years athletes believed that additional protein was necessary before heavy muscular activity. Many cavers follow the practice of eating more protein before a caving trip. During the past twenty years, this has been proven to be a false notion. The eminent Swedish physiologist, Per-Olof Astrand (1970) says, "There seems no doubt that it is proper to exclude protein from consideration as a fuel for working muscles." Work by Dr. Astrand has demonstrated that an athlete's energy comes from a combination of glycogen and fat. Glycogen, stored in the muscles and liver, is a product of carbohydrate foods. While carbohydrates are not essential to sustain life and a large amount may be harmful in a sedentary diet, they are important to the active person.

For long, difficult trips, you may find it advantageous to increase the percentage of carbohydrates in your diet. Many serious athletes who participate in endurance events practice a technique called carbohydrate loading. This involves a dramatic increase in the percentage of carbohydrates in their diets prior to strenuous competition. This technique is of limited value to cavers but

may be of some help when preparing for a very long, strenuous trip. For most trips, carbohydrate loading is unnecessary. Most good, modern books on athletic nutrition should give a summary on the advantages, problems, and procedures for carbohydrate loading for those serious cavers who may be involved in expeditions where endurance demands are great. Several of these books are listed at the end of this chapter.

Perhaps more important than what is eaten before the trip is what is eaten during a caving trip. Frequent light snacks are beneficial in providing energy to keep going and to maintain body temperature, thus preventing hypothermia. Foods high in carbohydrates are good for cave food.

Suggestions might include dried or fresh fruit, honey, hard candy, granola bars, and other quick energy foods. For the more creative caver, backpacking magazines often have recipes for high energy trail mixes and bars which can be prepared at home. One of the best foods which can be taken into a cave is fruit juice in eight or twelve ounce cans. Fruit juice cans tend to be a little bulky for a cave pack but they provide the simple sugars needed for quick energy and the liquid needed to prevent dehydration. Cans are sturdy and stand up well to being dragged through a cave. Glass containers should never be taken into a cave.

Cave foods need to meet several requirements. Here are a few features to consider.

1. The food should be simple and relatively neat to eat. When a caver is covered with a layer of mud, finger-lickin' chicken is not appetizing.

2. The food should not require refrigeration or cooking to be edible when needed.

3. Foods should be packaged in a way that will allow them to withstand abuse. Nothing breakable should be used. Sandwiches, crackers, grapes, and chocolate bars are often smashed so badly during the caving trip that little is left of their original form by the time you're ready to eat them. Food should also be packaged in waterproof containers or bags to help keep dirt and water away from the food. Air tight plastic containers (plastic baby bottles and Tupperware products, for instance) have been successfully used to carry cave food.

4. If the trip is a long one, it is best to pack food which can be eaten as several snacks throughout the day instead of as one large meal.

5. Food taken into the cave should be palatable. No matter how nutritious a food is, it helps only if it is eaten.

Take food into the cave that will be eaten and enjoyed.

6. Quick energy foods make the best cave foods. Protein seems to be of little value as a cave food. Foods high in carbohydrates seem best. Fruit juices, dried or fresh fruit, honey, and hard candy are some examples of quick energy foods.

7. If the food taken into a cave has waste left over, provision should be made for carrying this material out of the cave. Apple cores, orange peels, and oil from canned meats do not belong in the cave environment. If you bring something into the cave, you should also remove it from the cave.

It is always best to pack more food than you expect to need. Cave trips almost always last longer than expected. Also, should an accident occur or hypothermia become a problem, extra food could make a crucial difference.

Eating correctly both before and during a caving trip can add energy and increase the pleasure of a trip. On work trips or during difficult exploration, proper nutrition can help add to the amount of work accomplished. The results can be well worth the small amount of time needed to assure that proper food is eaten before and during a trip.

References and Additional Information

Astrand, Per-Olad and K. Rodahl. 1970. *Textbook of Work Physiology*: New York: McGraw-Hill, , pp. 453-488.

Bergstrom, J., L. Hernamsen, E. Hultman, and B. Saltin 1967. *Diet, Muscle Glycogen, and Physical Performance.* Acta Physiologica Scandinavica 71:140.

Cooper, K.H. 1970. *The New Aerobics*: New York: Bantam Books, 191pp.

Cooper, K.H. 1977. *The Aerobic Way.* New York: Bantam Books, 311pp.

Feuer, C. Undated. *A Nutritionally Adequate Cavers Ration.* Huntsville, AL: National Speleological Society Caving Information Series, 20:1-7.

Nieland, L. 1975. *The Backpacking Caver: Just Add . Water. NSS* News 33:98.

Strong, L.H. 1976. *Nutritional Aspects of Human Physical and Athletic Performance.* Springfield, IL: Charles C. Thomas.

FIRST AID

Eileen Carol
RN, FNP, MN
NSS 12945

An extremely important, yet often overlooked, aspect of caving involves first aid. The purpose of this section is to introduce the caver to the more common accidental threats and injuries prevalent in the cave environment. No step-by-step guide to treatment is intended here as entire books have been written for that purpose. However, an attempt will be made to offer some general guidelines for action. From that framework, it is intended that the caver will be motivated to obtain more specific knowledge and training in first aid. The responsibility for preparedness remains an individual and personal obligation.

Prevention

Prevention of accidents remains by far the most effective policy. This includes preparedness and knowledge in the areas of:

1. the caving environment to be encountered
2. the caving skills and techniques required for the specific cave (horizontal and vertical)
3. good physical condition
4. knowledge of your own ability and the ability of those members in the caving party
5. proper clothing and equipment (and maintenance of that gear)
6. adequate fuel for the body (food and water)
7. other associated stress factors such as minor illnesses and psychological elements
8. minimum number of three cavers on a trip.

Other considerations include:

1. prevention of overheating
2. prevention of hypothermia
3. abstinence from alcohol and drugs
4. sensory deprivation
5. knowledge of other cavers physical and/or mental disorders.

Preparedness also includes the consideration for specific injuries that might be encountered within a specific cave or caving locale. The importance of becoming knowledgeable about hazards before entering the cave cannot be stressed enough. The conditions of the hike to the cave must also be included. Forethought alone can often be enough to divert any possibility of accident or injury. Local cavers are an excellent resource in an area. They can provide information relating to the cave hazards, as well as the available first aid and rescue personnel and routine. They should be contacted prior to a trip into an unknown area.

First aid knowledge and skills are included in preparedness. The American Red Cross provides both standard and advanced first aid courses at minimal cost. Short courses in Cardio Pulmonary Resuscitation (CPR) are taught by either the Red Cross or the American Heart Association and are a necessity. Consult your local telephone directory. The NSS has the National Cave Rescue Commission (NCRC) for a resource. (See the current NSS Directory for the address of the NCRC.) Hopefully, cavers will pool their talents and resources to devise and offer caver-oriented first aid courses on a local level.

First Aid Kit

A basic first aid kit is an integral part of personal caving gear. This can be small and light enough to be unnoticeable, until it is needed. Contents should be placed in a waterproof or water-tight container (large-mouthed plastic water bottle, plastic case, metal tin, etc.). Contents should include:

1. 1 large heavy plastic garbage bag
2. a few large and small band aids
3. large paper clips, tongue blades, or pencils to be used as splints
4. 1-inch or 2-inch-wide rolls of adhesive tape
5. mixture of 1 teaspoon salt and ½ teaspoon baking soda wrapped in a plastic bag (used to make one quart of "shock" solution)
6. a few 3 x 3 or 4 x 4 gauze dressings
7. matches in waterproof container
8. a few aspirin (wrapped in plastic)
9. a clean handkerchief.

Optional items include:

10. a small elastic bandage
11. 1-inch-wide gauze roll or roll bandage
12. butterfly closures
13. a small bar Dial soap
14. small container of Betadine antiseptic solution.

A more complete first aid kit should always be kept in the car for severe injuries. The location of the car key should be known by all trip members. The kit should include the following items:

1. large-sized and more 4 x 4-inch gauze dressings
2. roll bandages of assorted size and lengths (can be made at home from prewashed cotton muslin)
3. triangular bandages
4. splints (pneumatic, wood, metal)
5. small camp stove and fuel
6. small pot and 2 cups
7. water
8. wool blankets
9. extra webbing, ropes, pulleys
10. spine board (for caving spine board plans, contact the NCRC)
11. heavy plastic.

Common Injuries

It is impossible to predict all the hazards and injuries that can occur in a caving situation. The trip locale will dictate specific possibilities. The arduous, arid hikes into the Sierra Madre Oriental of Mexico will offer varied hazards compared to the cold, wet caves of the mountains and northwestern U.S.

In general, the more common injuries to be encountered, in order of probability, include:

1. exhaustion
2. dehydration
3. wounds
    a) lacerations
    b) abrasions
    c) contusions (bruises)
    d) minor burns

the more serious,

4. hypothermia
5. sprains, dislocations (to be handled the same as a fracture)
6. fractures
    a) neck and spine
    b) femur and long bones
    c) pelvis
    d) other bones
7. shock
8. cessation of respiration
9. cessation of heart beat

non-trauma problems include:

10. insect and snake bites
11. infectious agents (rabies, histoplasmosis
12. food poisoning from improperly prepared caving food and/or contaminated water.

Often, injuries occur in combination and can aggravate each other. Some degree of shock and hypothermia should always be anticipated. The more significant and life-threatening issues will be dealt with separately.

Open Wounds

Open wounds include abrasions, incised wounds, lacerations and puncture wounds. Severe bleeding occurs with the most serious of these injuries. Management includes the control of bleeding, prevention of contamination and immobilization of the part involved.

Minor wounds generally need only to be covered with a clean dressing (handkerchief, cloth strips) and bandaged in place. Because these are not life threatening, treatment can be delayed.

Major, deep wounds require immediate action to stop severe bleeding. Bleeding from the arteries, if left uncontrolled, will result in heavy blood loss, shock and possibly death within minutes. To stop severe bleeding:

1. Apply direct pressure on the wound with a clean dressing. If one is not available, use your hand and apply firm pressure. Be sure you don't cut off the circulation.
2. Elevate the affected limb.
3. If bleeding persists, apply pressure on the pressure point nearest the wound but between the wound and the heart. See Fig. 14 for the location of the pressure points.
4. When severe bleeding is controlled, apply a compression dressing and tie in place (scarf, sock, webbing, strips of cloth). If blood soaks through, don't remove the dressing, but apply an additional dressing on top.
5. Apply a **tourniquet ONLY as a last resort. This may lead to amputation of the limb** later on. It should only be used as a life-saving measure when a limb has been destroyed or amputated. The simplest is to use a belt webbing or cloth wrapped about two inches above the wound and pulled just tight enough to stop the flow of blood. With a narrow belt, wire, or thin rope, you run the risk of cutting into the victim's skin. Do not cover the tourniquet as it could go unnoticed. Once a tourniquet is applied, never remove it for any reason. If it were loosened, clotted blood could enter the heart and lungs causing death.
6. Puncture wounds generally don't bleed freely. One of the most serious is to the chest wall, which may collapse the lung. Seal off a sucking wound as soon as possible. If clean dressings or bandages aren't available, use air-tight material such as plastic wrap, a baggie, or aluminum foil, and bandage in place. If no dressing is handy, use your hand. If a spinal injury is not suspected, turn the person onto his injured side.
7. When an object has penetrated into a person, never make any attempt to remove it. You risk severe hemorrhaging if you do. It is important to immobilize the object so it won't cause any further damage. Pack folded clothing around the object to keep it steady, and fasten in place with tape, elastic bandage or strips of clothing.

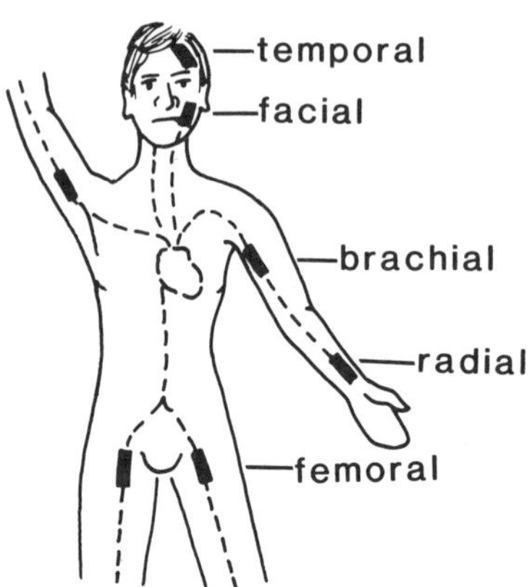

Fig. 14. Body pressure points.

Hypothermia

Hypothermia occurs when there is a fall in body temperature. When heat loss is greater than heat produced, the body defends itself in order to protect the vital organs. The first reaction is to shut down the circulation to the skin, the external muscles and the limbs. This is done to maintain the "core" temperature of the blood flowing to the vital organs. However, as the core temperature decreases from 98.6° F., the progression from drowsiness to coma can be very rapid, with death occurring in less than one hour. Never assume a hypothermia victim to be dead until attempts to revive him in a hospital have failed.

The wet and cold environment of most caves provides prime conditions to foster hypothermia. Water, whether from rain, snow or perspiration, conducts heat away from the body 200 to 250 times faster than air. Other aggravating factors include improper clothing, exhaustion, lack of food intake, drugs, and alcohol.

Hypothermia often gives little warning. Initial reaction to the cold is goose pimples and shivering. If the heat produced by shivering doesn't keep up with the heat being lost, the body's temperature will fall. With the slowing of the metabolic rate, mental and physical changes occur. As the victim drops out of conversation, he may appear discouraged or depressed. Uncoordinated, slow and labored movements may occur. Simple tasks become difficult, judgement will fail, and sleepiness may occur.

Try to prevent hypothermia before it occurs. Preventive measures include:

1. Proper clothing of several light, loose layers that will trap air and provide ventilation
2. Wool and polyester fabrics (PolarGuard, Dacron Hollofil II) retain some protective value when wet; whereas, cotton and bird down do not.
3. High heat loss areas such as the head and neck should be protected at all times.
4. Good physical condition is important.
5. Adequate food and water intake are fuel for heat maintenance.
6. Neoprene wet suits are a must for extremely cold and wet caves.
7. Pace yourself and avoid fatigue.

Know the early signs of hypothermia and leave the cave environment immediately. Symptoms of hypothermia in yourself are:

1. intense shivering
2. fatigue
3. numbness
4. stumbling
5. poor speech
6. poor orientation
7. careless attitude

Look for signs of hypothermia in others:

1. poor coordination
2. slowing of pace
3. stumbling
4. forgetfulness
5. hallucinations
6. thickness of speech
7. dilation of pupils
8. decreased attention
9. careless attitude

The darkness of the cave and spacing of party members may hinder the recognition of hypothermia. Long, waiting intervals at vertical drops and pitches can also aggravate hypothermia. If the condition is discovered early enough, leaving the cave won't present a problem. However, this decision must be made for each situation. Forcing someone to get out of the cave on his own may worsen hypothermia and add to the danger.

When being evacuated, the victim must be watched closely. He must be carefully protected from even minor hazards in the cave. Caution must be taken to belay even simple situations.

Removal may have to be delayed or stopped if the hypothermic condition worsens. If this happens, help should be sent for and other members must maintain the victim. Very wet top clothing must be wrung out and extra clothing put on from other party members—but not at their expense. Rubbing the limbs has no value. A garbage bag or space blanket is an asset, especially with the heat from a carbide lamp underneath aimed at the victim's chest. Insulate the victim from the cold, wet ground. Provide warmth from others huddled around him. Have him huddle, sitting in a thigh-to-chest position to maintain his body warmth. Feed him with any nourishment, especially hot and sweet things. Offer encouragement and reassurance at all times. Give absolutely no alcohol or drugs, as this increases the heat loss.

Injuries or shock aggravate hypothermia. Under any circumstance the condition of the victim dictates whether he can safely evacuate himself. If his speech is impaired, or if his muscle function is impaired so he is unable to move along the cave passage in a coordinated manner, then he should not be forced to move on. Outside the cave, warming should be slow and gradual, and may require medical assistance.

Know the factors that can lead to hypothermia—cold, wind, wetness and a likely victim. Prepare for the worst. Plan to refuel the body at regular intervals. Keep moving as much as possible.

Shock

Traumatic shock can occur from all types of injuries, even minor ones. If not treated, it can become life threatening. Once bleeding has been controlled, you must deal with assessing and treating shock. For assessing shock:

1. Checking the skin color and temperature will be a problem in a cave. Early signs of shock are clamminess and bluish or pale skin color.

2. Check the pulse. If the rate is over 100/minute, the victim is probably in shock. It may be too faint to be felt at the wrist, but, can be felt better at the carotid artery at the side of the neck, or in the groin.
3. Check the breathing. There may be rapid, shallow, irregular breathing.
4. A person in shock may also be restless, anxious, complain of thirst and become nauseated.
5. Check the pupils of the eyes (also a problem in the cave). If they are widely dilated (Fig. 15), he may be in severe shock.

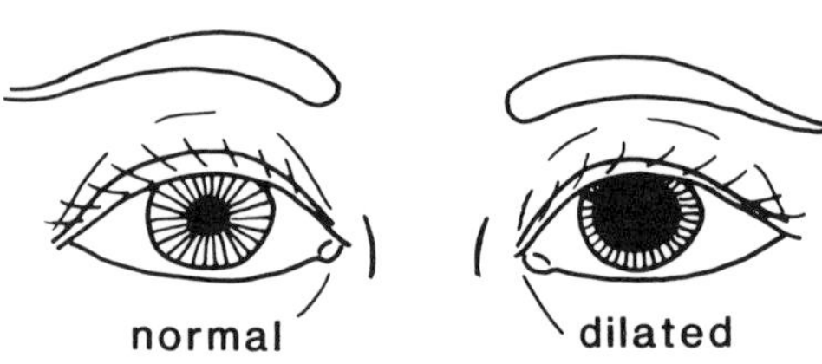

Fig. 15. Eye condition.

For treating shock:

1. Victims in shock should be kept lying flat, with clothing and blankets under and over the person. External heat applied at this time will draw blood away from the vital organs and to the skin and should be avoided. The lower limbs should be elevated slightly, about 8-12 inches. The exceptions follow.
   a) If a person has severe facial wounds or is unconscious, place him on his side to prevent the possibility of fluids being drawn into the lungs.
   b) If he has difficulty breathing, the victim may be placed on his back with his head and shoulders propped up—only if he doesn't have a spinal injury.
   c) With a head injury, the victim may be kept flat or propped up. Do not elevate the rest of the body higher than his head.
2. Fluids should not be given to a half-conscious or unconscious person, if help is immediate, or if the victim is nauseated. If rescue is more than an hour away, which is most likely in a cave accident, a "shock" solution of tepid temperature is recommended (1 tsp salt, ½ tsp baking soda to one quart of water, to be sipped, about ½ cup, at 15-minute intervals). If a person becomes nauseated, fluids must be stopped.

Closed Wounds

After bleeding and shock are under control, you can check for other injuries as internal bleeding, fractures and damage to the brain and spinal cord.

1. Gently feel the head for any depression or injury. If a hard hat is on, you may have to remove it to do this. Always suspect neck injury in persons with head injuries. Avoid moving them unless you must do so in order to protect them from further harm.
2. Check the neck, feeling for lumps and bony protrusions. If the victim is conscious ask him to:
   a) wiggle his fingers and toes
   b) squeeze your hand hard with each of his hands
   c) push against the palm of your hand with each foot. A weak or absent response indicates probable spinal cord injury.
3. When you suspect spinal injury, do not attempt to move the victim, bend his back, or raise his head.
4. If you must move him for further protection and don't have a spine board, use as many individuals as available for a six-man carry. Equal numbers of people should be on either side of the victim. Gently, the hands should be worked under the victim, to midline. Upon first command the victim should be lifted to waist level. On second command they should rise to their feet. The same procedure should be used in reverse to lower the victim to a safe location. When lifting, the rescuers should use their legs, not their backs.
5. Examine the eyes, nose, ears and mouth for blood or clear fluid.
6. Closed fractures and internal bleeding have the same signs as shock. In addition, the person may vomit blood and have a rigid abdomen. There is nothing you can directly do for internal bleeding in the field. You can insure a good airway, give nothing by mouth, and reassure the victim.
7. Gently check the ribs for fractures, asking if he has any pain or tenderness. Place in a comfortable position, generally on the side of the injury. If he has trouble breathing, raise his head and shoulders (or give artificial ventilation).
8. Feel the pelvic area for tenderness and deformity. With a pelvic fracture, the victim should be immobilized from his waist to his feet (rolled jackets, blankets). Then treat him like he has a spinal injury.
9. Check the limbs for deformity. Look for bones protruding through the skin. A clean dressing or handkerchief, moistened with clean water, can be placed over protruding bones to protect them. Do not attempt to straighten out any fracture. Keep the victim lying quietly.
10. Dislocated or broken fingers do not have to be splinted in the field. You can protect them by wrapping a clean cloth or handkerchief around the hand involved.
11. In the case of fractures, splint the involved limb in the exact position you found it. Use any

available materials. You may have to wait for these to arrive from outside the cave. You can use strips of cloth or rolled clothing to immobilize the fracture.

a) For fractures of the upper arm (humerus) splint to the side of the body.
b) For fractures of the leg (femur, tibia, fibula) splint to the uninjured leg.
c) Always immobilize the joint above and below the fracture. If no pulse is present, move the limb only enough for the pulse to return and then resplint in that position.

Though a good assessment of the victim is conducted with removal of the clothing, this is impractical and unwise in a caving accident. Leave all clothing and boots on the victim. Begin to treat and protect him from hypothermia.

First Aid Guidelines

Common sense knowledge is a basis for action in administering first aid. Several broad guidelines will be presented. These will provide a logical course of action for thinking through and acting in a first aid situation. Table 5 can be used as a learning tool to assist you in becoming knowledgeable in assessing an injured individual. These are also important factors medical personnel will want to know.

The goal of first aid is to administer first aid quickly, correctly and with calm assurance. One must assess the injuries, know what to treat first and know how to treat. The limitations of your own first aid ability must also be recognized. More harm can be inflicted if you are unsure of what you are doing.

Before a caving trip, it is important to determine what individuals will be in charge if there is an accident or injury. This will prevent dissent later on in the cave if such a situation does occur. The trip leader should also be made aware of any medical problems of the party members.

First and foremost, cardio-respiratory arrest (cessation of heartbeat or breathing) is life threatening and must be treated immediately. Before any other action is taken, all victims must be breathing and have a heartbeat. Only then can care be administered for shock, wounds, fractures and other injuries. In a cave, the situation is hampered by the darkness, the cold, the uneven passage and often by the long and difficult distance to the entrance.

In an accident situation, keep in mind the following:

1. The accident scene must be secured for the safety of the victim and the rescuer, and to prevent any further injury. If life-threatening hazards cannot be eliminated, the victim MUST be moved from further danger, regardless of the injuries or his condition.
2. The most knowledgeable, medically-trained individual should take charge of the victim.
3. The most experienced and best-trained first aid or rescue person should take charge of the situation. This individual may not be the trip leader or a doctor. (A doctor would be #2 above.) He can then delegate duties to other trip members.
4. Look for a Medic Alert tag on the injured person.
5. Look for the instrument or the cause of the injury, as this may give a better clue to the type of injury sustained.
6. If there is more than one victim, make a quick check of each person before beginning treatment. Quickly classify the severity of the injuries to your best ability. After checking a victim, assign someone to stay with the person and to inform you immediately of any adverse change in the condition.
7. Evaluate from the head and work down.
8. If the victim is conscious, ask him to describe his pain and sensations, and to give an evaluation of his own injuries. At this time, get a good history of the accident or injury.
9. NEVER move an unconscious person or one with a spinal injury unless his life is immediately threatened.
10. Always treat the worst-suspected injury first.
11. Never attempt to administer any liquids by mouth to a semi-conscious or unconscious person.
12. Respect the modesty of the victim.
13. Always be honest but positive with the person. Explain what you are doing and why.
14. Continue to check his condition until trained personnel take over.
15. If in doubt about a person's injuries or the proper position, keep him flat.
16. Insulate the person from the cold ground—shock potentiates hypothermia.
17. At least one person should stay with the victim while two others go for help.
18. The decision to move the victim is an individual one. It depends on the victim's condition and the ability of the trip members to handle the situation. The nature and location of the cave as well as the availability of rescue personnel will dictate what will be done.
19. Always anticipate some degree of shock and hypothermia with any injury.

Above all, stay calm. Psychological reassurance of the victim and other party members is just as significant as

Table 5*
Evaluation Checklist

Before caring for an accident victim, you must make a full assessment of his condition and injuries. This chart will help you to determine the most immediate hazards to him and to establish priorities in treatment.

FUNCTION	METHOD OF ASSESEMENT	OBSERVATIONS	POSSIBLE CAUSES
Respiration	Watch and feel chest for rise and fall; listen for breathing; check skin color	No respiration cyanotic,ashen, or general death-like appearance	Respiratory arrest - begin mouth-to-mouth resuscitation immediately, check for airway obstruction if resuscitation not effective
		Deep,gasping,labored, choking breathing	Airway obstruction,heart failure
		Rapid, shallow breathing	Hypertensive crisis, hyperventilation pain, hypovolemic shock, cardiogenic shock,pulmonary embolism
Pulse	Check carotid and femoral arteries	Absent	Cardiac arrest, death-begin CPR immediately
		Rapid, bounding	Fright, hypertension, hemorrhage, septic shock
		Rapid,weak	Cardiogenic, hypovolemic shock, hemorrhage
Level of consciousness	General observation history	Brief periods of unconsciousness	Simple fainting, concussion
		Confusion	Concussion,slight blow to head, psychiatric disorder,hysteria, alcohol or drug use or overdose, cerebral insufficiency
		Stupor	Concussion, brain damage, skull fracture, severe blow to head, diabetic shock, hysteria
		Deep coma	Severe brain damage, poisoning, drug overdose, diabetic shock, diabetic coma, hysteria
Ability to move	Ask conscious victim to move extremities, to describe any sensation; perform Babinski test on unconscious victim	Inability to move arms and hands	Injury to spinal cord in neck
		Inability to move legs and feet	Injury to spinal cord in lower back
		Limited use of any or all extremities	Pressure on spinal cord or in brain
		Paralysis limited to one side	Stroke, head injury with brain damage or hemorrhage
Skin color	Check extremities and fingernails; in dark pigmented patient, check fingernails, lips and palms of hands	Red skin	High blood pressure, septic shock carbon monoxide poisoning, heart attack, skin burn
		White skin	Cardiogenic, hypovolemic shock, heart attack, fright
		Blue skin (cyanosis)	Asphyxia, anoxia, heart attack, poisoning, electrocution
Skin temperature	Place back of hand on victim's forehead	Hot,dry	Heat stroke, high fever, dehydration, septic shock
		Cold, clammy	Cardiogenic, hypovolemic, insulin shock
		Cool,dry	Long exposure to cold
Pain	Query victim, observe general reaction of patient to gentle pressure	General pain at injury site	Injury to body but probably no injury to spinal cord
		Localized pain in extremities	Fracture, torn muscles or ligments and tendons, hematoma
		No pain but obvious injury	Spinal cord injury, vicient shock, excessive use of drugs or alcohol, hysteria
Pupil reaction	Lift victim's eyelids and check response to light	Dilated	Unconscioulsness, cardiac arrest, brain damage, drug use, shock
		Constricted	Disorder of the central nervous system, drug overdose or use
		Unequal	Head injury, stroke
		No pupil response to light, eyes rolled back in head	Death, coma, cataracts in older person

Refer to victim' history of the accident, other medical problems.

*from Nursing 1979, revised April 1979, used with permission of the publisher and author.

any first aid administered.

The environment of the cave offers potential of injury to those who are ill prepared or careless. It also presents a unique challenge for first aid and rescue. The responsibility for preparedness is an individual one. A good rule of thumb is to be prepared for the worst injury on any caving trip. It usually won't happen. If it does, you can be assured you have prepared and acted to the best of your abililty.

References

American National Red Cross. 1981. *Advanced First Aid and Emergency Care, 2nd Edition.* Garden City, NY: Doubleday & Company, Inc., 318pp.

American National Red Cross. 1979. *Standard First Aid and Personal Safety.* Garden City, NY: Doubleday & Company, Inc., 268pp.

Bangs, C.C. et al. 1975. *Winter Trauma: Help for the Victim of Hypothermia*: Patient Care 11(21):46-57.

Boericks, P.H. et al. 1975. *Emergency! Part 2, First Aid for Open Wounds, Severe Bleeding, Shock, and Closed Wounds.*. Nursing 5(3) : 40-47.

Clarke, C., M. Ward, and E. Williams, (Eds.). 1976. *Mountain Medicine and Physiology.* Proceedings of a symposium for mountaineers, expedition doctors, and physiologists sponsored by the Alpine Club, London, 1975. Seattle: Mountain Safety Research, Inc., 143pp.

Committee on Injuries, American Academy of Orthopedic Surgeons. 1978. *Emergency Care and Transportation of the Sick and Injured.* Menasha, Wisconsin: George Banta Company, Inc.,

Darvill, F. 1985. *Mountaineering Medicine.* Berkeley, California: Wilderness Press, 11th Edition.

Fear, G. 1972. *Surviving the Unexpected Wilderness Emergency.* Tacoma, Washington: Survival Education Association, 192pp.

Lathrop, T. 1975. *Hypothermia: Killer of the Unprepared.* Portland, Oregon: Mazamas.

Paton, B.C. 1975. *Cold, Injury, Hypothermia, and Frostbite.* Summit 21(12):6-13.

Wilderson, J., (Ed.)1975. *Medicine for Mountaineering* Seattle, Washington: The Mountaineers, Second Edition, 309pp.

ON THE UPS AND DOWNS OF VERTICAL CAVING

Bill Steele
NSS 8072F

Fig. 16. The "hot-seat" (body) rappel.

Introduction

I leaned back in the pose shown in the book.

"Yeah, that's the way they show it," Pete said, "a hot-seat rappel." Around my chest was a second rope, a belay for safety, manned by two friends who had it wrapped around a tree and were letting me down slowly.

"O.K., here goes," I said. Leaves and dirt fell into the pit as I inched backwards over the edge.

"More rope, more rope," I begged, as I got below the lip of the pit and felt the extent of the pain in my right thigh and left shoulder from the friction of the rope.

Soon I was on the bottom. There were no passages leading from the pit bottom. I could barely hear the muffled voices of my friends some 50 feet above. "O.K., pull me out!"

As the rope dug into my armpits, I left the ground in short jerks. I would go up five feet and then back down one. The higher I got, the slower my five friends pulled. Finally, I was at the top. Here, I had to climb hand-over-hand over the lip while my buddies tugged.

"Never again," I swore. "I am going to learn how to do it right!"

I lived through my first trip to a vertical cave. My second and third trips were not much better. Eventually I joined the NSS and was exposed to accepted and safe techniques for descending pits and getting back out again.

American vertical cavers consider the father of their techniques to be Bill Cuddington of Huntsville, Alabama. Early in the 1950s while the NSS was beginning its second decade, Cuddington was starting to explore caves near his home stomping grounds of Roanoke, Virginia. He was well versed in the practice of cable ladders used with a belay line from above, but figured that there had to be a better way. Cuddington began to apply mountain climbing rope techniques to caves. He began to use only one rope and would rappel down this rope with the rope wrapped under one leg and over the opposite shoulder: a hot-seat rappel (Fig. 16). For ascent he would use prusik knots. Soon, he and his associates progressed to carabiner rappels and rappel spools. The game of innovation of vertical caving methods was on.

Bill Cuddington met with a great deal of guff over his revolutionary approach to pit caves. The caving establishment chastised him at the time for his unorthodox techniques, predicting his demise. But, instead, he began to win over converts one after another to his way of doing things.

Cuddington kept at it for many years and was the first person down scores of pits in the southeastern states. People who followed him into these same drops duplicated his means and ideas spread. They were further spread at demonstrations and contests held as a part of the annual NSS convention.

In 1961 Bill Torode of Huntsville, Alabama, discovered Surprise Pit in Fern Cave, near Huntsville. The 437-foot drop was much deeper than anything else known at the time. Bill Cuddington showed up and descended Surprise Pit first. Two others also did it that summer, two the next, then only one person in 1963. After 1964 Surprise Pit was done with great frequency.

Cavers were using nylon rope by this time. Goldline had been developed during and after WWII and was being purchased for pit rope. Rappel devices were either double brake bars on carabiners (Fig. 17) or a rappel spool. By 1964 the unorthodox methods of getting into and out of pits that Bill Cuddington had adapted from climbers and developed for caving were now widely accepted practices.

A "great leap forward" in pit caving occurred in early 1968 when an issue of the *NSS News* came out with the account of the first (1967) descent of the Sótano de las Golondrinas, Mexico. There, in black and white, was a photo of two American cavers ascending out from the awesomeness of the 1094-foot pit. A wave of consciousness swept the caving mind. Deep caves.

One member of the first group to descend Golondrinas, John Cole, had invented a new rappelling device for long

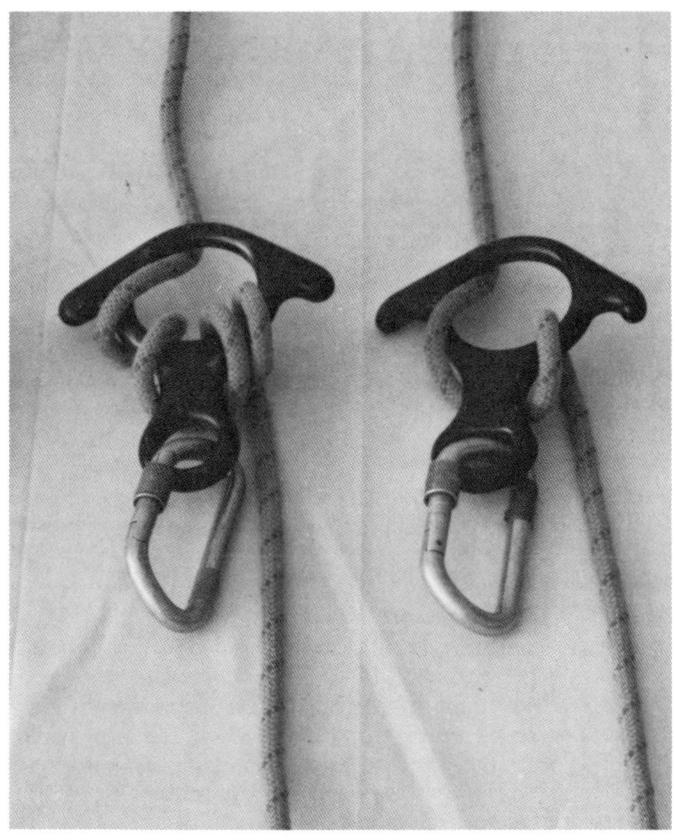

Fig. 17. Figure 8 descender (which has largely replaced double brake bars) is now widely used for drops up to 100 feet. At left, second wrap provides more friction. Figure 8 is safer than brake bars because bars put severe stress on gate, weakest part of carabiner.

Fig. 18. Six bar rappel rack. Rope runs across top bar, not against rack body. Braking hand cradles rack to control descent. Bars at left squeezed together to stop. Center, bars spread for descent. (hand not shown for clarity). Right, rack being locked off for resting.

drops (Cole, 1966 and Hughes, 1981). It was called the "rappel rack" (Fig. 18). This innovative new device has yet to be surpassed in design and function. Its versatility makes it useful in the deepest of pits, the shallowest, and most variations in between.

So You Want To Do A Pit

I initially learned to do pits on my own with the aid of illustrations in a book. **I would never recommend this course to anyone.** The proper and safe way to go about learning the techniques of vertical caving is to seek out someone who has experience in this field. Many NSS grottos conduct vertical practice sessions during the year to train newcomers in rope work as well as to give the experienced cavers a chance to improve their techniques and to exchange ideas on new methods. If your grotto does not hold such sessions, or if you do not belong to a grotto, seek out someone who is knowledgeable in vertical work and learn from that person. Regional meets in various parts of the country, plus the Vertical Session and the Vertical Workshop at the annual NSS convention, are excellent

There are no short cuts to learning vertical rope techniques and no short cuts in the quality of equipment used. Your life, as well as that of others, depends on your knowledge, your equipment and your judgement in the use and care of equipment and of yourself.

Books such as *Single Rope Techniques* (1977), *On Rope* 1987), and *Adventure of Caving (1986)* are valuable to the newcomer. But these are no substitute for training with an experienced vertical caving instructor.

Accident accounts abound with examples of people who found a rope near a pit and decided to go ahead this one time. To descend a pit is a highly technical and dangerous undertaking. It should be done with painstaking preparation. First secure all the right equipment and practice on short drops above ground. Do this under the guidance of an experienced person, until you are proficient in the use of this equipment before heading for your first underground vertical experience.

Descending

Getting down a rope is done by means of rappelling. For short drops, 15 feet or less, the "hot seat" (Fig. 16)

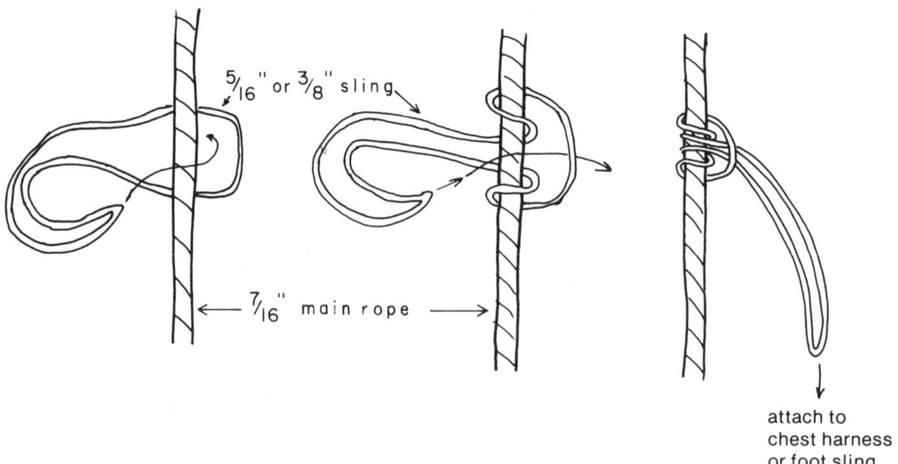

Fig. 19. The prusik knot. If the prusik slips, its grip can be increased by looping around the main rope a third time.

can be used. However, rappelling is usually done by use of the aforementioned double brake bar carabiner rig (Fig. 17) or, for better control, the "rappel rack" (Fig. 18). Before heading off to a pit, or a cave with a pit, you should practice rappelling on a cliff or a wall. On your first descent, and during all that follow, a bottom belay should be maintained if possible. This is done by a person stationed at the bottom of the rope who can halt an out-of-control rappeller by simply pulling hard on the rope. The additional weight acts to brake the person by increasing the friction against the brake bars. A bottom belay is given only when the belayer is able to find a safe place to stand.

The acceptable signal for announcing that one is beginning the rappel is to shout, "on rope." This should be acknowledged from below before the rappeller starts the descent. If a rock is dislodged by the rappeller or anyone else, a loud call of "ROCK" should be yelled as a warning to those below. This call of "rock" should be used no matter what object is falling. "Canteen" may not solicit the correct action below (that is—get the hell out of the way). When a person gets to the bottom and removes his rappel device from the rope, he or she should shout "off rope" to the next person coming down. This means **both** that the **rope is available** and that the person shouting **has sought shelter** and is away from the base of the drop. If the end of the rappel rope becomes coiled and kinked due to the action of the rappel device, the rope should be shook out before the command "off rope" is given.

Ascending

As with rappelling, it is a must that beginners practice ascending before heading off to a pit that they must get themselves out of. One should be able to ascend up the same wall or cliff that the rappel was practiced on.

Cavers will tell most anyone they should learn to use prusik knots first (Fig. 19). These basic knots can be made from three slings with either tenstron, polypropylene, or nylon rope of 5/16-inch diameter and are attached separately from the main rope to a chest harness and one to each foot. These knots can slide up and down the main rope when there is no weight on them. The technique is to stand, loosen the top knot and slide it up, hang by the chest harness fastened to the top knot, move the foot slings up and then stand in the foot slings and repeat.

Mechanical ascenders are predominantly used for ascent these days. Two ascenders lead the field and are known as Gibbs ascenders and Jumar ascenders (Fig. 20). Both grip the rope with eccentric cams having teeth and do not damage the rope fibers. Jumars are normally used in pairs with a length of rope from each

Fig. 20. A Gibbs ascender on the left and a Jumar on the right.

Jumar to a foot. One is short so that the Jumar is just above the knee, while the rope for the other sling is long enough so that the top of the Jumar is about chin-high. The sling from the high one passes through a carabiner at the chest on a chest harness (all carabiners used in caving, except with brake bars, are of the locking variety) and down to the foot. The main rope is also engaged within this carabiner. A chest box, a device which is designed specifically for housing the main rope and the rope from the top Jumar is more efficient to use. Fig. 21 shows this system which is referred to as the Mitchell system (Mitchell, 1967).

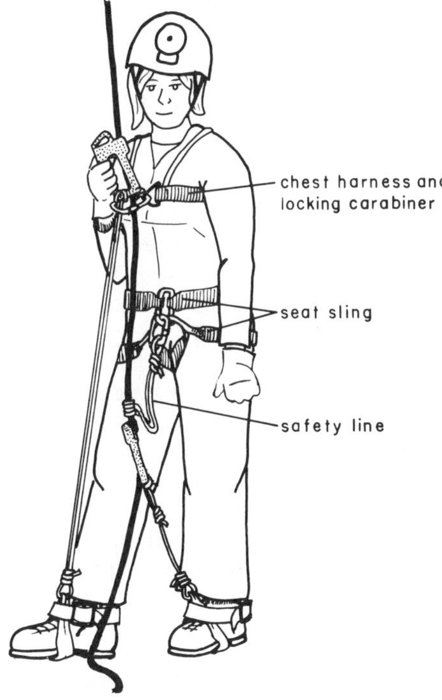

Fig. 21. Mitchell system using two Jumars. A third attachment to the main rope with either a mechanical ascender or a prusik knot from the seat sling should be used for resting and a safety.

Gibbs ascenders are normally attached to the body at the upper torso, i.e. shoulder or chest, and at one knee and the opposite ankle. It is possible to "walk" right up a rope using this technique. One would be hard pressed to estimate if more cavers prefer Gibbs or Jumars.

The specifics of these techniques for ascending and rappelling should be sought from a competent person well versed in their use.

Belaying

Elsewhere in this discussion (under rappelling) is a mention of "bottom belaying." A top belay is a separate rope that is tied to the climber and is let out or taken in as he moves either up or down a rope, cable ladder or a free climb. The belayer is the person who handles this safety line. This person must be on the constant alert for the calls of the climber as to whether to take in rope or let it out. The commonly used calls are:

belay on—(from the climber) the climber is tied into the rope and is ready to ascend.

climb—(from the belayer) means the belayer is in a secure position and ready to handle the rope as needed.

climbing—(from the climber) he is starting to climb.

rope—(from the climber) short for up rope or to take in the slack.

slack—(from the climber) means the climber wants a little slack in the rope.

tension—(from the climber) means to hold the rope tight enough to support part of the climber's weight.

rock—(from anyone) a warning that some object is falling.

off belay—(from the climber) means that the climber no longer needs or wants the belay, usually at the finish of the climb.

belay off—(from the belayer) means that the belay has been dispensed with.

off rope—(from the climber) means that the climber has finished the climb, is in a safe area away from the climb and has untied the rope.

The belayer chooses a spot above the descent route or to the side of the climbing route to avoid dislodging rocks. His stance must be "bomb-proof" so that he could catch a falling climber without being pulled off, thrown or rolled over. To achieve this, the belayer must tie himself securely to a rock or some other solid object. The belayer should be wearing protective leather gloves to prevent possible rope burn. The belay rope runs around the back of the belayer, above the tie-in when the climber is below. As the climber moves up the belayer takes in the belay rope with one hand pulling the rope from around his back and then laying the rope into his other hand which is guiding the rope to the climber and clasping it. He then slides his hand back along the rope and again pulls up any slack. This hand that pulls up the slack from around the belayer's body is the braking hand. It never, NEVER, leaves the rope. If the climber should happen to fall, the belayer does not try to grab the rope to catch the falling climber, but rather quickly wraps the belay rope across the front of his body with the braking hand and allows the friction between the rope and the belayer's body, hopefully covered with clothing, to stop the rope and climber.

This takes practice, lots of it, that must be had before belaying a climber for real. There are mechanical devices to help in belaying but the body belay, always there, is easy to use and has the least number of parts to fail.

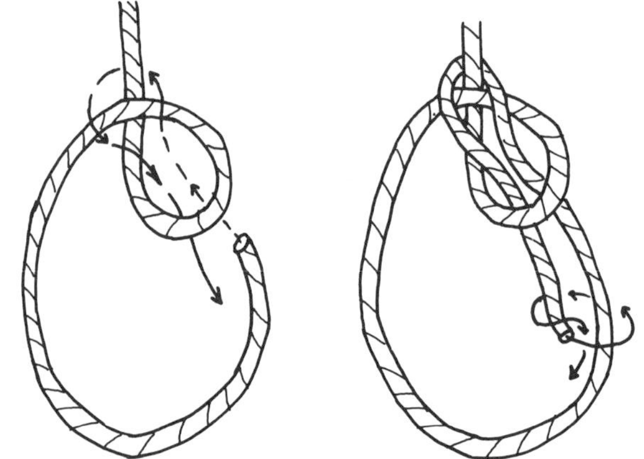

Bowline secured with an overhand knot.

Double fisherman's knot, or grapevine, secured with overhand knots. This is a good knot for joining two ropes of different construction but of the same diameter.

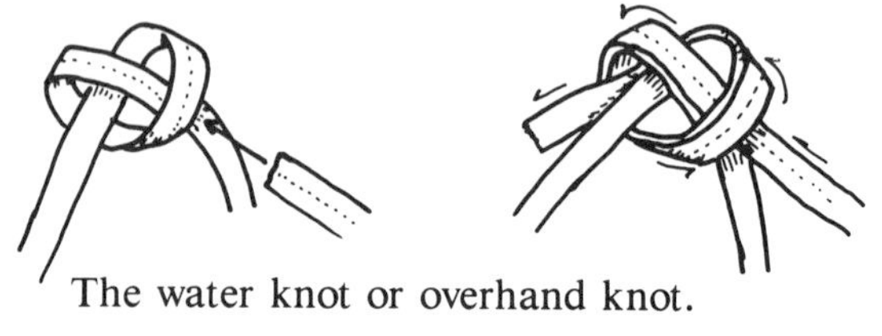

The water knot or overhand knot.

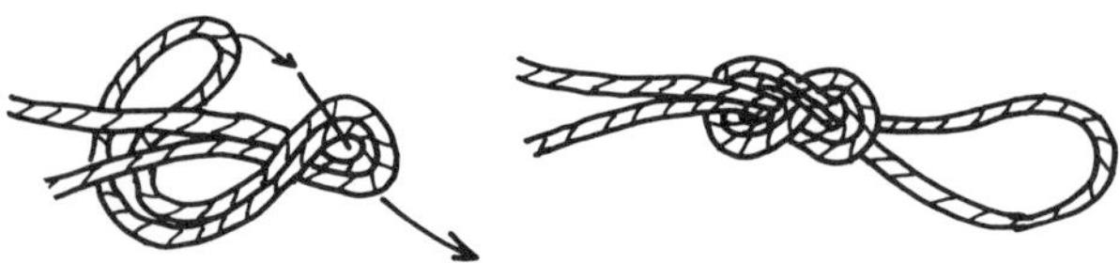

The Figure-eight knot.

Fig. 22. Four commonly used knots for vertical caving.

When You Get There

So, you have practiced the rappel and ascending on a cliff and you are now ready for your first cave with a **short** vertical drop. Very often a group which includes a beginner or several beginners goes off to a cave intending to share vertical equipment. The reason for this can be readily understood: maybe the novice will decide on a different technique after using someone else's system; maybe the novice will find out he has a fear of heights (or is it depths?); maybe the people without vertical gear are going to do only this one drop and do not want to lay out the cash for mechanical ascenders. Whatever the reason, **it is not good enough**. For the maximization of safety, **everyone along should have their own** vertical equipment, even if borrowed. Too often the only set of ascenders gets caught on the wall while being sent back down, or dislodges rock onto those below, or the person in charge of the gear forgets something and everyone is caught on the bottom with no way back up.

Rigging

The pit, or pits, are either in one of two places. It is either in the cave or at the entrance. More often than not, a pit at the entrance has a tree nearby to rig around, a truck or a boulder. If the pit has been done many times, look for rope marks on a tree's bark to indicate a tried and true rigging spot. Any rigging point used should be secure and fail-proof.

The loop that goes around the tree normally would be secured by a bowline knot. Though any Boy Scout book can show knot after knot, cavers normally rely on one of four knots (Fig. 22) to handle everything. The bowline is used around trees, boulders, logs and climbers on belay. The figure-eight is used to tie a rope to a carabiner and in spots where a loop in mid-rope is necessary. The double fisherman's knot (also called the grapevine) is preferred for joining two ropes together. The water knot (overhand) is used for tying two ends of webbing together. After the rope is tied off, padding is placed under the rope at spots where the rope comes in contact with sharp rock edges. The padding is also tied to a rigging point.

Carrying a rope through a cave can be a "drag" if it is not properly coiled. A "caver's coil" (Fig. 23) has come to be used primarily, and is done by sitting cross-legged on the ground and looping the rope around both

Fig. 23. Rope coiled in a "caver's coil."

knees. The aspect of a "caver's coil" that distinguishes it from other coils is that enough rope is kept from the coil to tightly spiral around the main body, forming a solid coil that is just right for the shoulders. It will not snag if tightly wrapped.

A Word To The Wise

This brief treatise about vertical caving has not been meant in any way to be instructional in how to accomplish the successful descent and ascent of a pit. **There is no substitute for instruction from a person well-versed in vertical caving.** A high percentage of accidents in caves occur in and around vertical drops. The descent and ascent of pits is a highly technical undertaking that requires proper equipment and practice with this equipment before the first drop is encountered.

Nylon rope under tension cuts like butter. It sometimes happens during a rappel that some item of clothing, or even your hair, becomes caught in the rappel device, preventing any further descent. **Do not** use a knife to cut the material from the device. Switch over to an ascending rig with the ascenders above the rappel device to relieve the tension. Then unjam the rappel rig. Several accidents have happened when people tried to cut the material from a jammed rappel rig under tension only to cut the main rope instead because it was under tension.

While caving is generally known as an inexpensive endeavor, vertical caving necessitates an outlay of funds that can be considerable if the deepest of caves are to be in one's repertoire. The basic vertical gear of a rappel rack, seat harness, chest harness, mechanical ascenders, and all the necessary carabiners and webbing can run $150 to $200 plus. And this is the minimum gear.

Some caves can take a fortune in rope to rig. The Sotano de Agua de Carrizo in Huautla, Mexico, if fully rigged down its three ways of going deep, would take 6367 feet of rope. At today's prices this amounts to nearly $3000 worth of rope.

References

Cole, J., (1966)— *New rappel device:*: NSS News 24:154-155.

Hughes, D., (1981)— *An Interview with John Cole:*. NSS News 39:145-147 and 158.

McClurg, D.(1987) *Adventure of Caving.*. D&J Press, Carlsbad, NM 332pp.

Mitchell, D., (1967)— *Fastest method with Jumars:* NSS News 25:211-212.

Montgomery, N.R., (1977)— *Single rope techniques—a guide for vertical cavers:* The Sydney, Speleol. Soc. Sydney, Australia, 122pp.

Padgett and Smith (1987)— *On Rope, North American Vertical Rope Techniques:* Vertical Section, Nat. Spleological Soc., Huntsville, AL. 496pp.

Thrun, R., (1971)— Prusiking: Nat. Speleological. Soc. Huntsville, AL, 75pp.

VERTICAL CAVING CHECKLIST

Ray Cole
NSS 12460

Because of the potential for accidents in vertical caving situations and the technical nature of the equipment, you should consider the following points:

1. Persons inexperienced with vertical techniques and equipment should receive their initial training outside of a cave in a controlled situation.
2. Each caver on a vertical trip should have his/her own vertical equipment which includes seat and chest harnesses, ascending and descending equipment.
3. Only rappel devices that have adequate strength and range of control should be used.
4. Discard any item of vertical equipment that is broken or worn out. Black paint is often used to mark ropes and equipment no longer safe for vertical caving.
5. An ascending set of equipment should include a seat sling and provisions for resting with both hands free.
6. Visually and physically examine ropes prior to use.
7. Use a buddy system to check each other's personal rigging prior to use.
8. If you use an electric caving light with acid electrolyte, you should plug the vent holes to prevent acid leakage on nylon ropes and slings. Be sure to unplug the vent holes before recharging the battery! Duct tape works well in covering the holes.

THE SELECTION, USE AND CARE OF ROPES FOR VERTICAL CAVING

Kyle Isenhart
NSS 12327F

All cavers are eventually faced with the need for a piece of rope. They may need five feet or 1500 feet. They may need a handline or a main rappel and prusik line. They may be in free space or against a wall, dry or wet, clean or muddy. They may even be doing technical rock climbing underground. All these factors can affect the selection of the proper rope to use.

In many parts of the United States there are very few vertical caves and an active caver may spend many years underground and not need a handline, much less a rappel and prusik rope. However, in most caving areas at least a few caves with significant vertical development are found. This discussion is directed to novice cavers and the more experienced horizontal cavers who wish to enter these vertical caves.

In most cases an individual's introduction to vertical caving is under the leadership and direction of an experienced vertical caver. That individual or his club will usually provide the necessary ropes and equipment for the introductory vertical trips. During these trips the new caver can see what types of ropes and equipment his trip leaders are using.

After these first trips the decision should be made whether or not to enter the expensive area of vertical caving. While there are people who own very few ropes and mechanical ascenders, in the realm of vertical caving this condition is the exception rather than the rule. Most people who only vertical cave occasionally have well over $100 in their equipment. At one time the author had over $1600 worth of ropes, carabiners, mechanical ascenders, cable ladders, etc. Most vertical cavers are somewhere in between.

The most important item in all vertical caving is the rope. Whether it be a handline, belay line for a ladder climb, or rappel and prusik line, **it must not fail**. The selection of a high quality rope suited to the applications is a necessity. But acquiring a good rope is only the beginning. It must be properly cared for or it will deteriorate and become unsafe.

The selection of a rope, as mentioned earlier, depends upon many things. One thing it should **not** depend upon is price. Even the most expensive ropes are cheap when compared to medical bills, disability, or even death. Every person's life on a trip may well depend on the rope. At such times a few dollars are meaningless. Fortunately, the finest ropes available today are relatively inexpensive. Except for the specialized dynamic rock-climbing ropes, top-quality lines sell in the U.S. for around $42 per 100 feet. While there are hundreds of ropes on the market today, they vary in only two things: material of construction and type of construction. This discussion will address only three basic types of rope construction.

The oldest and most common type of construction is twisted, usually called laid (Fig. 24). The second and less common type, usually restricted to rope of ½ inch or less in diameter, is the solid braid. The third type is usually called kernmantle (Fig. 24). This type consists of two basic layers. The core or kern, and the outer, braided sheath called the mantle. The inner core can be braided, highly twisted, or have nearly parallel strands. In some cases combinations of two or even all three core methods are used in a single rope. This discussion will be limited to the laid and kernmantle ropes of nearly parallel core construction as they are the most common caving ropes. Both types have advantages, but due to the low stretch and non-twisting characteristics of the kernmantle ropes, they are more popular for main rappel and prusik lines.

There are more laid ropes available than kernmantle ones on the general market, but fewer laid ropes suitable for caving, so we will examine them first. Their main advantages are as follows:

1. Low cost and ease of manufacture, hence a lower potential selling price.
2. They are easily inspected for damage. However, since under high loads, tensile failure usually occurs first in those filaments closest to the center of the rope, it must be untwisted slightly to inspect for this type of damage.

Their main disadvantages are listed below:

1. They twist or spin in free space when a weight is suspended from them.
2. They have high stretch which is not easily controlled.
3. Their outer surface is rough due to the three or four strands used to make up the final rope.
4. Since all filaments in the rope make up the main load-bearing unit, loss of strength from abrasion can be rapid.

The first two disadvantages listed have been the major reasons for laid ropes losing their position of leadership in caving use to the kernmantle ropes.

The other type of construction we will examine is the

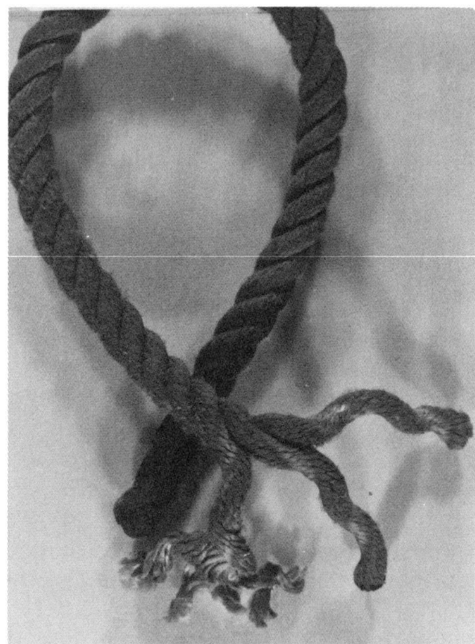

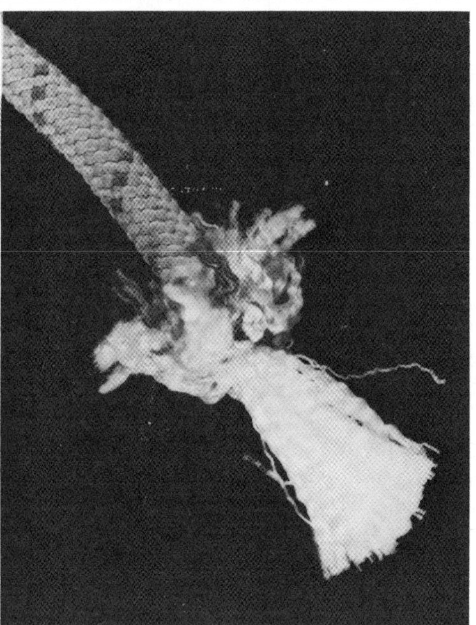

Fig. 24. A twisted Goldline on the left and a kernmantle Blue Water II on the right with the outer sheath pulled back.

kernmantle. Its main advantages are as follows:

1. Very little or no tendency to spin in free space when a weight is suspended from it.
2. Controlled stretch, usually quite low.
3. High abrasion resistance. Almost all the load on a kernmantle rope is carried by the core. Therefore, abrasion of the sheath has very little effect on the total strength of the rope.
4. The outer surface of the rope is smooth.
5. There is a high strength for a given diameter.

Main disadvantages of kernmantle are listed below:

1. Tendency to have tensile load failures in the core strands before any visible failure occurs in the sheath.
2. Due to the tightly braided sheath, it is not possible to visually examine the core strands for damage without ruining the rope.

These two disadvantages are still major problems for manufacturers and users of kernmantle ropes and are mainly responsible for their failure to totally displace the laid ropes in this country as rappel and prusik lines.

Within the laid and kernmantle categories, there are also individual differences. Within the laid ropes the main differences are the rate of twist in the strands, the direction of the twist (left or right), and the tension under which the twisting was done. For caving purposes a rope of hard-lay construction is preferable to a rope of standard ("marine") lay. A hard-lay rope is much stiffer than a standard-lay rope. It usually has less stretch and improved abrasion resistance. This hard-lay characteristic is achieved by increasing the rate of twist and tension during the manufacture of the rope.

There are a large number of variables in the manufacture of kernmantle-type ropes. This paper will only deal with a very few which in the author's opinion relate directly to the rope's utility in most caving activities.

For caving, a kernmantle rope should have high abrasion resistance. One method of accomplishing this is by adjusting the tension, braiding pattern, strand size and/or denier so more yarn can be put into the sheath, making it thicker and hence more abrasion resistant. Some people feel it may also be accomplished by using a large denier yarn of high quality and twisting it at a high rate before braiding the sheath. The problem that happens with a too heavy sheath is that an imbalance between the sheath and core can occur causing all sorts of stretch and load-absorbing problems to crop up. Also the sheath can start carrying too much of the tension loads and premature tensile failures of the sheath can occur.

Another desirable characteristic in a caving rope is high strength. All good quality kernmantle ropes have very high strength. But again, as previously mentioned, the balance between the load-absorbing characteristics of the sheath and core must be maintained for optimum strength.

Another important characteristic of rappel and prusik ropes in particular is low stretch. When compared to laid ropes at loads between 200 and 600 pounds, kernmantle ropes have much less stretch. However, when subjected to shock loading, such as someone falling several feet and then the rope coming suddenly tight, low stretch can be a major disadvantage. Since this type of shock loading can occur during caving activities, the rope should have enough stretch to have some shock absorbing ability. For rock-climbing activities there are special ropes with low stretch under low loads and extremely high stretch when high loads are required. **Low stretch ropes** made for caving **are not suitable for belaying** where the climber may fall several feet before being caught by the rope.

The next area of importance in ropes is the material of construction. Because of their tendency to lose strength rapidly and to rot, natural fiber ropes should not be used for caving activities. Ropes made of cotton, manila, sisal, etc. are no longer used for caving.

Due to their higher strength and overall better resistance to deterioration, synthetic fiber ropes have replaced natural fiber ropes for caving use. Synthetic fibers that are commonly used for ropes include nylons, polyesters, polypropylenes and various types of polyethylenes. There are many types of each of these synthetic fibers. In general, ropes made of nylon, polyester and polypropylene have all found some acceptance in caving circles. The polyethylene ropes are usually too weak, stretchy and melt at too low a temperature to be used. There are many world-wide polymer manufacturers. These polymers then are made by manufacturers into synthetic yarns which are made into rope by even more manufacturers. So, getting a rope made of the right type of the right polymer from the right size of yarn into the right type of rope construction for your use can be a complex problem. Fortunately, the rope manufacturers usually sort through all the various materials available and select the ones they feel are best for a particular type of rope. As a consumer you must trust the rope manufacturer to make the right decisions. In different parts of the world different synthetic yarns are available to the rope manufacturers. Because of this, the type of rope in use in various areas may be different. Also the machines used to manufacture the ropes themselves are different in various countries.

In the United States the preferred material for caving rope construction in 1978 was type 6-6 nylon. This could change soon. Even within the broad class of this type of nylon, there are many different grades for various uses. In the U.S. polyester ropes are not popular for caving, but they are used quite a bit in Europe. In many caving areas inexpensive polypropylene ropes are used for handlines and in some cases for short rappel and prusik lines. Small diameter polypropylene ropes are popular for prusik knot construction. The nylon ropes generally have a better balance of strength, elongation and abrasion resistance than those made of other materials. These improved properties are more than enough to offset their greater cost.

When deciding what rope to choose for a handline, consider how often one certain length will be needed and if it is worthwhile to buy a special rope for that purpose. If a rope will be used exclusively as a handline, it should be large enough to get a good grip on and usually of laid construction. The laid rope is rough on the surface and facilitates gripping by hand. I use ½-inch polypropylene laid rope for handlines. It is sufficiently strong, easy to grip and inexpensive. A handline is usually short, 15 to 50 feet in length. If you only need a 25-foot handline, it isn't very practical to carry a 150-foot main prusik line instead. Active vertical cavers often have to cut their long main prusik lines due to

Table 6. Characteristics of Caving Ropes*

Rope Identification	*Construction Type***	*Cost Per Foot*	*Weight Pounds Per 100 Feet*	*Tensile Strength Pounds*	*Abrasion Resistance*
Blue Water II	Kernmantle	.42	6.5	7000	Excellent
Blue Water Super III	Kernmantle	.44	6.5	7000	Excellent
PMI Pit Rope	Kernmantle	.42	6.7	7000	Excellent
Speleo Static Master	Kernmantle	.36	6.5	7000	Excellent
Goldline II	Hard Laid	.45	6.2	5600	Good
Sampson Two in One	Braid over Braid	.50	7.0	6000	Fair
West 707	Kernmantle	.40	6.5	6000	Good
Wall	Kernmantle	.40	6.5	5400	Fair

* All data is based on similar tests. This table should be used for comparison purposes only and not considered absolute.

** All ropes are 7/16-inch diameter nylon.

excessive wear on ledges, etc. In this way a number of short ropes of handline length are acquired by many cavers.

The selection of a main rappel and prusik line is a little more complicated. Kernmantle ropes are currently in vogue for this purpose. Many people still prefer hard-laid ropes, especially in very muddy conditions and against a wall. In free space the kernmantle ropes are much preferred. Their lack of spin and low stretch make them immensely better on long, free drops. On wet drops the laid ropes tend to splash more water on the rappeller than kernmantle ones, but when coated with a sheath of ice, the increased stretch and spin characteristics of the laid ropes help them to de-ice and be easier to ascend. At the present time in the United States, over 90% of the main rappel and prusik lines in use by cavers are of kernmantle construction. Whether the main line be of laid or kernmantle construction, the most popular diameter worldwide is 7/16 inch (11 mm). Ropes from 3/8 to ½ inch are used, but 7/16 inch diameter is the standard. Ropes of 5/16 inch diameter are sometimes used doubled and when long pack trips are encountered, the weight savings is significant. However, because the thin sheath is susceptible to abrasion, and the small diameter is sometimes not gripped as tightly by ascenders, I do not feel that 5/16-inch diameter ropes should be used as main rappel and prusik lines for caving.

The most important thing to remember when using a rope is that it must be protected from damage. Ropes should not be overloaded with extreme weights. They should be protected by sturdy pads wherever they contact rough surfaces and could be abraded. Whenever possible, extremely tight bends and knots in the loaded portion of a rope should be avoided. Ropes should never be walked on or drug along the ground. They should be kept clean. A dirty rope is not a status symbol. Mud and dirt on a rope not only destroy the rope, but damages expensive descending and ascending equipment.

Ropes should be washed regularly. Use either one of the special rope washers available or wash the rope in a large front-opening washer. Use a good detergent, warm or hot water, and a fabric softener, which is also helpful to re-lubricate the yarn filaments that make up the rope. The importance of taking care of a rope cannot be over-emphasized. The rope should be inspected inch by inch after being cleaned following each trip and before storage. Store the rope in a cool, dry place out of direct sunlight. Protect the rope from exposure to acids and alkalines. Remember that a rope you trust your life to is for that purpose only. A rope used to tow a car is a tow rope, not a rappel and prusik line or a handline.

Where to purchase a rope for caving is the final question. If you are looking for a handline, you might find one at a local hardware or marine supply store. If you want a rappel and prusik line or a special dynamic rock-climbing rope, you will have to go to an outdoor sporting goods store or a mail-order catalog. In recent years some people affiliated with caving in the United States have set up small "travelling stores" from which they sell all sorts of supplies for caving, including ropes. Their addresses are given in the appendix. When you buy a rope, try to make sure it is of high quality. Companies such as West, Sampson and Wall have been making good ropes for many years. For those people desiring a hard-laid nylon rope, Goldline has always been the standard. Originally manufactured by Plymouth, later by the Cordage Group, it was dropped as a product. It has been recently reintroduced as Goldline II. Kernmantle type ropes especially designed for caving use such as Blue Water II, P.M.I. pit rope, Speleoshoppe Static Master and Blue Water Super III are all excellent ropes. The specially-designed dynamic kernmantle ropes for rock climbing are nearly all manufactured in Europe. They are available by mail order and at some outdoor sporting goods stores.

Always buy the best rope available, use it only for its intended purpose, protect it from damage, keep it clean and inspect it regularly. Get proper training in rope work and don't take chances. Remember, it's your life on that line.

READING CAVE MAPS

Langford G. Brod, Jr.
NSS 5329F

Introduction

Cave maps are somewhat like road maps in that they depict a geometrical arrangement of routes and features in a cave. Some cave maps will show a single passageway, much like a highway traversing a sparsely-populated area; other maps of more complex caves will show multiple interconnections, somewhat resembling a network of city streets. All of these maps give some idea to the reader of how the explorer can travel through the cave, what routes he can follow. However, only a small percentage of cave maps are made with the express purpose of displaying a route and most of these maps have been prepared for commercial caves. Most cave maps are produced by unpaid cave surveyors for their own purposes.

Probably the greatest number of cave maps are prepared specifically for the purpose of determining the relationship of room and passages with each other and with surface features. Such maps will reveal potential connections between adjacent passages or even between separate caves, assuming both caves have been mapped and the relative positions of their entrances is accurately known. There is a thrill and a sense of discovery associated with the map preparation, first in seeing the skeletal development of the survey lines as they are laid out line by line, next in seeing the fleshing out of the map as walls and details are added, and finally laying this completed segment on the main map and properly orienting it. Suddenly, that large, blank area on the main map is no longer blank; there is now a passage in that space, filling in the blank area with unforeseen detail. Your just-completed large side passage isn't at all heading in the direction you thought it was going. No, it's heading more easterly, nearer the main passage. You check the alignment to see if the segment has shifted. No, it's good; the alignment is correct. Suddenly, you see a verification: the previously-mapped, tiny side passage with a small stream is only a few feet away from the terminal room of your just-completed side passage—that's where the waterfall runoff is going! You have a sense of satisfaction; two previously unrelated hydrologic features are now united and you know the map is right. This insight is the payoff, the reason that cave surveyors labor under cold, dirty, poorly lighted conditions for no pay to survey a cave, to make a map.

Thus, in reading a cave map, one must bear in mind that the map is, for the surveyor, a highly personal creation and, within the limits of permissible variation allowed by the cave map format, is a product of his own personal creative biases. Features of little general interest may be shown, while other information of more importance may be omitted. Alternatively, such additions and omissions may not necessarily reflect the surveyor's bias, but may represent a regional standard followed by all the mappers in a certain locality. Names of features in the cave, of little or no significance to the casual reader, may evoke deep feelings in the surveying crew and others familiar with the cave, especially if the cave is a challenge. To these cavers, the names bring back memories of campsites, crises, pinnacles of achievement, milestones of penetration or, in less frequent instances, a breakthrough into virgin passage. Notable exceptions are provided by those cases where the map is accompanied by an account of the exploration and surveying, such as in the case of Jewel Cave (*The Jewel Cave Adventure* by Herb and Jan Conn) and the Flint Ridge-Mammoth connection (*The Longest Cave* by Roger Brucker and Richard Watson). There is a growing number of such publications and, hopefully, many of the larger caves will be similarly documented in the future.

In addition to the personal bias of the surveyor, there are a number of drafting styles. Despite the restrictions imposed by the cave map format, individual styles and techniques are evident. Furthermore, there is a great variety in the quality of the maps, depending on various factors such as the size of the cave, its complexity, the surveying difficulties encountered and the survey leader. As a consequence, maps range in quality from rough sketch maps to precise and highly detailed cave cartography. It should not be inferred that less detailed or less accurate maps are necessarily inferior. There is no formal standard of excellence to which all maps must comply. Whether or not the map pleases the reader is a secondary consideration; the primary question is: did the map serve the purpose intended by the person who drew it? All cave maps should be observed with this question in mind rather than a critical appraisal of style or technique.

The Various Views

Cave maps are drawn in three principal views: the **plan view**, the **profile view** and the **cross section** (Fig. 27). If we imagine the cave to be a straight horizontal tube, the **plan view** will correspond to an outline of the cave in the horizontal plane, as viewed directly from above. The **profile view** is an outline of the cave in the vertical plane as viewed from the side, while the **cross section** is an outline of the cave passage viewed end on. Thus the three views in this case correspond to three slices taken through the cave in three mutually perpendicular planes.

Actual caves are much more complex and are seldom linear or horizontal; consequently, the maps differ from the simplistic explanation given above. Though not horizontal, many caves dip at low inclination angles and are approximately horizontal. Rather than showing an outline along the actual floor, the plan view in this case is a projection of the cave passage onto the horizontal plane and tilted features are slightly foreshortened.

Similarly, profiles may consist of projections of the cave passage into a vertical plane generally parallel to the passage. Frequently, because of bends in the passage, it is impractical to project into a single vertical plane; in this case, the profile is made up of a series of short profiles strung together to form a single profile. The bends where the profile segments join may be marked or unmarked, depending on the preference of the map draftsman. In some instances, the profile is not a vertical projection, but a trace of the ceiling and floor along a particular plane, most often along the station line which serves as the skeleton upon which the plan view measurements are made. Frequently, there is little difference between the two methods; in cases where there is a difference, features out of the plane are shown with dashed lines. Some mappers show entering side passages in a quasi-pictorial style on the profile, with the actual side passage shape shown in solid black. Of course, the profile can be drawn from either side of the main passage and the correct view must be chosen so that the side passage appears in the background.

Section views are generally shown as an outline formed by the intersection of the cave passage with an arbitrary section plane. The section plane is generally vertical and is usually roughly perpendicular to the axis of the passage, but not always. Cave passages in some cases are so irregular that an axis is undefinable. In other cases, such as a large room, it may be more feasible to take the section along the length of the room, similar to a profile view. In general, however, sections are taken across the passage, more or less perpendicular to the long dimension.

The alignment of the section plane is shown on the plan view by a line, either continuous across the passage or broken in the middle. In most cases, this line is broken where it crosses the plan view so that it does not interfere with plan view details. This line is either connected to the section view by an auxiliary line or is marked with letters corresponding to identifying letters on the section. Section views are usually drawn at the same scale as the plan view, but in some cases it may be necessary to enlarge some or all of the section views. In that event, the enlargement factor is indicated somewhere on the map or adjacent to each enlarged section.

Section views may be taken across pits, in which the section plane is horizontal or nearly so. These section views should complement a profile view. The pit may exhibit unequal development in different directions, so that two or even more profiles may be required to show the configuration, as shown in Fig. 33. The profile planes are usually, but not necessarily, vertical. The alignment of the profile planes is indicated on the plan view by linear line segments exterior to the wall outline, identified by appropriate letters or numbers, as in the case of the cross sections. If the profiles are not vertical, the line segments indicate the alignment of the profile plane at floor level.

Types of Maps

The Rough Sketch Map. The rough sketch map depicts only the most significant relationships in a cave. There has been no attempt to depict dimensions and directions in their true relationships and the map is frequently much distorted. The primary utility of this map is to depict the sequential arrangement of rooms or other interesting features, which are frequently named on the map. Thus, this type of map is often accompanied by a verbal description or a written description and loses some of its utility without this information. The rough sketch map is frequently used to describe a new find or to plan an exploration or survey trip.

The Detailed Sketch Map. The detailed sketch map is similar to the rough sketch map in that it is simply a sketch and is not based on surveyed dimensions. However, greater care, has been devoted to its preparation. The map is roughly to scale and has approximately the correct alignment. This map is usually intended to illustrate some particular detail or relationship.

The Compass and Pace Map. The compass and pace map is similar to the detailed sketch map, except that it incorporates a very crude survey technique which provides rough measurements of distances and directions. This type of map is used principally to find out how far and in what direction a passage extends. A relatively large amount of effort in relation to the useful data is required for a map of this type, so that it is not often made.

The Line Map. The line map, Fig. 26, consists of a sequence of straight-line segments corresponding to the surveyed distances and directions (station lines) between consecutive survey points (survey stations) in the cave. The line map does not depict any features such as the width of the cave, but it does give some idea as to the size of the cave and the direction and orientation of its passages. Unless specific features are named on the map, it cannot serve as a guide. The map is as dimensionally accurate as a fully detailed map and thus can provide directional and distance data between various cave features if they are noted on the map. Because of their limited utility, line maps are not frequently made as a specific end product. One principal exception to this general rule is the case of the computer-generated stereo

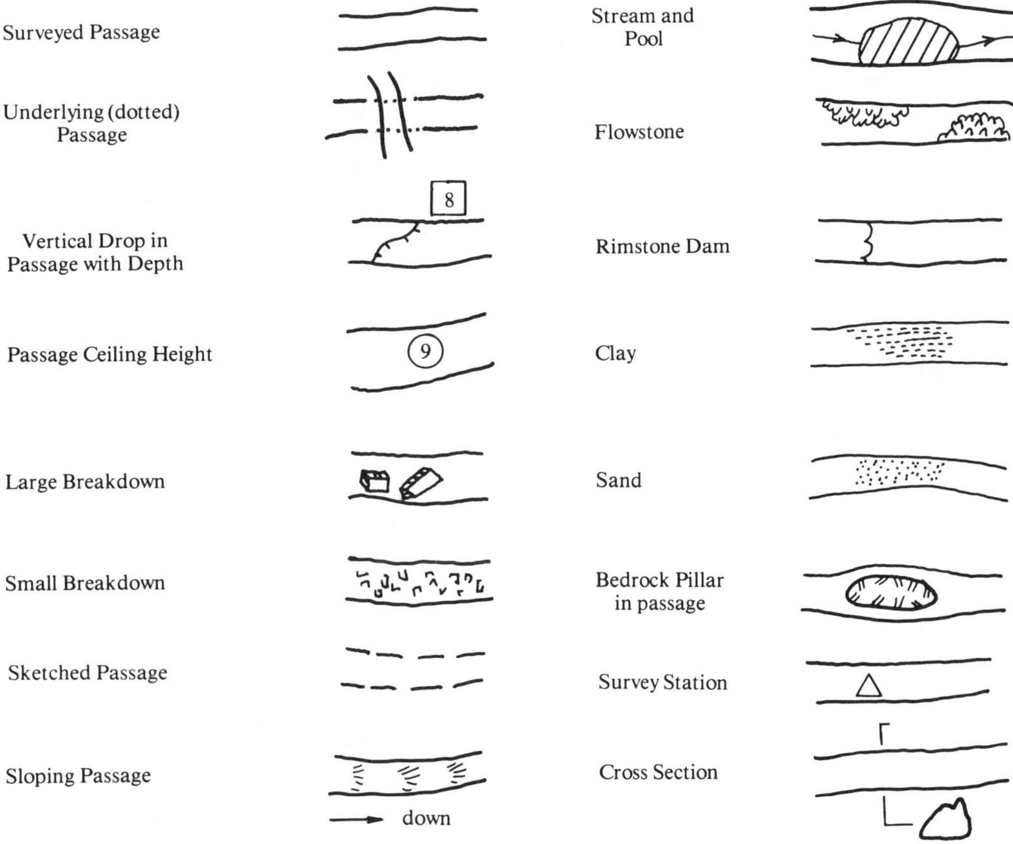

Fig. 25. Common cave map symbols from The 1976 NSS Standard Map Symbols in *The NSS Bulletin*, v. 41, no. 2, April 1979, pages 35-48.

maps in which two maps generated in different colors are viewed as a stereo pair with appropriate colored glasses; this arrangement provides a visual three-dimensional view of a complex cave developed on multiple levels.

Line maps are most frequently encountered as intermediate stages in the survey of large cave systems, where they are produced by computers using the survey data. The computers are programmed to correct for closure errors produced in surveying around a complete loop of cave passage; the error is apportioned among the survey measurements so that the loop closes. The computer-generated line map then serves as a skeleton upon which the walls and other cave features are manually drafted.

The Solid Outline Map. The solid outline map, Fig. 28, is somewhat similar to the line map, but in addition the cave walls have been included; the entire cave passage is depicted by a solid black line of varying width. Solid outline maps are generally prepared when the cave is large compared to the size of the passages. In that case it would be difficult and probably confusing to show the adjacent cave walls by two separate lines; thus, the space between the cave walls is completely blacked in. This type of map is much superior to the line map as the size of passages and rooms are readily apparent. Dimensions and directions are to scale, so that significant rooms may be ascertained without additional captions. A variation of this type of map shows white cave passage on a black background representing the enclosing rock. In this type of map, features can be symbolically or pictorially depicted in the white region representing the interior of the cave.

The Detailed Map and Symbols. The detailed cave map, Fig. 31, is the most sophisticated of all cave maps in that it depicts significant features within the cave as well as the walls. Both the features and the walls are dimensionally to scale so that anyone reading the map can obtain a fairly accurate idea of what the cave is like. The various features are illustrated symbolically and some symbols are shown in Fig. 25. The NSS has published a list of standard map symbols (by the standing Committee on Cave Map Symbols, Cave Geology and Geography Section, NSS) for caves in *NSS Bulletin*, v. 41, no. 2, 1979, and is available from the NSS Office for $2.50.

It is recommended that these symbols be used in the preparation of cave maps. The cave walls are shown by lines, either solid, dashed or dotted, depending on whether the lines portray the main passage (solid), an underlying passage (dotted) or unsurveyed passage (dashed). Ceiling heights are shown by numbers inside circles; the number has generally represented height in feet, but may represent height in meters on more recent maps. Breakdown, which includes blocks of rocks fallen from the cave ceiling or tumbled in from the entrance, is pictorially depicted with angular, block-like outlines to resemble a rock. Larger blocks are usually illustrated with a shaded or blackened edge on one side, giving the block a three-dimensional appearance. Larger blocks may be drawn to scale, while smaller rocks are simply illustrated. Slopes, whether of clay, silt or talus, are shown by sets of radiating lines, with the divergence pointing in the downward direction. Ledges and drops are symbolized with the hachured line, a primary longer line representing the ledge edge with short line segments (tick marks) perpendicular to the primary line attached at closely spaced intervals. The tick marks point to the dropoff side.

Pools and streams are represented in several different ways. Probably the best symbolism is one in which the pool outline is drawn to scale and the interior region is shown by finer lines at an angle to the general passage. Flowstone and speleothems, where of significant size, are depicted by a series of small circular segments arranged so that the end of one segment joins another segment partway along its length. This connected series of circular segments represents the outline of the feature. That part inside the outline is represented by isolated circular segments with the area density of the segments being roughly proportional to the surface slope of the feature. An older symbol used for small speleothems is a small, black, arrow-shaped triangle. The symbol for rimstone dams consists of a series of very small semi-circular line segments joined at diametrically opposite points to form a chain of semicircles. The convexities point in the downslope or downstream direction.

Different symbols may be combined to illustrate composite features. For instance, the flowstone symbol and the breakdown symbol may be combined to show flowstone-covered breakdown. Talus can be shown by combining the slope symbol with the symbol for small rocks. Flowstone-covered ledges can be shown by drawing tick marks on the flowstone symbol.

Conventional plan view maps are often supplemented by profile and section views. Symbolism is less frequently used in these views, and the primary objective is to depict the actual physical outline of the cave chamber lying on or close to the profile plane or the section plane. These views are used to supplement the symbolism on the plan view and to clarify relationships not readily apparent on the plan view.

Once the symbolism is understood, it should be possible to read a cave map with some fair degree of comprehension. Problems arise, however, when the cave is complex. In that case, the only recourse is to study the map in great detail to distinguish the different levels and sublevels. In some complex caves the configuration has been clarified by depicting different passages in different colors. Thus, all passages at a single level are shown in a single color, overlying passages of a different color, and underlying passages of a third color. Unfortunately, this color technique cannot be duplicated by most types of reproduction equipment, so the technique is found exclusively on special one-of-a-kind maps.

Title Block

The symbolic representation of the cave is accompanied by the title block, which includes the name of the cave, the political province in which it is located, the names of the surveying crew or the group responsible for the map, and the date of the map. Other information is sometimes included, such as a precise location of the cave, the total surveyed length and the survey accuracy. Underneath the title block or in some convenient position is the bar scale, a line or a narrow linear strip of alternating black and white spaces marked off in feet and/or meters at the same scale as the map. A distance measured on the map with a ruler or a pair of dividers can be placed on the bar scale and the length in feet or meters can be read directly from the scale. On maps of small caves, the bar scale may be an appreciable part of the length of the cave or even greater than its length, whereas on maps of larger caves the bar scale is only a small fraction of the cave length. On some maps a scale factor, such as 1 inch = 50 feet, is included. It is only necessary to measure the distance on the map in inches (or whatever unit is used) and multiply by the scale factor to get the actual distance. This scale factor only applies to full-scale maps which have not been reduced (or enlarged) and therefore should be used with caution.

On the subject of reduction, it happens that cave maps are sometimes copied by Xerox copiers or similar machines. The copies are not only enlarged slightly but also are enlarged at slightly different factors along different axes. Thus, the map is distorted slightly, not enough to significantly alter the appearance of the map but enough to preclude accurate measurements.

A north arrow is included at some convenient place on the map, usually more closely adjacent to the plan view if a profile view is included. In some instances, the north arrow will point to magnetic north rather than true north. If so, the north arrow should be indicated as magnetic north.

In addition to the title block, bar scale and north arrow, cave maps sometimes include a list of symbols with an appropriate description for each symbol. This list explains the use of unusual or nonstandard symbols, or clarifies the usage for standard symbols as used on that particular map. Some map draftsmen include small human figures in their cross section or profile views; such figures, while not standard symbolism, are universally

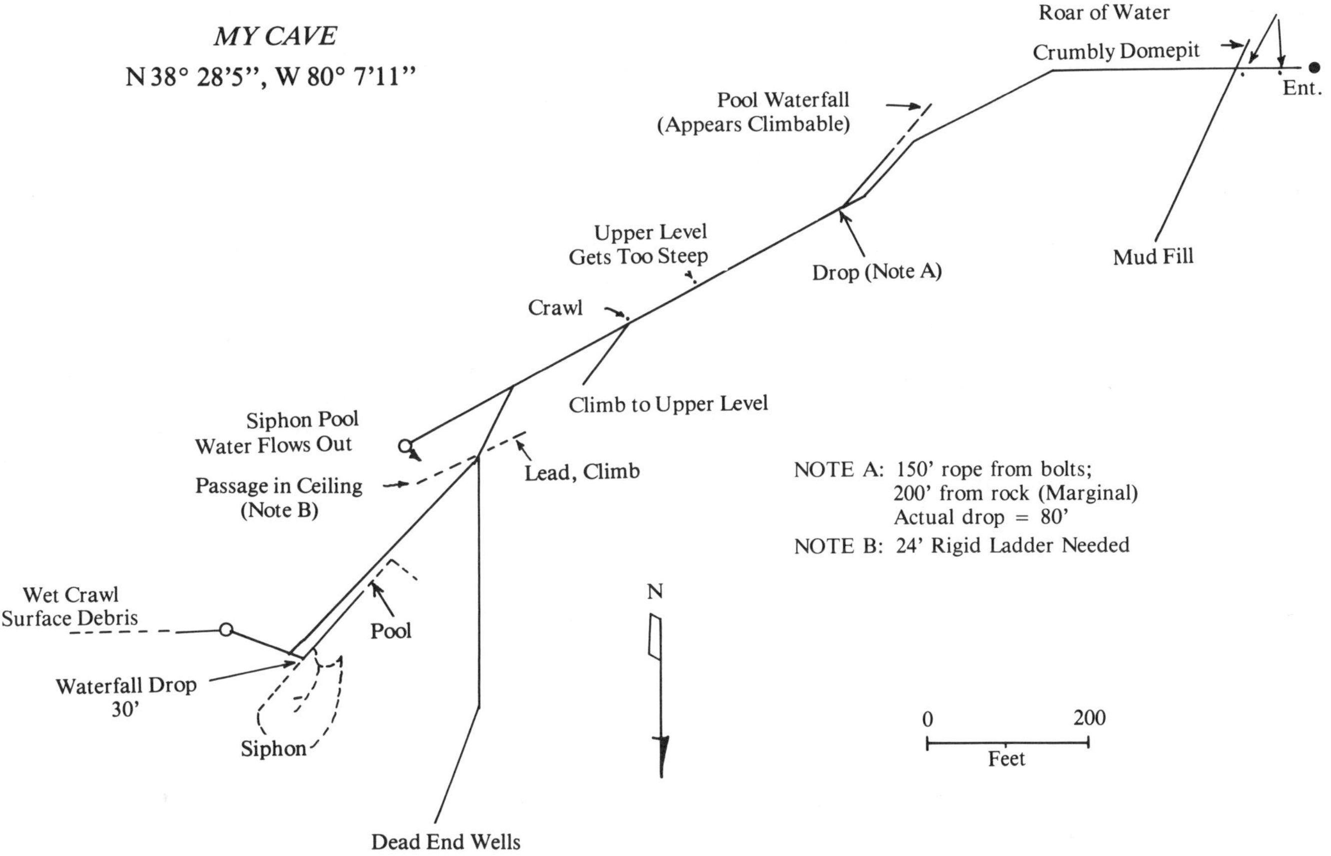

Fig. 26. Map of My Cave, West Virginia. (*The Potomac Caver*, 1966, v. 9 no. 1, page 6. Copied from the *1966 Speleo Digest,* page 1-135.)

recognizable and provide handy references for passage size and shape.

Using the north arrow, it is possible to align the map with surface features and determine the relationship of those features with the cave passages. If the map fortuitously happens to be at the same scale as the topographic map of the area, the cave map can be directly laid upon the topographic map for comparison. The cave entrance (or entrances) on the cave map can be superimposed on the entrance location plotted on the topographic map; the cave map can then be rotated with the entrance as a pivot point until the north arrows on both maps are parallel. The maps can be transilluminated with a strong light to view the cave and surface features together. It is, of course, necessary to mentally supply the missing third dimension by imagining the cave lying underneath the surface features, as if the earth were transparent and were viewed from a height.

Usually the scale of the cave map and available topographic maps are greatly different, with the cave map scale factor much higher than the topographic map. To illustrate the relationship of the cave to surface features, some cave maps include surface topographic contours and/or surface features enlarged from standard topographic maps or independent surveys.

The topographic additions illustrate the relationship of the cave to surface drainage routes, valleys, highways, mines, quarries, etc. The site of potential new entrances can be studied, and the feasibility of digging a new entrance can be evaluated. The possibility of a connection between adjacent caves or the possible extension of a terminated cave can be ascertained from the topographic data.

Despite the quality and accuracy of a map, people are disappointed when a map fails to describe a cave in terms which convey the "feel" of the cave. A map, however, by its very nature is a double abstraction: it reduces features to dimensional relationships and it portrays only two dimensions in any one view. This double abstraction is not a defect of the maps; it is, in fact, a deliberate objective so that dimensional relationships may be shown in a clear and unambiguous manner. It is possible, if desired, to abandon the three mutually perpendicular (or almost perpendicular) plan-profile-section views and combine the data into a single quasi-perspective (isometric) view which simulates a three-dimensional view of the cave. In doing so, the draftsman provides an illustration which may be more understandable in certain respects, but only at the price of deleting or obscuring other relevant data.

It should always be remembered that a map is, first and foremost, a scale drawing illustrating geometric relationships of the cave, usually in the three principal planes. Maps cannot and will not convey to the reader the majestic grace of a cathedral-like chamber or the yawning blackness of a deep pit. These visual impressions are better left to artistic renditions, cinematography or still photography.

Discussion of Cave Map Examples

Figures 26 through 33 show eight cave maps. A discussion of each map follows.

Map of My Cave, West Virginia, Fig. 26

This map is a line map of a moderately large cave in West Virginia. It is not clear from the map whether the lines are actual survey lines or merely average alignments. In any event, several lines are about 300 feet long and probably represent several individual measurements, even though the several station lines may have the same direction. Regardless of such details, the end result is a line map, which of course corresponds to a plan view of the cave. The map includes no passage details, no symbolism, no profile and no cross sections. Significant features are denoted by captions. The title block is the utmost of simplicity, including only the cave name and the latitude/longitude location. The bar scale, 0-200 feet long, is subdivided into 100-foot increments by a midpoint marker.

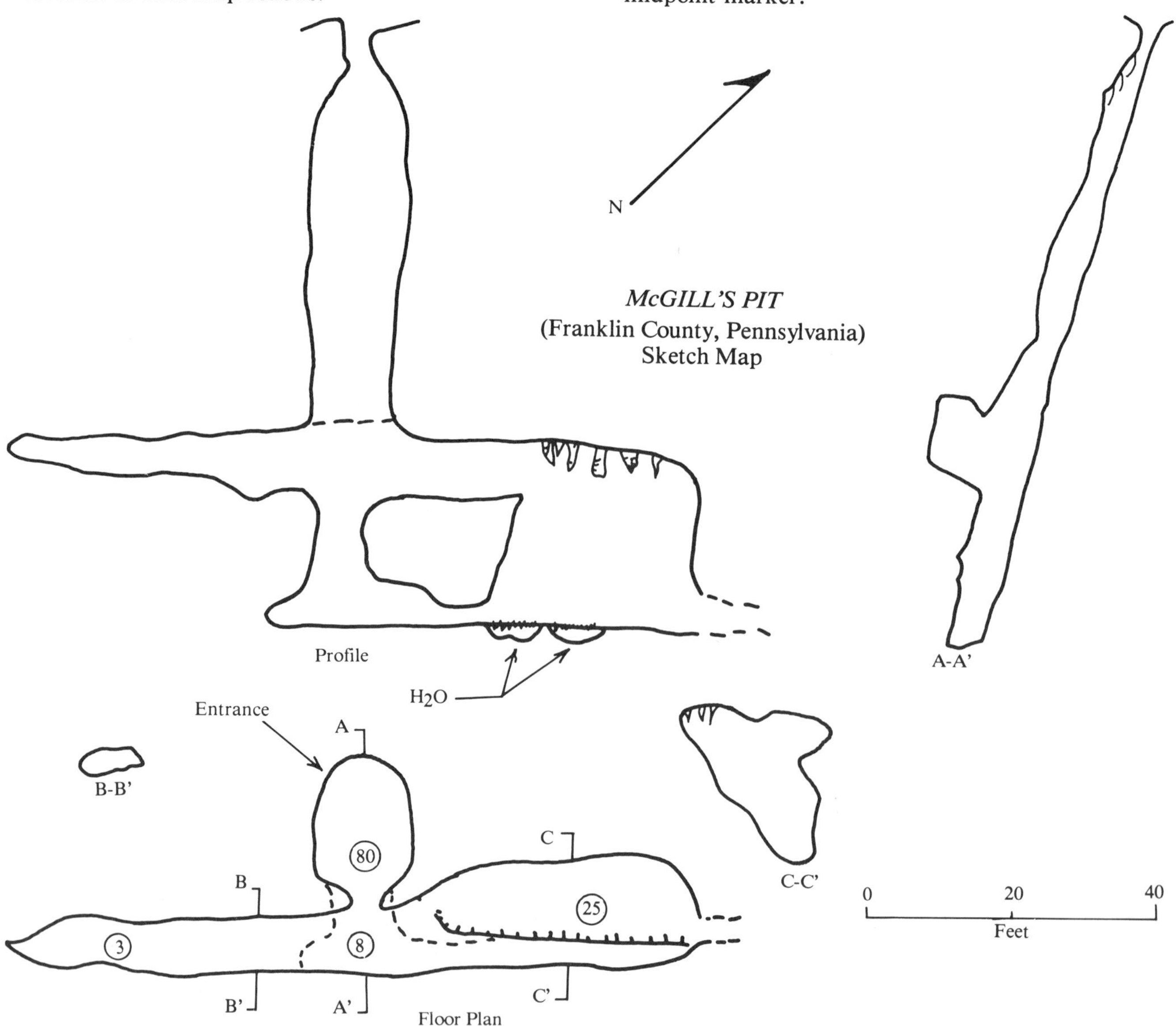

Fig. 27. Map of McGill's Pit, Pennsylvania (Copied from the *1962 Speleo Digest*, page 1-71.)

The map is not intended as a finished product, but rather as a schematic diagram for the accompanying article in the original publication. The article discusses eight potential places where the cave may possibly be extended. Despite the limitations of the map, it serves its intended purpose and clearly demonstrates the size and directional trend of the cave. Furthermore, the preliminary map could serve as the basic planning document for a more detailed survey, if one has not already been done.

Map of McGill's Pit, Pennsylvania, Fig. 27

This map of McGill's Pit is a well-drawn sketch map, a fact which is noted in the title block. The name of the draftsman and the source publication have, unfortunately, both been omitted, and there is no accompanying report. The map includes the plan view, two profiles and two cross sections which adequately define the major aspects of the cave's configuration. The plan view includes a ledge (shown with the hachured line), a breakdown block and four ceiling heights. The primary profile view shows two pools and a group of stalactites. This same profile also illustrates the cave's horizontal development along two principal levels, an aspect not apparent in the other views. The secondary profile, shown as section A-A', depicts some stalactites near the entrance and shows the tilted nature of the entrance pit. Whether this view is treated as a profile or a section is immaterial; the draftsman has chosen to show it as a section. Section B-B' and C-C' show the cross sections of the horizontal extensions.

There is so much detail here that one might think that the pit had been surveyed if the map were not specifically called a sketch map. In all probability, the explorers made at least one compass reading at the bottom of the pit to ascertain the primary alignment and estimated a number of pertinent dimensions, as implied by the north arrow and the bar scale. This relatively small cave is well suited to such a sketch. The technique is more difficult to apply in the case of a more complex cave.

Map of the Moore Cave System, Missouri, Fig. 28

This map depicts the plan view of two large caves considered to be segments of a single cave system. The map is an example of a solid outline map, where the cave passage is shown in solid black. The scale of this map, about 1200 feet per inch, is such that passages 15 to 20 feet wide are proportional in width to the width of an inked line. Some wider passages are indicated by a corresponding increase in the width of the passage shown on the map. Unsurveyed passages are shown by the small arrows. With these two exceptions, no other symbolism is employed. No cross sections and no ceiling heights are shown. Significant features are denoted by captions.

The primary objective of this map is to illustrate the geometry of the two caves, the relationship of the two caves to one another, and the position of notable features in the caves. The map is a reduction from a more detailed map drawn at a scale of 160 feet per inch, which in turn was prepared from map notes and detailed map segments at a scale of 16 feet per inch.

Map of Indian Rock Cave, Alabama, Fig. 29

This map of Indian Rock Cave, Alabama, Fig. 29, shows only a simplified plan view of a long and, in places, apparently complex cave. The map is fairly typical of the maps of long caves appearing in grotto newsletters, where the lack of sophisticated reproduction equipment and the restriction to an 8½ x 11-inch format size preclude showing much detail. Thus, this map is just about the simplest detailed map which can be found. There is no profile, no cross sections and no specific ceiling heights. One symbolized mud slope is shown. The lack of symbolism is partially compensated by the use of captions which indicate significant features in the cave. Interestingly, the name of the county in which the cave occurs is not listed in the title block information. The AL535 in parentheses is a unique serial number assigned to this cave for purposes of identification by the Alabama Cave Survey. The length of the cave is listed under the north arrow as 5300 feet, a large amount of passage to show on a single page. Despite its limitations, the map clearly shows the geometric relationship of its passages and salient features to one another. Note the three interesting captions at the bottom of the map, implying the distinct possibility of a connection to a cave 1800 feet away, or at least the possibility of finding another entrance. This map is probably a simplified version of a larger, more detailed map.

Map of Davis Cave No. 2, Missouri, Fig. 30

Fig. 30 shows a cave of moderate size (1460 feet shown) in Laclede County, Missouri. The map consists of a plan view and one section, and it is fairly simple for a detailed map. Two ceiling heights are shown, one of which is included in the section view, rather than the plan view which is customary. The use of symbols is limited to three on this map: breakdown, the hachured line for ledges and the symbol for streams and pools. A stream is shown running the length of the cave and forming a pool at the entrance with an arrow indicating the flow direction. In addition, the stream is shown exiting the cave and running overland a short distance to the Osage Fork River, thus showing the relationship of the cave to surface drainage. The stream is shown entering the cave via a low extension with a question mark beside it, indicating that the stream was not followed farther and that the continuation is unknown. An accompanying report (not included here) states that this extension is a water crawl. Another extension leading to low, unsurveyed passage is indicated by a second break in the wall line adjacent to the water crawl.

The title block information omits the state name, a common omission in *Missouri Speleology* maps. The north arrow indicates the true north direction. A border around the periphery of the map was cropped during reproduction. The map can be somewhat misleading if the reader does not pay close attention to the bar

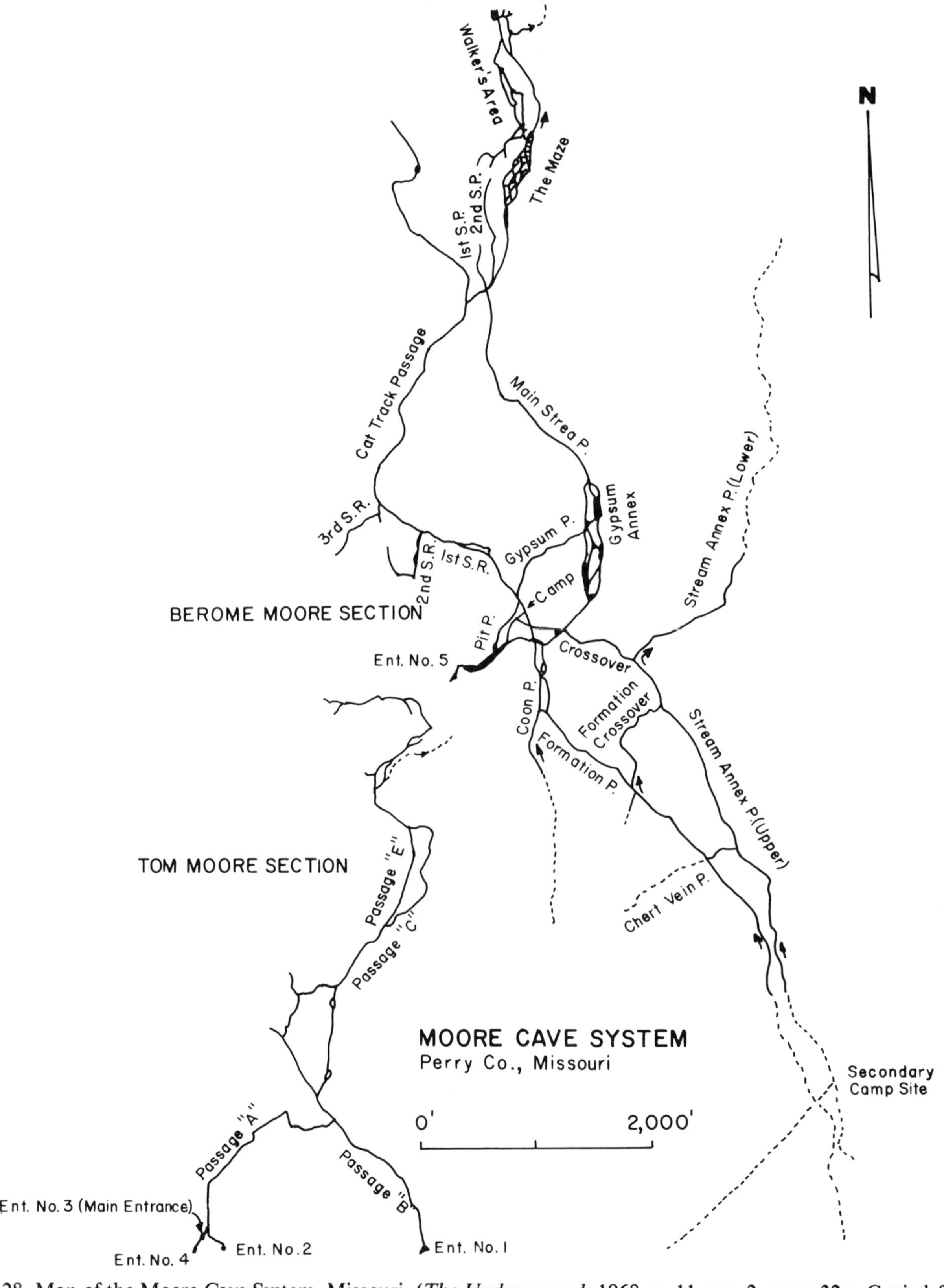

Fig. 28. Map of the Moore Cave System, Missouri. (*The Underground*, 1968, v. 11, no. 2, page 32a. Copied from the *1968 Speleo Digest*, page 1-80.)

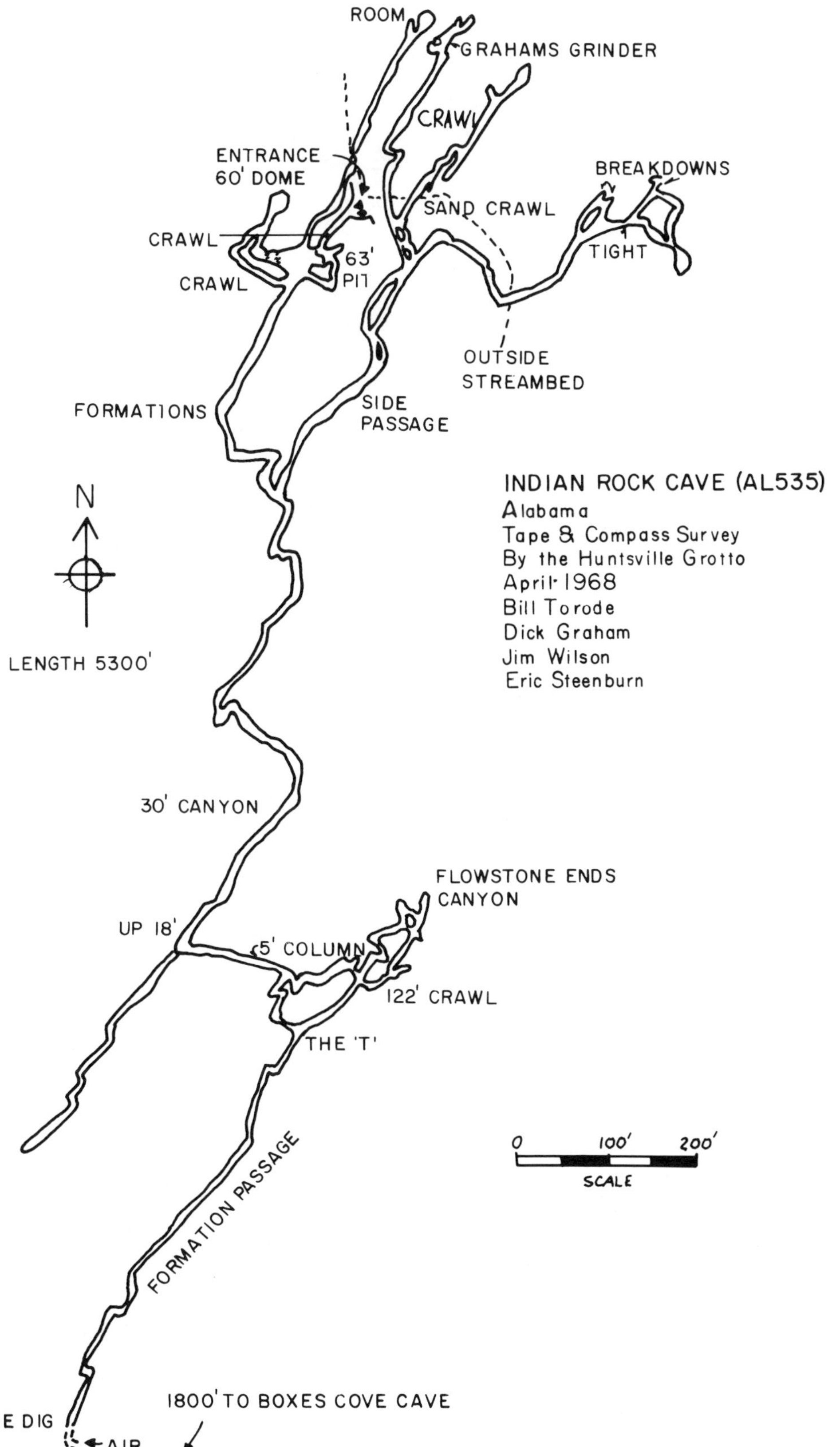

Fig. 29. Map of Indian Rock Cave, Alabama. (*Huntsville Grotto Newsletter*, 1968, v. 9, no. 5, page 72. Copied from the *1968 Speleo Digest*, page 1-8.)

Fig. 30. Map of Davis Cave No. 2, Missouri. (*Missouri Speleology*, 1973, v. 13, no. 1, page 14.)

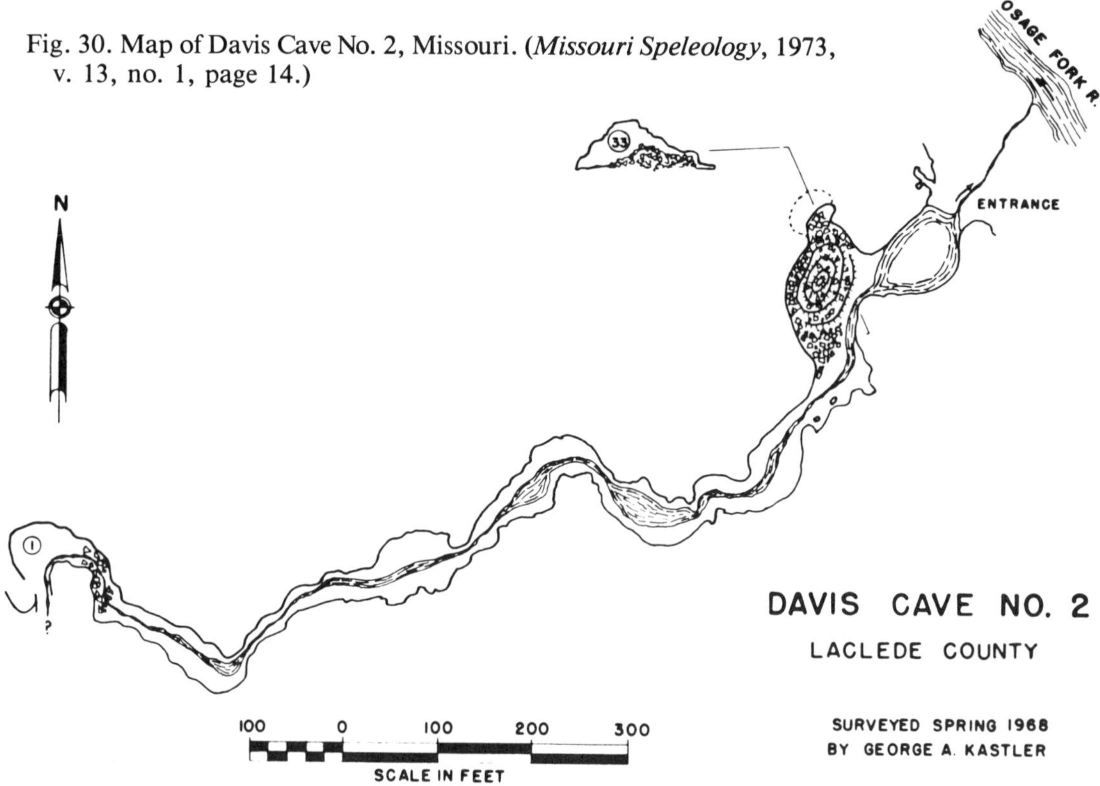

scale. The average width of the cave is 30 feet, and there are several places where the width exceeds 70 feet, reaching 100 feet at one point. These large widths cause the cave to appear more like a shorter, narrower cave at first glance.

Map of Smallin Sink Cave, Missouri, Fig. 31

This detailed map shows a moderate size cave (about 625 feet long) in southwestern Missouri. The map consists of the plan view and ten sections; no profile is included. The wealth of detail shown on this map permits the size and nature of the cave to be readily assessed. Note the use of breakdown symbolism, slope symbolism and hachured lines for ledges and domes. The drip line at the entrance has been depicted with a dotted line, and dotted lines are employed further back in the cave to show abrupt changes in ceiling elevation. Ceiling heights, shown by the circled numbers, are scattered throughout the cave. Decimal points on some ceiling heights have become obscured by photographic reduction from a larger original map; fortunately in the ambiguous cases the ceiling heights can be deduced from adjacent heights. The plan view is supplemented with several names and explanatory captions, and the caption of a large log points to a scale drawing of the log in its actual position. The large section view at the bottom of the map, actually a profile of the terminal room, includes symbolism showing the horizontally-bedded limestone which forms the walls of the cave. The title block lists both the primary name and an alternate name of the cave. The bar scale, included here in the title block, is simply calibrated from 1-100 in 20-foot increments. The north arrow shows N_M, indicating that the specified direction is magnetic north, not true north. Judging from appearances, the map has been photographically reduced by a factor of about four to five. The reduced map has no border, but it may have been cropped off during the reduction process.

Map of Antonia Pit, Missouri, Fig. 32

This map shows a pit 71 feet deep with a small entrance opening. Contrast this map with the map of Bonacker Pit, Fig. 33, in the same county. The map of Antonia Pit shows two profiles, termed "vertical sections" on the map. The two profiles are not taken perpendicular to one another as in the case of Bonacker Pit but instead are two views of a single profile with the background details of the two halves of the pit included in each profile. The profile plane is taken across the larger width of the pit. Note the extensive use of flowstone symbolism, especially in the lower part of the pit. The map is interesting for its display of horizontal sections, of which there are six, including the floor plan. The uppermost horizontal section, taken through the entrance, shows the numeral 71 enclosed in a square; this figure denotes the depth of the pit, a standard symbol on cave maps. Pool symbolism is shown in the fourth and sixth section, and the corresponding pool surfaces are

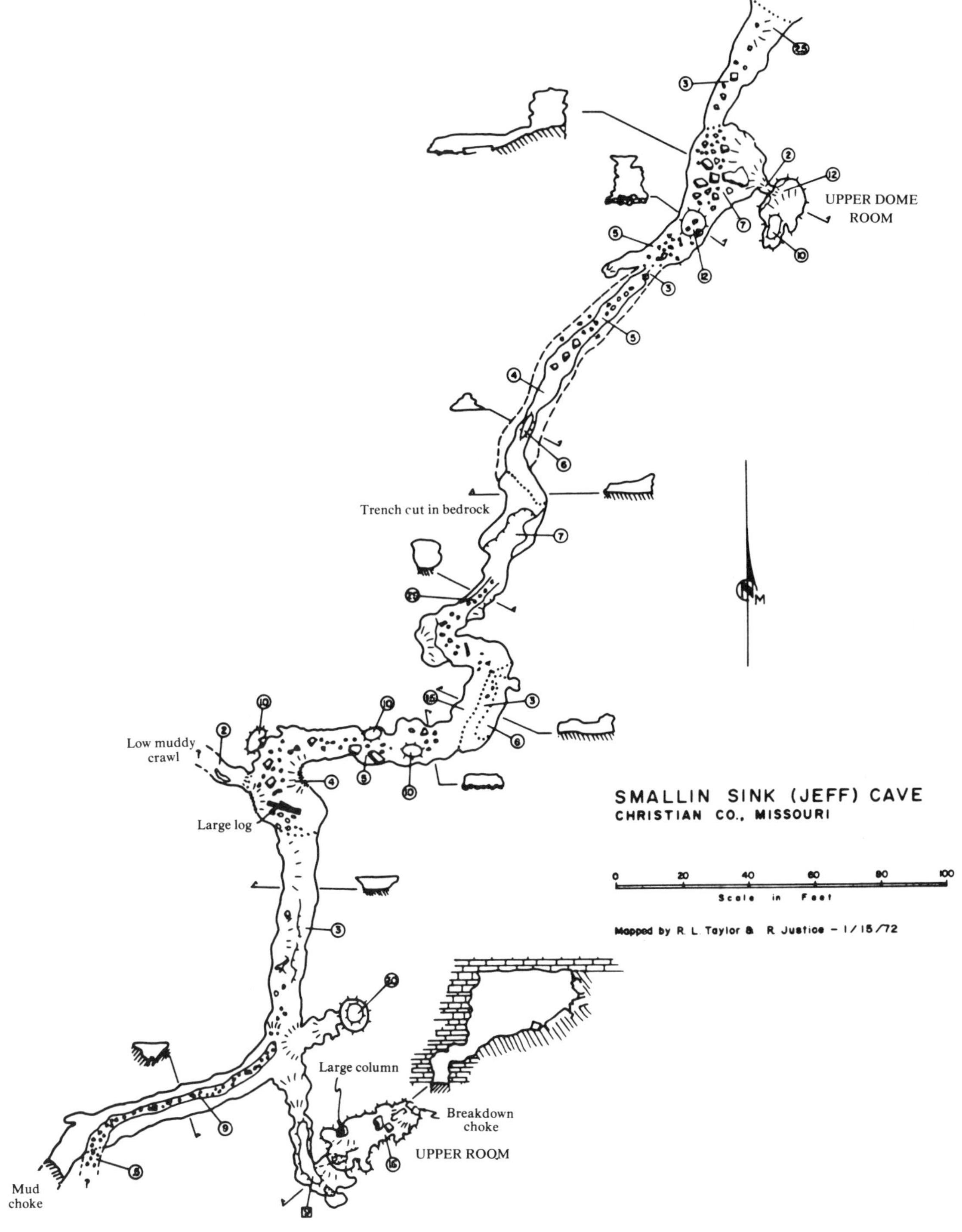

Fig. 31. Map of Smallin Sink Cave, Missouri. (*Missouri Speleology*, 1975, v. 15, no. 4, page 21.)

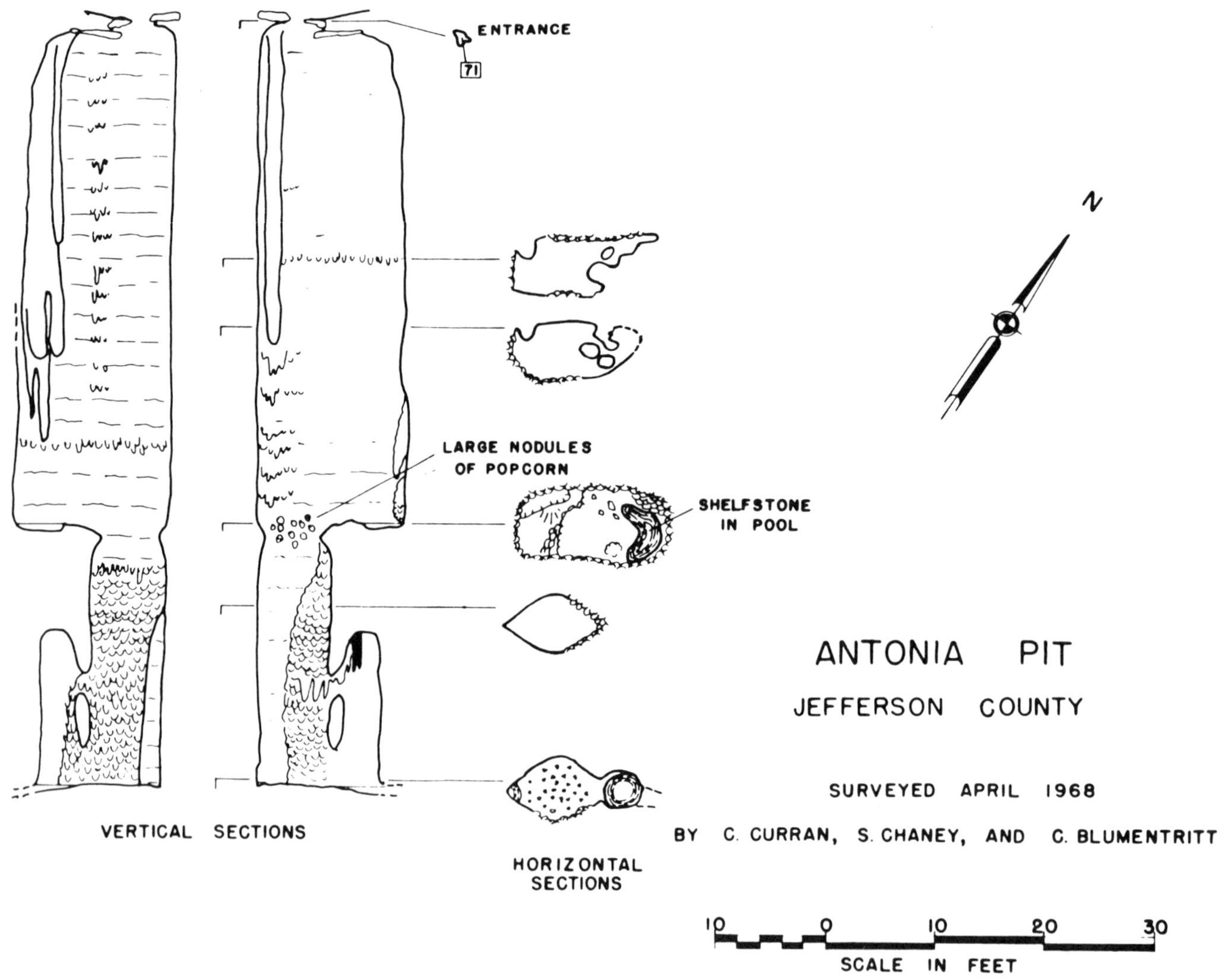

Fig. 32. Map of Antonia Pit, Missouri. (*Missouri Speleology*, 1971, v. 12, no. 2, page 36.)

shown as straight, thin, horizontal lines in both profile views. The bar scale in this map is horizontal. Note the ten-foot section subdivided into two-foot increments at the left side. In using the bar scale, this ten-foot section should not be included in the 30-foot length. The border was cropped off during reproduction.

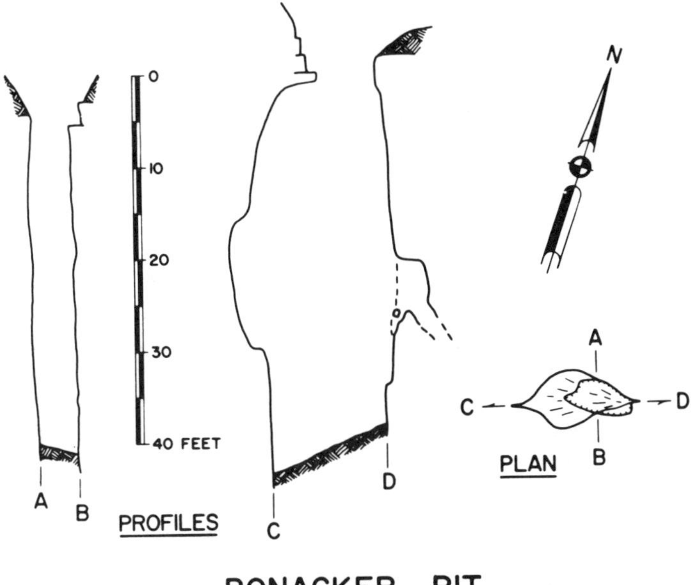

Fig. 33. Map of Bonacker Pit, Missouri. (*Missouri Speleology*, 1971, v. 12, no. 2, page 40.)

Map of Bonacker Pit, Missouri, Fig. 33

Fig. 33 shows a small, almost featureless pit about 40 feet deep. Because it had developed along a joint (Shown by half-arrows pointing toward C and D), it exhibits unequal development along the joint and across the joint, and it is in these two directions that the two profile views are drawn. Both profiles pass through the entrance, which is shown by the hachured line in the plan view. A small alcove is shown in profile C-D about 15 feet above the floor, but the alcove is not shown on the plan view. Thus, the plan view is only the floor plan of the pit with the entrance opening superimposed upon it. On this map, soil and talus are shown by a non-standard symbol consisting of small, cross-lined squares. This symbol is used to show soil at the lip of the pit and the talus covering the pit floor. The bar scale is drawn vertically, parallel to the longest dimension of the cave, but it obviously also applies to the plan view. The state name has been omitted in the title block; however, as the map was published in *Missouri Speleology*, there should be no problem arising from this omission. The map border was cropped during reproduction.

THE GEOLOGY OF CAVES

William B. White
NSS 2237F

Introduction

These notes are intended to provide an introduction to the descriptive aspects of cave geology. They tell something about the patterns and shape of caves and about the features found inside caves. They say little or nothing about the origin of caves or about the time scale and historical sequence of events that are recorded in the levels, sculpturing and sediments of individual caves.

The practitioners of cave geology usually operate from one of two viewpoints. They may be inwardly looking, concerned about some specific cave or cave system, its historical evolution in context of its geological setting, the minerals it contains, or the detailed processes of growth and decay that are the fate of all caves. Alternatively, they may be outwardly looking, concerned with the regional flow of groundwater in an aquifer that happens to contain caves, with the chemistry of the solution process by which caves are formed, or with the evolution of entire drainage basins and how the caves can be used as clues to historical events. Examples of the current state of cave geology may be found in the textbooks cited at the end, to which these notes may be regarded as an introduction.

Kinds of Caves

What is a cave? Some writers insist that a cave is a "natural cavity beneath the earth's surface whose dimensions are measurable in feet, whose walls are bedrock, and usually extending to absolute darkness." Quite a bit is wrong with this definition. There are caves in the mountains into which daylight may penetrate for hundreds of meters. There are caves in unconsolidated sediments or in glacial ice whose walls are not in bedrock. How many feet are required to qualify as a cave depends on the observer. The Alabama Cave Survey requires 50 feet; the New Jersey Cave Survey—6 feet. My favorite definition is: "A cave is a natural opening large enough to admit a human explorer and which some explorers, at least, chose to call a 'cave'."

Since caves, as seen from the viewpoint of the explorers, are primarily voids, we first separate caves into two broad classes: those that are formed by essentially chemical processes and those that are formed by mechanical processes. Within these two classes caves are listed by the major process which led to their formation.

I. Caves formed by mainly chemical processes: (Strongly dependent on the lithology of the host rock)
   1. Solution caves
   2. Lava caves
   3. Ice caves

II. Caves formed by mainly mechanical processes: (Essentially independent of the lithology of the host rock)
   4. Tectonic caves
   5. Eolian caves
   6. Sea caves
   7. Talus caves
   8. Caves formed by outwash and slumping (erosion caves)
   9. Suffosional caves

Solution caves are formed by the removal of bedrock by circulating groundwater and/or by underground streams. The water transports the bulk of the rock material out of the cave in solution. Most rocks, even the highly soluble ones, also contain a certain residuum of insoluble material which must be transported mechanically by the water. Most solution caves are in limestone. Less frequently they occur in dolomite, marble, or gypsum. Small caves form in massive salt deposits. The only requirement is that the bedrock be soluble. Limestone caves achieve the largest sizes and contain most of the interesting and attractive mineral deposits.

Lava caves form in pahoehoe basalt lava flows and result from the draining of moving subsurface streams of lava after the surrounding lava had solidified. In many instances, an outlet permits the draining of the tube and a conduit-like cave results. These can be of considerable length such as Ape Cave in Washington, more than two miles long. Many are single conduits, but multi-level development is not uncommon. Lava caves occur in many volcanic areas of the United States.

Ice caves are caves in ice. These occur in many glaciers throughout the world and form by the action of sub-glacial streams which emerge from the foot of the glacier. Ice caves consist of long elliptical tube conduits often with delicately sculptured walls. Exploration of

Acknowledgement

These notes are adapted in part from an article, **The Geology of Caves**, published by the Pennsylvania Geological Survey (White, 1976). Permission of the State Geologist to reproduce some of the figures from that work is gratefully acknowledged.

these caves is difficult since they are often completely flooded during part of the day and are only accessible when the water freezes at night. Explorations for distances to several kilometers have been conducted.

Ice caves can be confused with **glacieres** or freezing caves which are simply rock caves of some sort which contain perennial ice. The term "ice cave" in most American writing refers to this type of cave.

Tectonic caves are formed by actual movement of masses of bedrock. They can occur in any type of rock but are usually associated with hard, insoluble rocks where they are easily distinguished from caves of other origins. The type of bedrock movement is not specified. It might be slippage along bedding planes, parting because of intense folding, or a sudden splitting due to faulting. Tectonic caves are usually small, but examples are known that run into hundreds of meters of passage. One does not usually classify limestone caves in this group, but there is no reason that tectonic movement could not create caves in limestone without the action of solution.

Eolian caves are formed by the abrading action of wind-borne particles. They are common to desert regions where soft sandstones often have small caves carved into them. Caves which are apparently due to wind action have also been reported in loess, a homogeneous deposit of silt.

Sea caves (also called "littoral caves" in some literature) are formed by the milling of sea coasts by wave action. They occur in many coastal areas throughout the world. Some of the most famous caves known are sea caves, of which Fingal's Cave in the Hebrides Islands and the Blue Grotto on the Isle of Capri are examples. While some sea caves have formed along the rocky New England coast, the mid-Atlantic and southeast coasts of the United States are unsuitable for development of sea caves because of the low relief of the Coastal Plain. The West Coast in California, Oregon and Washington abounds with sea caves in a variety of rocks.

Talus caves are formed when masses of piled boulders or other rock debris arrange themselves in such a way as to leave explorable openings beneath and between the blocks. These caves are only of interest if they reach considerable size. Obviously, there are indefinitely large numbers of small openings in all boulder slopes. In a few instances, talus caves in sandstone and granite have interconnected passages of large extent.

Erosion caves—for the lack of a better name, we use "erosion caves" to describe minor openings formed by mechanical erosion of soft rock material. Mostly these are rock shelters that form when a resistant sandstone layer overlies a weaker shale horizon. Often small sandstone cliffs occur where minor streams flow down steep hillsides. The underlying shales are easily undercut and a combination of slumping and erosion cuts the shale back, leaving a sandstone overhang. While rock shelters formed in this manner wouldn't usually be considered caves, they are often referred to as caves locally, sometimes appearing on maps as caves, and are often listed as cave sites by archeologists or historians who are concerned with the human usages of such shelters.

Suffosional caves—There is a process called **soil piping** which is the process by which unconsolidated soils and sediments are transported by rapidly moving water. It is possible for the runoff from sudden storms to flush out underground openings entirely in unconsolidated material. These occur frequently in badland topography where there is little plant cover to protect the sediments from erosion. Suffosional caves are usually small.

The Shapes of Caves

Caves in Map View

Most caves appear complex when viewed either from inside or in map view. It becomes less difficult to understand this complexity if we use a building-block principle to describe the cave. Caves are made of **passages**. The passages have various shapes, various relationships to each other, may have formed at the same or at different times or may have been formed by a single water source or by different sources. Passages in the same cave may be genetically related or only fortuitously connected.

The pattern or map view of an individual segment of cave passage will be determined by the structural and stratigraphic factors controlling the route followed by the moving groundwater. End-member types are illustrated in Fig. 34.

A **linear** pattern is simply a straight reach of passage without bends. Linear caves nearly always appear oriented along the strike in steeply dipping limestones.

Angulate patterns are good evidence for some sort of joint or other structural control. In regions of dipping limestones, long reaches of the passage may be oriented along the strike while the short segments cut across the bedding. These patterns also develop in flat-bedded limestone where presumably the hydraulic gradient was oriented diagonally to the regional joint set. The groundwater flow used first one set and then the other to carve a zig-zag course through the joint blocks. In the few cases that have been measured, the rosettes of orientations of the angulate cave passages have been found to parallel the rosettes of the joint system for the area.

Some passages, particularly in regions of flat-bedded limestones where long conduit-like caves are common, have a **sinuous** pattern. Instead of sharp angle bends with straight stretches of passage between bends, the sinuous passage has broad sweeping curves and relatively few really straight reaches of passage. Passages with this pattern have at least a superficial resemblance to meandering surface rivers.

A cave consisting of a highly interconnected set of passages can be said to exhibit a **maze** pattern. The labyrinthine character of the maze cave is the result of simultaneous, rather than sequential, enlargement of

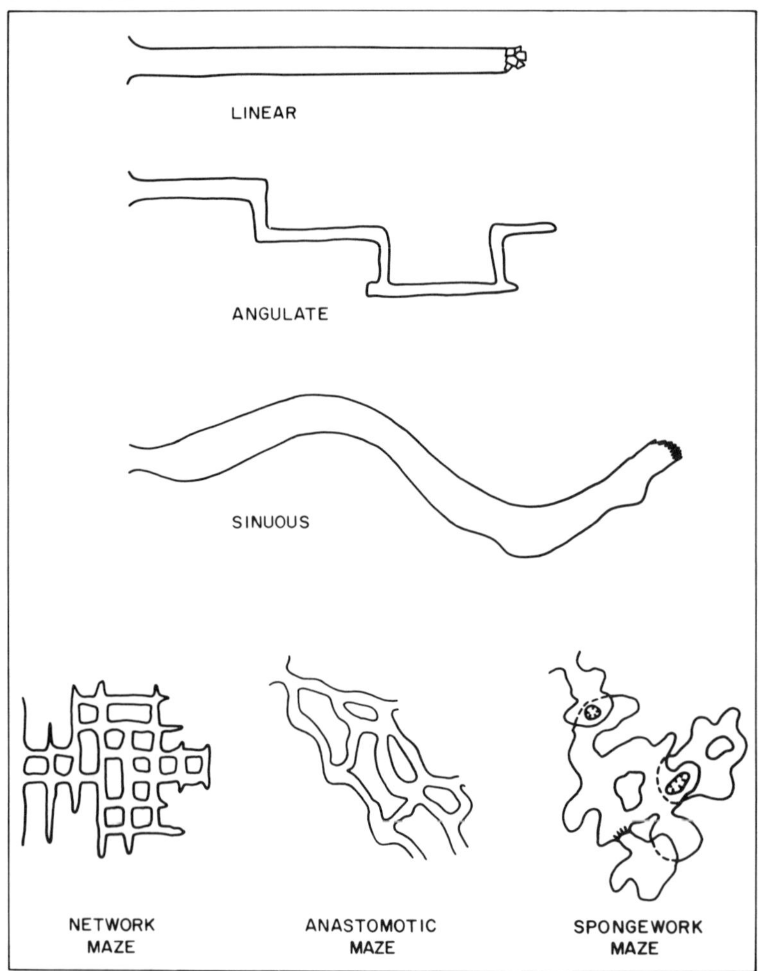

Fig. 34. Plan view of several basic types of cave passage patterns. (From *Geology and Biology of Pennsylvania Caves*, by Penn. Geol. Survey)

joints, bedding plane partings or other routes of groundwater movement. Thus, we consider it to be a single passage element just as the other patterns were considered single passage elements. It might be regarded as the underground equivalent of a braided river.

Art Palmer (1975) has distinguished three sub-types of maze pattern:

1. **Network mazes** consist of an angular grid of intersecting fissures that form by solutional widening of nearly all major joints to roughly the same size openings.
2. **Anastomotic mazes** are formed of curvilinear tubes, typically or circular or elliptical cross section that intersect in a random or braided configuration.
3. **Spongework mazes** consist of interconnected, non-tubular solution cavities of varied size and irregular geometry arranged in an apparently random, three-dimensional pattern.

Network pattern caves usually occur in flat-lying limestone and the plan and spacing of the net are determined by the regional joint pattern. There is no reason why the network must occur at right angles, although rectilinear patterns seem to be the most common. In an ideally developed network, every joint is opened and the passage spacing is the same as the joint spacing.

Passage Cross Sections

The cross sections of cave passage represent a compromise between hydrodynamic forces that tend to shape the passage into smooth, streamlined forms and the variations in solubility of the bedrock and the shape of the initial guiding joint or bedding plane, which often generate more complicated shapes. We can, therefore, subdivide cross sections into those that are primarily determined by the flow hydraulics and those whose shapes are structurally determined. High velocities and thick, uniform limestone tend to promote the hydraulic forms while low velocities, non-uniform bedding and lithology enhance the formation of channels with complicated cross sections. Some of these are illustrated in Fig. 35.

Mainly, hydraulically controlled passages trend to two end-member types—the canyon and the elliptical tube. Canyons are typically higher than they are wide, have near-vertical walls with little variation in passage width, and may show evidence of fast-flowing water. Canyons are of at least two origins. They may be formed by small streams gradually downcutting through the limestone or by solutional widening of a very regular joint that is completely filled with water. The canyon shape itself is not conclusive proof of the type of flow. Downcutting streams may meander and the meanders drift downstream as the canyon deepens. This may result in a sinuous cross section. Elliptical tubes are more or less regular pipes and presumably formed by groundwater flowing under pipefull conditions. These vary in size from tiny openings too small to enter, to perhaps 30 meters across.

An intermediate geometry is the rectangular passage also illustrated in Fig. 35. It can form as a wide canyon in a flat-bedded sequence with a relatively insoluble roof bed or it can form from an elliptical tube by breakdown of the projecting beds. Since both forms may be floored with an unknown depth of sediment, the origin of the passage may not be self-evident from casual examination.

Passages controlled by rock structure can be extremely complicated in cross section, depending on whether joints or bedding planes or both were the primary groundwater routes. Dip of beds usually has a considerable influence (Fig. 36).

In some caves a complex cross section occurs that is a combination of the various sections shown in Fig. 37. These may be called **composite cross sections** or **composite passages**. A common form is the T-shaped passage with an elliptical tube at the top and a canyon cut into its floor. Sometimes there is a canyon in the ceiling with a tube below. Still more complicated combinations exist. The components of the composite passage are really independent passages. They overlap in one reach of the passage to give the composite cross section and diverge either upstream or downstream.

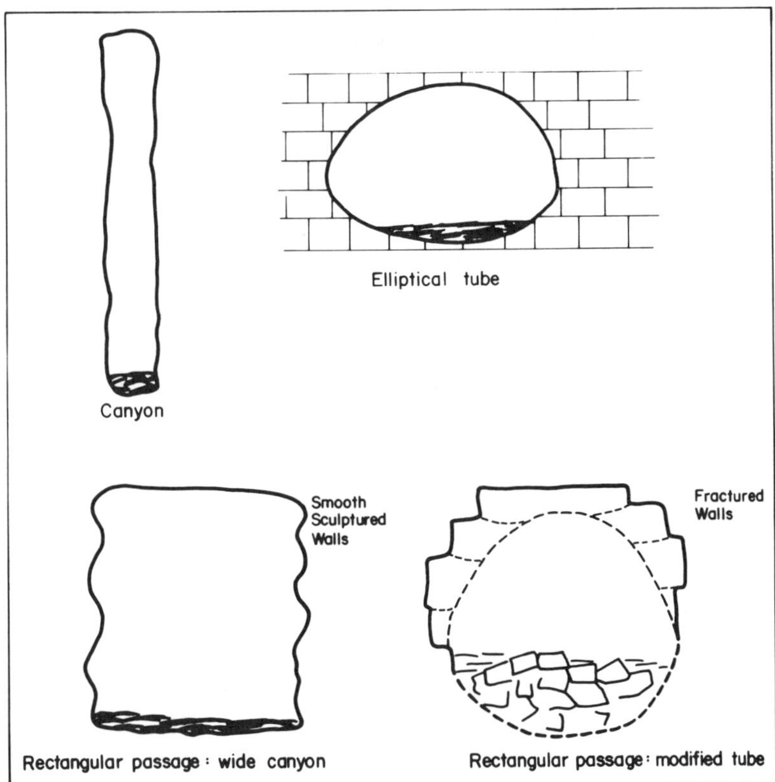

Fig. 35. Several cross-sectional passage shapes which have been controlled mainly by flow hydraulics. (From *Geology and Biology of Pennsylvania Caves*, by Penn. Geol. Survey)

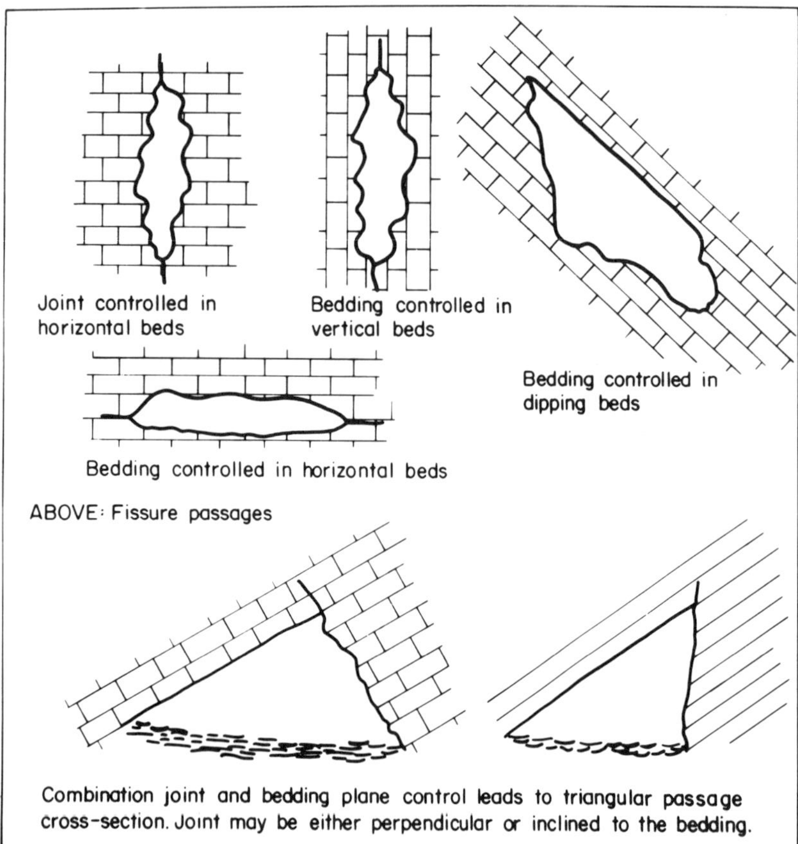

Fig. 36. Cross-sectional passage shapes which have been controlled mainly by the structure of the surrounding bedrock. (From *Geology and Biology of Pennsylvania Caves*, by Penn. Geol. Survey)

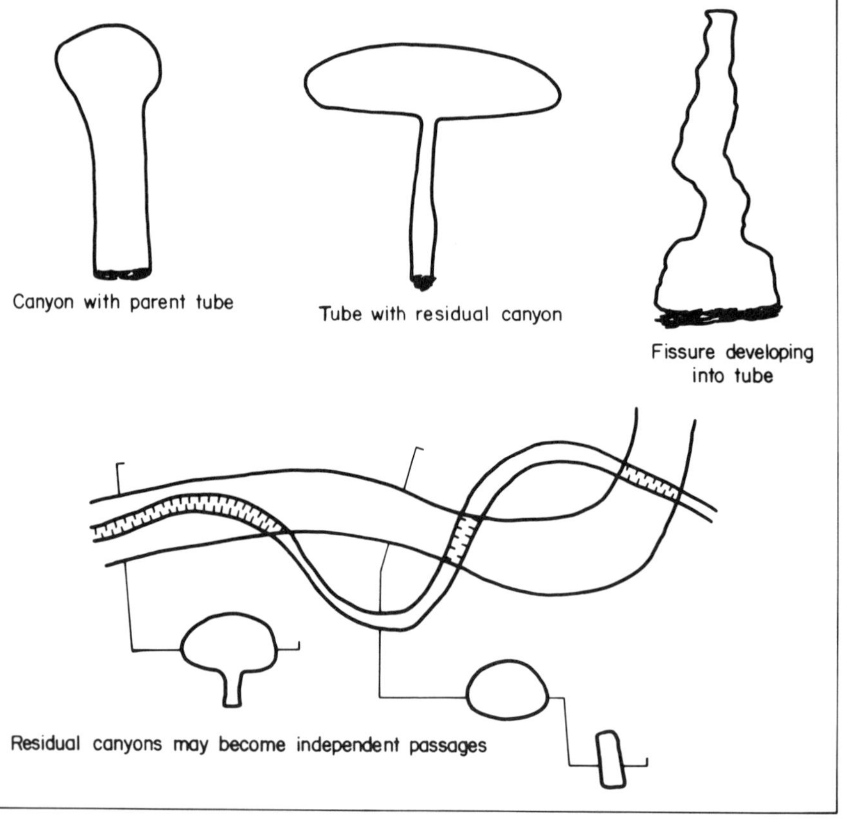

Fig. 37. Composite passage cross-sections that form as a result of a combination of structurally controlled features. (From *Geology and Biology of Pennsylvania Caves*, by Penn. Geol. Survey)

Pits

A remarkable aspect of most caves in regions of moderate-to-low relief is that the principal passages are either nearly horizontal or almost vertical. The vertical features may be conveniently divided into three types: **solution chimneys, vertical shafts** and **subsidence shafts** (Fig. 38).

Vertical shafts are cylindrical voids with vertical walls. In Kentucky, they range from five to 60 meters in height and to 15 meters in width. The base of the shaft is often a shallow basin in bedrock. The walls are often fluted. Shafts are formed by films of water moving down their sides at very high velocities. A few shafts contain waterfalls, but that is uncommon. The accumulated water leaves the bottom of the shaft through a very small passage usually of dimensions much less than the shaft itself.

Shafts form at the edge of a resistant caprock where a source of low pH water is available. The relationship to underlying cave passage may be fortuitous or the drain from the shaft may be part of the cave drainage system. Sometimes shafts and horizontal passages suffer a near miss and the shaft is seen cutting out a slice from the cave wall, just as a giant auger might do.

Shafts are very common features in all the plateau karst regions of the Appalachians and they reach their maximum development in the southern end of the range in northern Alabama and Georgia, where some shafts such as in Fern Cave, Alabama, and Ellison Cave, Georgia, have depths of over 120 meters. In the Appalachian plateaus, shale horizons serve as the resistant caprock.

There is no well-defined term for irregular vertical solution openings, and here we use **solution chimney** in a general sense to include those vertical openings that do not have the diagnostic features of the vertical shafts. Chimneys typically are solutionally widened joints of fissures, or solution passages extending along bedding planes in near-vertical limestone.

Subsidence shafts are formed by a combination of solution and mechanical stopping. Imagine a large cave passage with a flowing stream at some depth below the surface. The gradual widening of the passage weakens the ceiling and breakdown occurs. The fallen breakdown blocks are dissolved by the stream allowing more blocks to fall and the ceiling of the cavity migrates upward until it breaks through to the surface. The result is a deep pit with irregular, often overhung, walls. The floor is a rubble of fallen blocks and if the stream has not been effective in removing all of the fallen material, the pit may bottom out many meters above the solution cavity that gave birth to it. The deep Mexican pits, such as El Sótano and Sótano de las Golondrinas appear to be of this origin as do some large collapse chambers such as Devil's Sinkhole in Texas.

Many of the deep pit caves are made up of a mixture of vertical passage types with solution chimneys along

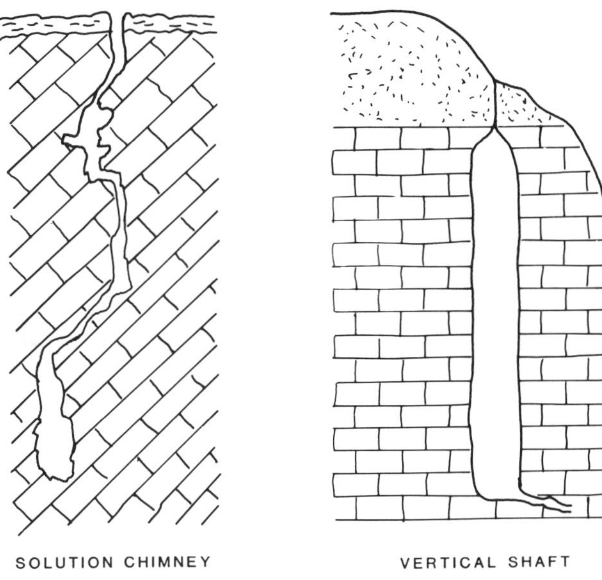

Fig. 38. Three types of vertical passage.

fractures or vertical bedding planes often opening into vertical shafts. Subsidence also plays a role in the creation of the vertical openings.

Rooms

A common feature shown on most cave maps is the cave "room." Cave rooms are a very diverse class of features about which relatively little can be said. The usual "room" is a place in which the cave widens or heightens above the average passage through which the explorers have been traveling. Among the many diverse origins for rooms may be listed:

1. Intersections of several passages.
2. Places where breakdown has fallen while groundwater was actively circulating. This stopping process leads to some very large dome-shaped rooms.
3. "Rooms" consisting of a fragment of large conduit reached through a cave system consisting of much smaller conduits.
4. "Rooms" formed mainly by vertical solution and intersected by smaller horizontal passages. Various dome rooms formed by shafts or complexes of shafts are of this type.
5. Actual widenings of horizontal passages. Such irregularities in the shape of cave passages occur but the causes are usually not known.

Thc cavc room is much likc thc ovcrall cavc pattcrn itself. Any particular room is a feature unique to that particular cave and must be interpreted on the basis of local conditions.

How Caves Are Put Together

Caves are found in an amazing variety of sizes and shapes. There are a few extremely large caves with total passage lengths of ten kilometers or more. There are a reasonable number of modest-sized caves with passage lengths on the order of a kilometer and there are a very large number of small caves with lengths from a few meters to a few hundred meters. The cave, as seen by the human explorer at some chosen instant of geologic time, is an accident, the net result of competing processes of growth and decay. The cave is not a representation of the drainage routes of the groundwater that dissolved the rock, but is a fragment cut from perhaps several drainage paths by processes of breakdown and siltation. And to explore the cave at all, there must be an entrance. For the most part, entrance formation is part of the overall process of truncation and decay and not part of the process of cave enlargement. There is much evidence that many caves exist with no entrances at all.

Entrances are found in many forms: in sinkholes, at the bottoms of chimneys and shafts, on hillsides where passages intersect the surface, as spring mouths, and in roadcuts and quarries. The common feature to almost all cave entrances is that they are the results of statistical accidents. Except for entrances in sinking streams and springs, the entrance is not an intrinsic part of the drainage system that forms caves. The cave forms without an entrance. The entrances are developed later as the downwasting of the landscape dissects and truncates the cave system. Entrances are closely related to the truncation processes that break up caves (Fig. 39).

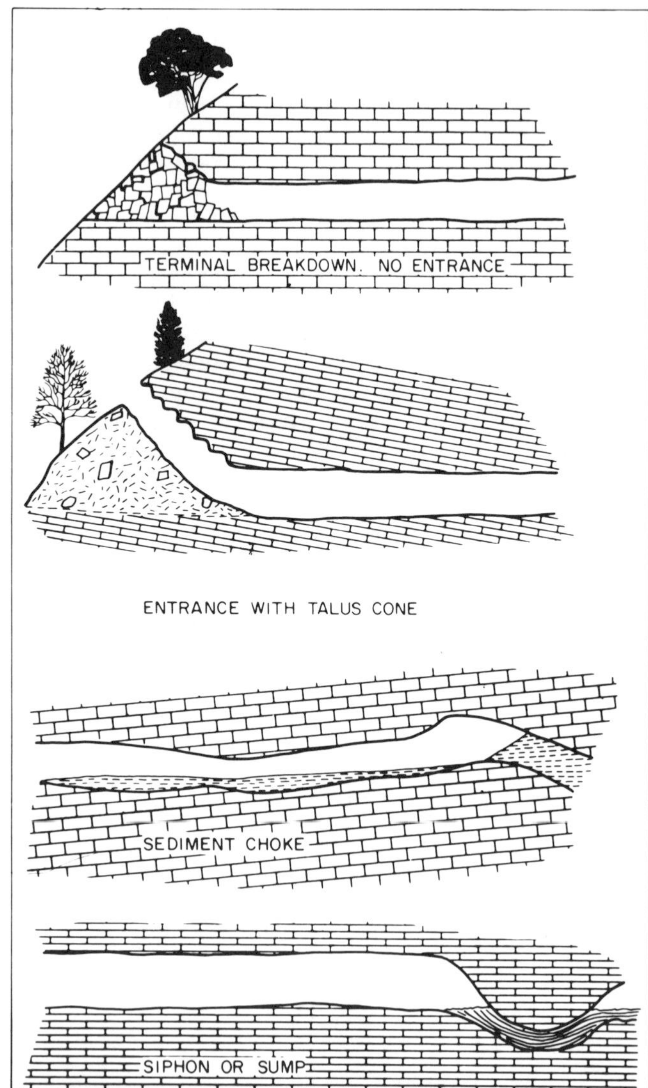

Fig. 39. Several types of cave passage truncations. (From *Geology and Biology of Pennsylvania Caves*, by Penn. Geol. Survey)

If we accept the premise that caves form by moving groundwater, it follows that passages cannot have blind bedrock terminations. Only in the case of network patterns where water is circulating simultaneously through all joint openings could a few of these have blind ends. Caves, however, do have ends. Roger Brucker (1966) very carefully pointed out that most of the big trunk conduits of the central Kentucky cave systems end in terminal breakdowns. The terminal breakdowns cut the once-continuous conduits into truncated passages. By careful examination of all available cave maps, it is sometimes possible to reconstruct the conduit by the alignment in plan and in elevation of the truncated fragments of passage and by agreement in general passage cross section and morphology. Such analysis sometimes also predicts the existence of previously unknown passages if these are necessary to complete the pattern. Much of the Mammoth Cave System was integrated by finding bypasses for these terminal breakdowns.

Caves under limestone valleys, at shallow depths and without any protective caprock, are usually highly truncated. Instead of miles of interlacing passages and tunnels, typical caves in folded limestones have lengths of hundreds of feet. Often a single fragment is all that is accessible. Some are terminated by breakdowns but many more terminate in clay chokes. The caves all contain layers of silt and clay on the floors, and in places these fill deposits reach the ceiling and effectively block the passage, although presumably it was open to groundwater flow at some earlier time.

Another effective termination is the sump, which is a place where the passage ceiling dips below water level. Some sumps have been bypassed by diving, but that is a dangerous undertaking in small, cramped cave passages and only a limited amount of underwater exploration has been carried out.

A cave is that sequence of entrance, passages and rooms that can be traversed continuously by a human explorer. Thus, a single long conduit that has been broken by entrenchment of a minor surface valley so that the entrances to the two fragments are 100 meters apart is considered to be two caves. On the other hand, two parallel conduits, on different levels, related to different drainage lines but which happen to be fortuitously connected by hundreds of feet of painful crawlway, are considered parts of the same cave.

If we are to have a scientific understanding of caves and cave processes, it is necessary to regard real caves as assemblages of passages that may have different histories and to try to interpret the way in which these passages are assembled and truncated to form the final cave as it is now observed.

The overall pattern of the cave can be classified in terms of the number of individual drainage lines present, and according to the geometry of the passages. We may call a cave pattern **simple** if it contains only one drainage line and **complex** if it contains more than one. Simple patterns would include fragments of single conduits and would also include network caves. In spite of the network cave having a large number of individual passages, the evidence points to the flow having moved along all of these simultaneously and so it is in effect a single drainage line much in the way that a braided river is still considered a single stream.

Complex systems seem to fit into three basic categories, although there are no sharp lines of demarcation between them. These are:

1. Networks
2. Conduit systems
3. Branchwork systems

Network systems are simply large network caves. The key feature is the multiconnecting passage arrangement. Conduit systems are those that have interconnecting channels on a larger scale than the networks, certainly with a wider spacing than the regional joint system. Some parts of the conduit system may represent the drainage line that was used during the earlier history of the cave and is now abandoned. Other passages may be cut-around routes, spill-over routes, piracy routes to lower levels and the like. A conduit system, in essence, is what would be expected from a surface stream if all the previous history of the valley were somehow preserved as downcutting took place. Branchwork systems are those in which a well-defined tributary system can be established. This means that several feeder conduits must be active at the same time.

From the above, it is clear why such classification schemes can only be applied to moderate-sized cave systems. If we consider entire drainage basins and are able to reconstruct all cave passages that at one time or another played some role in the movement of groundwater through the basin, we would probably find all the categories represented somewhere in the drainage net. The conduit systems might be in the downstream portions near the spring discharge point and the branchworks upstream in the headwaters. Networks are often included with more complex cave patterns.

Solutional Sculpturing of Caves

Few caves are bare rock tunnels like mines, subways and storm sewers. The water that created the passages in most caves left behind a variety of solutional sculpturings carved into the bedrock walls. These are a sort of hieroglyphic in which can be read something about the past history of the cave and the behavior of the water that made it. The list below contains only the more common of these sculpturings.

Anastomoses—Bedding plane and joint plane anastomoses are tiny networks of tubular openings usually occurring along bedding planes. They are of great complexity and differ from spongework in being nearly circular in cross section and actually resemble a miniature cavern system. They are usually seen only in cross section where slabs of rock have broken away and exposed the bedding plane. The openings are rarely large enough to crawl into.

Spongework is a highly complicated system of tiny holes and interconnected cavities found on cave walls. It gives the wall a very definite swiss cheese effect. An explanation for its origin is the differential solution of limestone by the etching action of nearly stagnant water. This great complex of holes within holes may extend many meters into the wall. Spongework is not common in caves, although Carlsbad Caverns, New Mexico, and Wind Cave, South Dakota, have extensive areas of it. Spongework can enlarge to become a cave itself with the pattern of the spongework maze.

Pendants are vestiges of bedrock hanging below the ceiling or a flat-bottomed ledge. They usually occur in groups and grade laterally into smooth ceiling. They are believed to be the remnants of an older ceiling and to be formed by solution or abrasion of the ceiling during times when the vadose stream flooded the passage.

Floor slots and **stream-cut canyons**—Narrow grooves, slots and canyons appear in the bedrock floors of passages. Some are mere narrow cracks of uncertain depth (marvelous traps for lens caps, carbide lamps and compasses). Others are wide enough to permit exploration and, at the upper limit of their size range, blend into the canyon cross section part of the composite passage described earlier. Such slots usually arise from the downcutting of a small residual stream flowing on the floor of the passage above.

Ceiling channels are what appear to be upside-down streambeds in the roofs of passages. If a passage were to be filled nearly to the ceiling with sand and clay, the stream would be forced to flow on top of the fill and thus might well completely fill the passage. If the stream did not have a high gradient, its power of solution would be greater than its power of abrasion and it would dissolve a course in the soluble ceiling faster than it could abrade a course in the insoluble floor. Later, as the channel enlarges, flow would increase and the fill would be gradually removed, leaving a ceiling channel behind.

Horizontal wall grooves in cave walls are formed by a cave stream cutting its way laterally into the wall, usually along a bedding plane. Sometimes it will leave the main passage completely and will be found flowing parallel to the main channel in a low-roofed passage extending some distance to one side.

Incised meanders in cave walls occur when a small stream is flowing in the clay fill of a large passage. The streams will meander back and forth and will sometimes cut both laterally and vertically into the rock wall of the passage. Thus, at the extremes of its meander loop, the stream will disappear into a conical trench in the wall, reappearing a few meters farther on. Occasionally, these meander loops become large enough to walk through and one can leave the main passage and return to it by completing a half circle.

Joint-determined wall and **ceiling cavities** are deep, narrow slots extending along a joint, often for many feet. They tend to widen at the intersection with the cavern passage and to narrow farther along the joint.

Wall and **ceiling pockets** are larger than spongework cavities and are usually separated by stretches of unaffected rock. The pockets differ from joint-controlled cavities in being more circular and in the absence of a guiding joint. They resemble kettleholes and are usually circular or elliptical in outline. They may be deeper than they are wide and have smooth sides with no indication of the reason for such deep penetration.

Potholes—High gradient streambeds in caves are often eroded into complex forms of which circular basins called potholes are the most common. These vary in size from a few inches to many feet. Usually associated with the potholes are other etched and eroded pinnacles in the limestones very similar to forms found in surface streambeds.

Scallops are cuspate pockets that form on exposed bedrock surfaces by the differential dissolving action of eddies in moving water. A related form is the flute. Scallops are pocket-like. Flutes are asymmetric grooves which, in ideal cases, completely encircle the cave passage. Scallops form under either free-surface stream or pipefull passage conditions. In a few cases elliptical tube passages have been observed with a uniform scalloping on floor, walls and ceiling.

Both flutes and scallops can be used to determine the direction of past water flow. The steep side of the asymmetric cusp is on the upstream side. The size of the scallop is inversely related to flow velocity. Small scallops are formed by high velocity flows and large scallops by low velocity flows. Roughly, 10 cm (centimeter) scallops indicate a channel velocity of 30 cm per second, whereas one meter scallops indicate a one cm per second velocity. Scallop measurements allow us to determine a flow rate of the waters that cut passages that are now dry.

Water in Caves

Caves are abandoned water courses. Limestone was removed by flowing water to create the pipe-like openings that we see as caves. Caves are not generally explored during the water-filled phase (although some caves in Florida are an exception); they are entered after the down-cutting of surface streams has lowered water levels and left an air-filled cavern behind. However, most caves contain some water and it comes from several sources.

Streams flowing in surface channels often sink underground at the edge of limestone regions and many of these streams can either be followed directly into the caves or can be shown to connect with cave streams by dye tracing experiments.

Rain falling in a region underlain by limestone is held for a short while in the soil before it percolates through and enters the limestone beneath. Water that migrates directly from the soil through small joints and fissures to the cave below is termed **vadose seepage**. Vadose seepage waters absorb carbon dioxide from the soil zone and the resulting carbonic acid dissolves the limestone at the base of the soil. Vadose seepage waters lose their carbon dioxide when the waters enter the cave and the dissolved limestone is redeposited as dripstone and flowstone.

Surface water accumulated by sinkholes or by collection areas on other rocks above the limestone enters the limestone at inlet points determined by joints and fractures. This water is usually somewhat acid and the acid is not neutralized by reaction with the limestone because of the short period of contact. Such waters are called **vadose flows** and they dissolve limestone in the cave to form vertical shafts, solution chimneys and other open pathways through the limestone.

Small streams are seen in caves that obtain their water from sinking streams or from the accumulated drainage from vadose flows. Sometimes the underground streams can be followed all the way to the surface again where they emerge through limestone springs. In other situations, exploration downstream is halted by sumps. Some of these are truly sumps, simply water traps in the passage, which could (in principle, at least) be dived and the passage beyond followed again. Others seem to be placed where the open cave stream merges with the larger body of groundwater that lies below. The surface of the sump in these cases would mark the level of the **water table**, the surface extending through the rock that marks the boundary between the upper or **vadose zone** where cavities are at least partly air-filled, and the lower or **phreatic zone** where all cavities are water-filled.

Some limestone springs are the mouths of caves and the source of the water can be determined by direct exploration. Other springs, perhaps the more common situation, well up from pools or flow from under hillside talus. Some of these drain cave systems; others are the discharge points of the main body of groundwater or some combination of the two. It is generally not possible without dye tracing or chemical analyses of the water to determine whether an open cave lies behind a flooded spring or not.

Many cave systems in Florida and in other coastal regions have been reflooded. At the time when glaciers covered much of North America, sea level was about 100 meters lower than it is at present. Caves formed in the coastal limestones, some of them became air-filled, and stalactites and stalagmites were deposited. When the glacial ice melted, the release of water raised the level of the sea to where it is today. The sea level rise flooded the caves and provides choice opportunities for underwater cave exploration.

Cave Sediments

Caves become filled with material originating from inside the cave or with materials which have been transported from someplace else. The most important of these are breakdown and clastic sediments, the latter having both local and distant sources.

Breakdown is a residual pile of bedrock fragments that results from the failure of cavern roofs and walls. Failure of massive beds along bedding planes or failure of whole sequences of beds at once give rise to block breakdown. Failure of single, thinner beds yields slab breakdown. Small shards and fragments that have not separated along bedding planes constitute chip breakdown. Block and slab breakdowns often break along joints or other pre-existing structural weaknesses. It is possible to analyze roof failure by the mechanics of fixed and cantilever beams. For any given thickness of bedding, there will be a maximum span (passage width) beyond which the ceiling bed will not support its own weight. A passage 30 meters wide would typically require a meter thick bed for the roof to support its own weight. The bedding thickness provides a limit to the width of cave passages. Caves in folded rocks are more susceptible to breakdown. In the ceilings of strike passages in dipping beds, the bedding plane forms one plane of weakness, the perpendicular joint another, and long, triangular prisms of rock easily detach themselves from the ceiling. This type of breakdown is common in caves in folded limestone and gives rise to a characteristic triangular cross section.

There are several processes that trigger breakdown. Some are: (1) initial draining of the cave with resultant loss of buoyant support; (2) undercutting of walls by free-surface streams that later make use of the open passages; (3) action of surface waters weakening roofs in the later stages of the cave's history when the land surface is lowered; (4) action of vertical shafts which may remove parts of walls and other breakdown which may be supporting the roof; (5) wedging and chemical attack by minerals, mainly sulfates, forming in the bedrock; (7) frost wedging near entrances.

Clastic sediments are of two main types: weathering detritus and transported or fluvial sediments.

Weathering detritus is the residual material left behind when the limestone walls are dissolved. The main mineral constituent is quartz. Quartz occurs as chert nodules common in many limestones, silicified fossil fragments, and grains of quartz sand. Indeed, examination of a number of fills reveals that the bulk of what cavers call "mud" is actually quartz. Clay minerals, kaolinite, montmorillonite and illite, occur but are a smaller fraction of the bulk sediment.

Broadly, there are two ways in which insoluble materials can be transported into a cave depositional site: horizontally and vertically. The infiltrates are clastic materials transported vertically under the direct influence of gravity with or without the aid of flowing water. Soils in karst regions are washed, piped or slumped into open crevices and sinkholes. They are eventually discharged into the cavern system without much chemical modification. Solution crevices, chimneys and vertical shafts reach through the cavernous bedrock and break through to the surface. Fragments of overlying bedrocks and surface debris fall down these openings to become part of the infiltrate sediment. Cave entrances are also sites of intense erosion because of frost pry and freezing and thawing of the rocks and soils upslope. Horizontal entrances usually lead to the top of an entrance talus cone of varying height down which one must descend to the cave passage. Entrance talus materials are a mixture of breakdown and infiltrated debris. The infiltrates are exceptionally important sediments because they contain most of the fossil and archeological remains. Animals fall down sinkholes and become buried in the accumulating sediment. The gradual accumulation of entrance talus buries the camp sites of primeval man.

Fluvial sediments, stream-borne deposits, which may be transported through filled pipes as well as in open channels, make up the greatest part of most cavern sediments. They are derived from many sources. Some are re-worked weathering detritus, some have been derived from rocks higher in the stratigraphic column, and some have been transported from non-karstic border lands by sinking streams. The material usually consists of stream-rounded rock fragments, sand, silt and clay. The finer grain-size material cannot usually be distinguished from weathering detritus or the infiltrates without extensive analyses. The composition and grain size merely reflect the character of the surrounding bedrock and the load-carrying capacity of the cavern streams. In many cases, sandstone, cobble and boulder fills occur in thickness of tens of meters.

Fluvial sediments occur in stratigraphic sequence and these strata are sometimes exposed where later free surface streams in the cave cut through them. The Appalachian sequence is frequently one of silts, sands and gravels in various combination, but the topmost bed is often a fine clay reflecting quieter water conditions as the passage filled with sediment. It would be pleasing to think that the complex sedimentary record in many caves could be used to decipher the Pleistocene history of the region. Unfortunately, such attempts as have been made have not come to any useful conclusions. A careful examination of the clastic sediments of a single passage in the Mammoth Cave System of Kentucky showed that the section changed continuously. Individual beds could not be traced very far.

Organic debris is the droppings of birds and bats which in some caves make up a distinct stratigraphic sequence and has in addition a distinct phosphate mineralogy where the leaching solutions interact with the limestone wall rock. Guano caves are common in the southwest, in the Caribbean and in South America.

Cave Minerals and Speleothems

Cave Minerals

Perhaps the most attractive features of caves are their mineral deposits. In the constant environment of the cave, mineralization processes can proceed uninterrupted over long periods of time. The result is a wide variety of mineral features known as **speleothems**. Minerals are naturally-occurring chemical compounds of specified chemical composition and crystal structure. Nearly 3000 such compounds have been identified in the earth (and a few on the moon). Of these, perhaps 80 or 90 occur in caves. However, many of the cave minerals require very special conditions for their formation. The chemistry of limestone caves is really rather simple with only a few metallic elements (calcium, magnesium, sodium, strontium and iron) occurring commonly and only a few anions (carbonate, sulfate, phosphate and hydroxide) available for the cations to combine with. As a result only a few minerals are expected to form in the "normal" cave environment. Nineteen of these are listed in Table 7. Many of the minerals even on this restricted list are not very common and only three, calcite, gypsum and aragonite, account for most of the speleothems seen by cavers.

Speleothems

Mineral-depositing solutions move vertically through the vadose zone under the influence of gravity. The mineral deposits left behind by dripping or flowing water, therefore, tend to take on shapes in which the gravitational control of the solution is much in evidence. Each mineral, however, has a characteristic growth habit. Certain crystal forms are preferred above others and certain crystal directions grow faster than others. Modification in the chemistry of the solution or in the rate of deposition can modify the habit or can change the relative rate of growth in different crystallographic directions. There is, thus, a competition between shapes guided by the flow path of the solution and shapes guided by the particular mineral and its crystallization habit. This gives rise to two broad classes of speleothems: dripstone and flowstone forms, and erratic forms. Within the context of these basic mechanisms, there is an immense and indeed continuous variety of shapes for the travertine (calcium carbonate) deposits depending on the vagaries of exact flow path, flow rate, chemical characteristics of the water, and relative humidity and carbon dioxide pressure of the cave atmosphere.

Because caves, particularly commercial caves, derive much of their charm from speleothems, these deposits have gained many fanciful names. Rather complete descriptions of speleothems may be found in Carol Hill's (1976) guide to cave minerals. We use here a two-level system of classification and speak of the **form** of a speleothem as the shape that can be distinguished by growth habit or depositional mechanism. **Styles** are variants of the forms and can be described by adjectial modifiers in as much detail and complexity as seems useful. In this system a stalactite is a form, whereas a soda straw stalactite refers to a specific style.

A listing of the most common speleothem forms is given below:

A. Dripstone and Flowstone Forms (gravity controlled)
   1. Stalactites
   2. Stalagmites
   3. Draperies
   4. Flowstone sheets

B. Erratic Forms (crystal growth controlled)
   1. Shields
   2. Helictites
   3. Botryoidal forms (popcorn, grape, etc.)

Table 7. A Listing of Cave Minerals

Name	*Formula*	*Mode of Occurrence*
Carbonate Minerals		
Calcite	$CaCO_3$	Flowstone, dripstone, pool deposits, helictites and many other forms
Aragonite	$CaCO_3$	Anthodite, flowstone and dripstone
Magnesite	$MgCO_3$	Rare, moonmilk and wall crusts
Dolomite	$CaMg(CO_3)_2$	Rare, mostly crusts and crystal coatings
Huntite	$CaMg_3(CO_3)_4$	Moonmilk
Hydromagnesite	$Mg_5(CO_3)_4(OH)_2 \cdot 4H_2O$	Moonmilk
Evaporite Minerals		
Gypsum	$CaSO_4 \cdot 2H_2O$	Flowers, crusts, crystals, dripstone
Epsomite	$MgSO_4 \cdot 7H_2O$	Flowers, crusts, dripstone
Mirabilite	$Na_2SO_4 \cdot 10H_2O$	Flowers, crusts, dripstone
Celestite	$SrSO_4$	Rare; crusts
Halite	NaCl	Flowers, crusts
Phosphate and Nitrate Minerals		
Hydroxyapatite	$Ca_5(PO_4)_3(OH)$	Reaction zone between dripstone and guano
Whitlockite	$Ca_3(PO_4)_2$	Reaction of guano with limestone
Brushite	$CaHPO_4 \cdot 2H_2O$	Reaction of guano with limestone
Nitrocalcite	$Ca(NO_3)_2 \cdot 4H_2O$	Dispersed in cave soils
Nitre	KNO_3	Nitre moss, dispersed in cave soils
Oxide and Hydrate Minerals		
Ice	H_2O	Permanent deposits in alpine caves
Goethite	FeO(OH)	Crusts and coatings
Wad"	$(Ca,Na,K)_2O \cdot xMnO_2$	Black "manganese" coatings

4. Anthodites
5. Oulopholites (gypsum flowers)
6. Moonmilk

C. Sub-Aqueous Forms
1. Rimstone dams
2. Concretions of various kinds (including cave pearls)
3. Pool deposits
4. Crystal linings

Water emerging from joints in cave ceilings hangs there in drops for a short time before the drops fall to the floor. During the time in which the drop hangs, carbon dioxide is degassed, the solution becomes supersaturated and a small amount of mineral matter is deposited in a ring with a diameter similar to that of the drop. This ring grows downward at constant diameter as more material is deposited until a slender tube of calcite known as a soda straw stalactite is formed. The tube is somewhat porous, and water can seep between grains and along cleavage cracks to deposit minerals on the outside as well. Additional fluid from other joints may stream down the outside of the straw and also build up additional layers.

The natural evolution of the stalactite is from the primary tube to a pendant form. As the stalactite grows, the central canal may become clogged and filled in, but some trace of it usually remains. In cross section, stalactites have a series of concentric rings representing different concentrations of impurities and different rates of growth. They are not annual rings and in spite of several efforts, no good interpretation has been placed on them. Long-term climatic variation in the cave region would be the most probable guess. Many minerals other than calcite occur in stalactite forms; both aragonite and gypsum occur this way.

Stalactites fed by more than one drip point may grow into quite complex shapes. Water flowing over the outside builds up ribs and folds to yield the form known as the drapery. Water that trails along the underside of ledges or of other stalactites may build up a sort of unfolded stalactite in which the growth layers are linear and parallel to the ledge and which is known colloquially as the "bacon strip."

Water dripping to the floor of the cave loses more carbon dioxide, deposits more minerals and builds up the mound-like masses of travertine known as stalagmites. If the cave is not at 100% relative humidity, evaporation will contribute to the $CaCO_3$ deposition also. Stalagmites have no central canal. In longitudinal section they appear to be built up of superimposed caps, thicker in the center and thinning toward the edge as the solution flowing outward from the drip point gradually is depleted in dissolved calcium carbonate. If the drip rate is constant, there will be an equilibrium diameter for the stalagmite determined by the drip rate and the amount of calcium carbonate in solution. Stalagmites are not limited by the amount of weight that can be suspended as stalactites are and can grow to quite large sizes. Many are fed by more than one drip point and can take on more complex shapes, or there can be one large core stalagmite with smaller stalagmites growing on it.

Solutions flowing down walls and over ledges deposit masses of travertine with the appearance of a waterfall of rock. These deposits are called flowstone and can be of very large volume.

Shields are massive plates or slabs of travertine that jut out from cave walls at angles apparently determined by the arrangement of joints. They are rare speleothems but occur in great numbers in some caves such as Grand Caverns, Virginia, and in Lehman Caves, Nevada.

Fig. 40. Flowstone, turning to draperies with bacon strips below.

Fig. 41. A mass of helictites.

Helictites are smooth-surface stalactitic forms that grow in curved paths instead of hanging vertically. Helictites have a central canal and appear to grow from the tip. They appear to form when flow rates through the canal are too slow to permit the formation of drops and are therefore controlled by the shifting orientation of the fast growth direction of the calcite crystal.

Botryoidal forms are small bead- or knob-like projections from cave walls. Globulite, or cave coral, is a term used for the smaller ones. They are usually of calcite and are layered structures. However, the center of the layering is a small projection of growth point on the wall of the cave. Growth mechanisms are unknown except that they seem to be associated with fast-moving films of water on cave walls.

The term anthodite has been applied to radiating clumps of crystalline aragonite. Typical anthodites grow in tufts of elongate acicular crystals radiating from a common center. Dendritic growth of individual crystals is common, resulting in a spiky appearance. It is not known how anthodites grow, although their appearance suggests that they must grow from the tip, otherwise the dendritic pattern is difficult to explain. Likewise, there are transitional forms between anthodites and helictites with calcite overgrown on aragonite. Some contain tufts or lumps of moonmilk on the tips of the crystals, suggesting that the magnesium is the last material to precipitate from the evaporating solutions.

Oulopholites (gypsum flowers) are a form apparently unique to the sulfate minerals and require the different growth habit of the sulfates. In their most spectacular form, oulopholites consist of petals of gypsum growing outward from a common center. The petals are curved and are made up of bundles of individual gypsum crystals. They have much in common with the anthodites except that growth is almost certainly from the base. The petals of the flowers spread outward because of faster growth at the center of the cluster. This speleothem is best developed in the Mississippian limestone caves of Kentucky and Tennessee.

Concretions are roughly spherical, unattached deposits that occur in pools or shallow basins. Several styles are found of which the smooth, polished variety known as "cave pearls" have received most attention. The other common style is a rough, rather porous, structure. Both are layered structures and growth appears to take place around some piece of foreign material that acts as a nucleus. Concretions vary in size from fractions of a centimeter to several centimeters in diameter. The water dripping into the basins in which they form must agitate the water sufficiently to keep the speleothem from becoming cemented to the bottom. Other restrictions on flow rate or chemistry are not known.

Water collecting in pools continues to degas CO_2 from the pool surface. The supersaturated solution deposits calcite on the walls of the pool, sometimes as rough, rather spongy deposits and sometimes as well-developed calcite crystals. A remarkable feature of cave pools is that some of them tend to be self-damming. Rimstone dams are travertine deposits, usually much thinner than they are high and often with a complex, convoluted pattern. Typical dams are perhaps 10 cm in height. Dams are known, however, that reach heights of several meters. Calcite also tends to deposit outward over the surface of the pool forming lily pad-like masses.

A few instances are known in which a cave has been completely re-flooded after the excavation of the cave itself. If the re-flooding waters are supersaturated with respect to calcite, the entire cave interior may be lined with crystals. The caves of the Black Hills of South Dakota are particularly noted for crystal lining.

References and Additional Information

The following books will give more information on the topics discussed in these notes and on other aspects of cave geology not discussed here. The references in these sources are a useful guide to the quite extensive primary literature on cave geology.

Brucker, R. W. (1966)—Truncated cave passages and terminal breakdown in the central kentucky karst: NSS Bull. **28**:171-178. (An investigation of truncated cave passages.)

Ford, T. D. and C. H. D. Cullingford (1976)—The Science of speleology:Academic Press, 595pp. (A somewhat advanced work. Good discussion of chemistry and hydrology of caves. Includes biology.)

Hill, C. A. (1976)—Cave minerals: Natl. Speleol. Soc., 137pp. (A comprehensive treatment of cave mineralogy.)

Jennings, J. N. (1971)—Karst:M.I.T. Press, 252pp. (Good introductory text. Much on surface landforms.)

Moore, G. W. and G. N. Sullivan (1978)—Speleology: the study of caves (2nd Edition):Zephyrus Press, 150pp. (Good introduction to geology and biology of caves.)

Palmer, A. N. (1975)—Origin of maze caves:NSS Bull. **37**:57-76. (Classifies maze caves into various categories.)

Sweeting, M. M. (1972)—Karst landforms:Macmillan, 363pp. (Comprehensive, if classical, discussion of both surface and underground karst landforms.)

White, W. B. (1976)—The Geology of caves:Pennsylvania Geological Survey, General Geology Report 66, pp. 1-71. (Introduction to cave geology. Emphasis on Pennsylvania caves.)

AN INTRODUCTION TO BIOSPELEOLOGY

William R. Elliott
NSS 10847F
Photographs by **Robert W. Mitchell**

What Biospeleology Is

Biospeleology, the study of cave-dwelling life, is the full-time pursuit of relatively few professional biologists. However, it has interested many biologists from time to time for various reasons. It is actually a multidisciplinary science encompassing aspects of zoology, zoogeography, taxonomy, evolutionary biology, ecology, genetics, population biology, physiology, ethnology, developmental biology, mycology and other disciplines. Many of our professional cave biologists developed their interest as young cavers. Others, such as many systematists (people who describe and classify species), became interested in biospeleology through their study of particular animal groups on which they specialize—groups that may be well represented in caves. Thus, a biospeleologist may not be a full-time devotee of the science, but he may have a continuing interest in one or more aspects of it.

One does not have to be a professional biologist to become involved in biospeleology. This article will describe how the ordinary caver can, and often does, make a real contribution to the study and conservation of cave life. Observation, documented collections and photographs of cave life by cavers can be a great help to the professional who is in contact with the caving community.

What Inhabits Caves?

A general terminology has developed among biospeleologists to describe ecological types of cave animals.

A "troglobite" is an animal that is an obligatory cavernicole (cave-dweller), that is, it can only complete its life cycle underground. Most troglobites exhibit varying degrees of depigmentation and eyelessness as a result of many generations of evolution. A few do not appear markedly different from closely-related species that may be found above ground, but are nevertheless limited to caves for biological reasons. Some arthropod groups are entirely eyeless (some millipedes, insects and arachnids) wherever they are found. Some aquatic troglobites, such as amphipods and isopods, are occasionally found in springs and wells that communicate with cave systems. Such forms are often called "phreatobites" because they inhabit phreatic waters. Troglobites often display other characteristic adaptations to their habitat such as increased appendage length, greater chemosensory and tactile sensitivity, lowered metabolic rate, greater locomotor and feeding efficiency, and smaller clutch sizes made up of larger eggs.

"Troglophiles" are a second major ecological category. Troglophiles may be found primarily in caves but also in similar habitats such as under rocks, in crevices or burrows, or in soil and leaf litter. Many troglophiles exhibit adaptations that grade into those of troglobites. Some may be incipient troglobites which, though isolated in caves, have not had sufficient evolutionary time to develop an obviously troglobitic appearance. Others are opportunistic species that may be found in caves and similar habitats across entire continents.

"Trogloxenes" (Fig. 42) are species that use caves for part of their activities but which are not limited to caves. Examples are cave crickets and bats, which roost and even reproduce in caves but which feed outside, or even certain species that specialize in the twilight zone habitat near the entrance. In many instances the biology of a particular species may be too poorly known to make a sure ecological designation. In such cases the general morphology (form and appearance) of the animal and the habits of its closest relations may serve to make a tentative designation.

Photosynthetic plants, which require sunlight to grow, cannot exist in the total darkness of caves. Their seeds may sprout in darkness but die after using their food reserves. However, the entrance sinks and twilight zones of caves often harbor plants that are rare in the surrounding countryside. The botany of cave entrances is poorly known and may someday provide fruitful work for

Fig. 42. *Ceuthophilus* sp., trogloxenic cave cricket.

plant geographers. One might expect to find some relictual (remnant) forms there which have become extinct elsewhere because of climatic changes. Likewise, the bacteria and fungi of caves are poorly known, but they may have some ecological importance since they require no light and are rather common in some cave muds, rotting debris and animal feces. Troglobites, such as some collembola and millipedes, may graze almost exclusively on bacteria and fungi.

Many animal groups have troglobitic forms. It would be impossible to discuss here the hundreds of cave-adapted species known in North America alone. Undoubtedly, many more species remain to be discovered, especially in the western U.S., Mexico and Central America. Instead, let us take a look at the major taxa (groups) that inhabit caves. A general survey of the world cave fauna may be found in Vandel's *Biospeleology* (1965), but it is already somewhat out-of-date. An excellent introduction to the cave life of North America is Mohr and Poulson's *The Life of the Cave* (1969), which contains many fine photographs.

Almost all major freshwater and terrestrial taxa contain cave-adapted species, and some predominantly marine (saltwater) taxa also have representatives. By far the most important phylum, in caves or elsewhere, is the Arthropoda, which includes arachnids, crustaceans, centipedes, millipedes and insects. Probably the second most important group is the Vertebrata (troglobitic fishes and salamanders), then the Platyhelminthes (planarians, Fig. 43), then a few Mollusca (aquatic and terrestrial snails and even some freshwater clams!). Some large groups have essentially no cave forms: Cnidaria (except for a few freshwater *Hydra*) and Echinodermata (starfishes and their allies, which are all marine). The Aschelminthes probably have some cave-adapted species in the form of nematodes (roundworms), but it is difficult to distinguish them from common, soil-dwelling nematodes. Some Onychophora (clawed worms) and Annelida (earthworms) are cave-adapted.

Fig. 43. *Sphalloplana zeschi*, a troglobitic planarian group feeding on a dead cave cricket.

Since most significant cave systems are formed in limestone by the action of fresh groundwater, it is not difficult to see why there are few marine groups with troglobites. However, some marine forms have been able to adapt to freshwater conditions and have given rise to troglobites. Good examples are some amphipod and isopod crustaceans and blind fishes of the families Synbranchidae (eel-like) and Brotulidae (catfish-like).

No two caves are exactly alike, so it is difficult to discuss what inhabits a typical cave. For the sake of example, we can imagine an idealized American cave and note what life we would encounter.

The plants in a sink entrance may differ from those of the surrounding area because of the different micro-climates. Ferns are commonly found at cave entrances. Certain birds nest at cave entrances: phoebes in some areas and cave swallows in many southwestern caves. Pits in Mexico commonly house swifts and parakeets. Guacharos (oil birds) nest in the dark of some South American caves. Even vultures have been found roosting in some entrances. They have an all too frequent defensive response: vomiting upon the intruder. Contrary to popular belief, snakes are infrequent in cave entrances and are rare in the dark zone. However, certain frogs, toads and salamanders frequent entrance areas. Depending on the nature of the twilight zone, one may find an abundance of trogloxenic insects and arachnids that exploit this limited habitat, which is all too often ignored by collectors. At this point one often encounters dense populations of trogloxenic harvestmen ("daddy-long-legs") and cave crickets on the walls and ceiling. Harvestmen are eight-legged arachnids but they are not spiders. They are non-poisonous and quite harmless, although they can be annoying. In some southwestern caves they form dense, undulating blankets that, when disturbed, fall off the ceiling in masses and on to cavers. There are many species of cave (camel) cricket throughout the U.S. but most California caves seem to lack them even though there are some camel crickets found above ground there. Some Mexican caves harbor true crickets (Gryllidae), a few of which are eyeless troglobites. Some caves in the Northwest U.S. have rare grylloblattids, a group similar to both roaches and crickets.

If there is a stream in the cave, you may find eyed crayfishes and amphipods in the twilight zone. During the winter many of the above-mentioned species may be found deeper in the cave where it is warmer.

The zone of total darkness and relatively constant temperature is where one most often sees troglobites. Several families of beetle (Carabidae, Leiodidae, Pselaphidae) have many different troglobitic species throughout the U.S. (Fig. 44). Some are specialized predators on cave cricket eggs or on other arthropods; others are scavengers. Dermestid beetles are common in bat guano (feces), although not strictly cave-limited.

Fig. 44. *Rhadine subterranea*, a troglobitic carabid beetle.

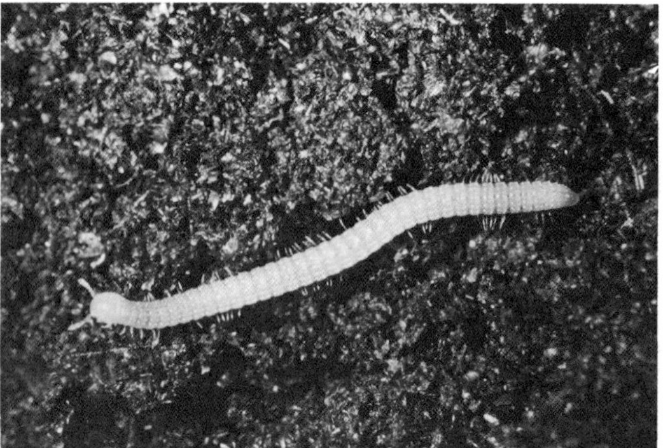

Fig. 45. *Cambala speobia*, a troglobitic cambalid millipede.

Their larvae feed on dead bats so efficiently that a bat skeleton can be "cleaned" in a few minutes. Incidentally, few troglobites are found in the vicinity of large bat guano deposits—the conditions are usually not right. Guano communities have their own cast of characters, "guanophiles", which may reach incredible densities. Some bat fleas have been known to reach densities of 11,000 per square meter in the vicinity of dying bats, and dermestid larvae, gnats and pseudoscorpions can also be quite abundant. Some of the large bat caves of the Southwest and Mexico are intriguing ecosystems that deserve more study. However, the heat, stench, flies and ammonia can be quite disagreeable to any but the most devoted student. Bats will be covered more fully below.

In a more typical, food-poor cave, one often finds small troglobitic millipedes feeding on organic detritus. They are harmless and should not be confused with centipedes. Millipedes (Fig. 45) are slow moving and have two pairs of legs on most body segments. Centipedes (Fig. 46) are rare in caves, generally are fast moving and have one pair of long legs on each body segment. They also have poison mouthparts (but no poison leg claws, as commonly believed), but most are too small to inflict a bite on a person. Some groups of millipedes and centipedes are naturally eyeless whether they inhabit caves or not. The cave forms of many parts of North America are poorly known.

Arachnids are a class of eight-legged arthropod. Many families of the Order Araneae (spiders) have troglophilic and troglobitic species: Agelenidae, Leptonetidae, Nesticidae (Fig. 47), Pholcidae, Telemidae and even a few tarantulas of the family Dipluridae. Spiders, like most arachnids, prey on other arthropods and are important members of most cave ecosystems. We have mentioned trogloxenic harvestmen, and there are troglobitic ones as well (Fig. 48). Harvestmen (Order Phalangida) can be distinguished from spiders by their lack of a constricted waist between the prosoma (anterior part of the body) and opisthosoma (abdomen). While trogloxenic harvestmen are often scavengers, many

Fig. 46. A geophilomorph centipede.

Fig. 47. *Nesticus* sp., troglobitic spider.

troglobitic ones seem to be predators on microarthropods, such as collembola. The scorpions have few truly troglobitic forms—several species are known from Mexico. Pseudoscorpions (Fig. 49) form an order separate from scorpions. They are minute forms that have the claw-like pedipalps of a scorpion, but no tail and sting. Some forms are adapted to bat guano communities, others are troglobites. All are predators. There undoubtedly are many unknown species of troglobitic mites. Even the best known mite family in caves, the Rhagidiidae, has been studied only recently in North America. Some cave rhagidiids are among the giants of the mite world: up to two millimeters body length with legs almost twice the length of the body. Even so, they are so tiny that they have sometimes been found sitting on the surface film of quiet water. They, too, are predators. In the tropics there are cave forms from other, less commonly known arachnid orders: Schizomida, Palpigradi, Amblypygi and Ricinulei. Until about 1968, the Ricinulei were thought so rare that just about every specimen that had ever been collected (a few dozen) could be accounted for. Abundant populations of several species of these reddish, tick-like creatures have been discovered in Mexican caves. Ticks themselves, which are closer to mites, have no troglobitic forms, but are common in bat caves.

Fig. 48. *Texella reddelli*, a troglobitic harvestman.

Fig. 49. A troglobitic pseudoscorpion.

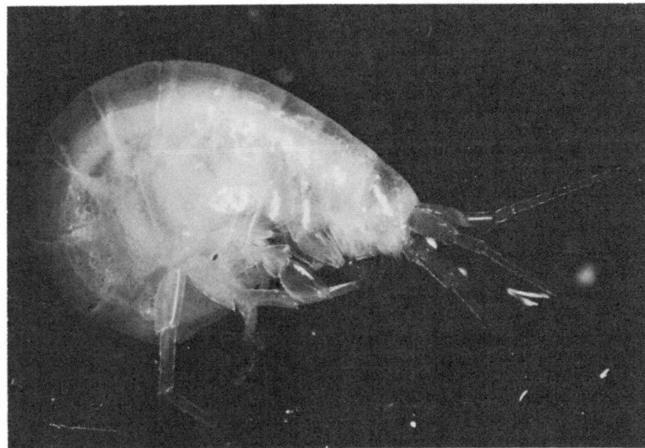

Fig. 50. *Stygobromus russelli*, a crangonyctid amphipod.

The large and complex Class Crustacea has many troglobitic species, mostly in the orders Decapoda, Amphipoda and Isopoda. There are a few among the more primitive orders Copepoda, Ostracoda, Thermosbaenacea, Speleograephacea and Mysidacea. Many American caves have troglobites of the amphipod genus *Stygobromus* (Fig. 50). These small, aquatic creatures look like shrimp with the tail bent forward under the body. They are scavenger/predators and, as with most cave-adapted crustaceans, the exoskeleton is so thin and colorless that the internal organs often can be seen. Decapods are represented by atyid shrimp (which are found in the Southeast U.S., Yucatan, Cuba and Puerto Rico), palaemonid shrimp (Fig. 51) (Texas, Florida, the Antilles and Mexico), crayfish (Mid-west and Southeast U.S. and parts of Mexico), and even a blind land crab of the genus *Typhloseudothelphusa* from Mexico and Guatemala. Three isopod families are common in American caves. Cirolanid isopods (Fig. 52) are all aquatic and mostly tropical (one species occurs in Virginia, another in Texas and several in Mexico). Cirolanids are generally elliptical and dome-shaped and usually crawl on the bottom, but occasionally swim if disturbed. Asellid isopods are also aquatic, crawling forms, but they look like centipedes, being long and narrow. There are many species of asellids in caves across the U.S. Some are over a centimeter long while others are tiny and cling to pieces of wood or the undersides of rocks. Trichoniscid isopods look more like the "pillbug" isopods familiar to most people. Many white, eyeless species of the genera *Brackenridgia* (Fig. 53) and *Miktoniscus* are found in North America. Some are aquatic, some terrestrial, and many seem capable of an amphibious existence. Grayish, trogloxenic forms of the pillbug, Armadillidiidae, are often found in entrance areas.

Fig. 51. *Palaemonetes antrorum,* a palaemonid shrimp.

Fig. 52. *Speocirolana pelaezi*, a cirolanid isopod.

Fig. 53. *Brackenridgia bridgesi*, a trichoniscid isopod.

North America has many different species of blind cave fish while Europe has none. The family Amblyopsidae has four cave species distributed from Alabama to Indiana and Kentucky to Oklahoma. *Amblyopsis* and *Typhlichthys* are the more common genera; *Speoplatyrhinus* is known from one cave in Alabama. These fish are among the more highly cave-adapted vertebrates in the world. In Texas two blind catfish species are known from deep artesian wells near San Antonio (they have never been found in accessible caves). In Mexico there are five families of fish having troglobitic forms—the number of species is currently in doubt and may range from six to eight or more. Cave fish in the U.S. generally have small populations and should not be collected unless for very good reasons. In parts of Mexico, blind cave fish of the genus *Astyanax* are so astronomically abundant that some cavers feel it is all right to take a few home for their aquaria. At the worst, this is merely a bad example to set and it is difficult to make a strong case against such collecting, except that it is against Mexican law to collect without a permit.

Fig. 54. *Typhlomolge rathbuni*, the famous blind salamander from San Marcos, Texas.

On the evolutionary scale, the highest group to contain troglobites is the Amphibia. No frogs are troglobitic, only a few salamanders. Texas has the majority: five described species and about 35 known populations of the genera *Eurycea* and *Typhlomolge* (Fig. 54). Like most troglobitic salamanders, they retain their gills and live in water all their lives, a "neotenic" condition. The Ozark blind salamander, *Typhlotriton spelaeus*, occurs in the Ozarks but is not an advanced troglobite. The juveniles live at cave entrances and have functional eyes and some pigment. The adult loses its gills and penetrates deeper into the cave, losing some pigment and eye function. If kept in the light, the retina still degenerates but the eyelids do not fuse as usual. The genus *Gryinophilus* has two troglobitic species: one from Tennessee that is neotenic, and one from West Virginia that undergoes metamorphosis. In Florida and Georgia there is a troglobitic, neotenic salamander, *Haideotriton wallacei.* The only other troglobitic salamander in the world is the famous *Proteus anquinus*, a neotenic form from southeastern Europe.

Bats (Order Chiroptera) are the only true flying mammals and form an important component of many cave ecosystems. Of the sixteen families, three occur in in the United States:

1. Pyllostomatidae (Leaf-nosed bats)—Mainly tropical in distribution; five species range into the Southwest U.S. (all are cave bats and three are nectar feeders); migratory.
2. Vespertilionidae—World-wide distribution; most hibernate; twelve of the twenty-nine U.S. species use caves; common cave forms are *Myotis lucifugus, M. velifer, M. sodalis, Eptesicus fuscus* and *Plecotus townsendii.*
3. Molossidae—Distributed from the tropics into southern U.S.; two of the six species use caves; *Tadarida brasiliensis mexicana* is the most common bat in southwestern caves and migrates to Mexico.

About half of these forty species utilize caves in some way at some time—for day or night roosting, hibernation or reproduction. Most of our bats are insectivorous. Summer colonies of *Tadarida brasiliensis mexicana* number in the millions in some southwestern caves. On their nightly forays, bats devour many tons of insects and are one of our best natural controls of pests. Over the past twenty years our bat populations have undergone an alarming decline. Disturbance by humans probably has affected many species, but there is good evidence that insecticide poisoning (via insects) is a major cause. Biologists have largely stopped banding bats as this too has been suspected as a minor cause of mortality.

As one moves into Mexico, the number and diversity of bats increases dramatically. The family Desmodontidae is composed of three species of true vampires. *Desmodus rotundus*, the most common vampire, inhabits many caves. Its guano is familiar to many cavers as a dark, molasses-like fluid which may harbor many tiny beetles.

A General Ethic for Collecting

For many years the NSS has had a general rule against cavers disturbing or collecting cave life. This rule often takes the form: "Do not collect cave life except under specific direction of a scientist" (e.g., see Moore and Sullivan, 1978). Many biospeleologists would probably agree that this rule is a bit too strict and needs elaboration. What the NSS should discourage, of course, is the unnecessary disturbance of cave life, especially if it is for no scientific or conservationist gain. Thus, personal collections of cave animals as mere curiosities should be frowned upon unless obtained under special circumstances. For instance, certain Mexican cave fish (Astyanax) can be purchased from aquarium shops and have been bred from a small beginning stock that was collected decades ago. The cave ecosystem from which they were taken (Cueva Chica in San Luis Potosi) was not adversely affected and thrives to this day.

Over the years cavers in all parts of the country have aided biospeleologists by making small collections of cave animals wherever they have explored new caves or studied known caves that were poorly known biologically. Such collections are frequently sent to biospeleologists who have ongoing research projects on certain regions or animal groups. For example, much of what is known about the vast and diverse cave faunas of Texas and Mexico would still be unknown if none of the members of the Texas Speleological Association and the Association for Mexican Cave Studies had made routine collections whenever they explored and mapped. Even the most staunch conservationist might agree that we cannot adequately protect cave life until we know what is living in the caves. There must be published scientific information on the cave fauna of any region before one can really begin to see what is there to protect. Moreover, such scientific documentation is necessary before legal action can be pursued to good effect, say in the protection of a possibly threatened or endangered species. The cave fauna of many regions is too poorly known to yet say what is endangered.

At one extreme some might equate the collecting of a cave animal with breaking and removing a stalactite. This viewpoint does not take into account the enormous amount of scientific information that even one specimen of an unknown species can contain or the fact that living things can reproduce themselves, unlike speleothems. Although some species of cave animal may have very small populations and thus be endangered by collecting, the popular notion that all cave populations are small and vulnerable is unsupported by hard evidence. Cave species are most often endangered by the loss of habitat and pollution, not by small-scale collecting. To quote James Reddell (1976), a leading American biospeleologist, ". . . the type of collecting that cavers do will in no way endanger the cave forms they may find or interfere significantly with the cave ecology."

No general rule for collecting will apply in all situations. The amateur collector should not collect in caves that have been well-studied or ecologically damaged, unless at the specific request of a scientist who knows the situation and asks for specific numbers of a certain species. If the caver is in serious doubt about the conditions, he should not collect, but he should make observations and notes. No collections should be made unless the caver already knows a scientist who will take the collections and put them to good use. This is not exactly the "supervision" in the rule of old.

In some instances just visiting certain bat caves can be harmful when the bats are hibernating during the winter or giving birth in the spring. Over the years bat biologists and cavers have identified certain caves that should be considered "off-limits," at least for part of the year. No doubt many more such caves will be identified in the future. Accidentally stirring up bats during their hibernation may cause them to deplete their fat reserves, which may mean death or reduced reproductive capacity later on. The collecting of bats by amateurs should be discouraged in most cases, especially since some bats carry rabies. Most cavers are thoughtful conservationists and can apply their own informed reasoning ability to each situation.

How to Collect

The simplest collecting kit one can carry into a cave is a one or two-ounce screw-cap jar containing 70 to 80% ethyl or isopropyl alcohol. Isopropyl (rubbing) alcohol is cheap and can be bought in most drug and grocery stores. Baby food jars work nicely if they have screw lids (snap lids should be avoided). Most animals can be preserved in alcohol, but formaldehyde is preferred for fish, frogs, salamanders and earthworms. Drugstore formaldehyde is usually 40% and should be mixed one part to ten parts water. Small, plastic baby bottles are best for formaldehyde (the lid should be taped shut). Planarians (aquatic flatworms) are best taken alive and air mailed immediately in some original cave water in an insulated container to a specialist.

Collecting tools are not absolutely necessary. Most arthropods can be picked up with light finger pressure. Crickets require quick aim and a firm grasp, or they can be trapped under the cupped hand and then brushed into the jar. For very small insects you can wet your finger with alcohol, touch the animal gently, and then stick your finger back into the alcohol so as to wash off the insect. A fine paintbrush is useful for microarthropods, insects in small crevices and for picking up planarians off the surface film of pools. Most tweezers and forceps are too stiff and will only crush the specimens. I make very light, flimsy forceps by cutting them out with scissors from a flattened aluminum drink can, in paper-doll fashion. Such forceps often require rebending to keep the tips aligned, but they can be used on all but the tiniest and largest of insects. Small insects on rocks or sticks can be tapped over or dipped in the jar. Creatures on the ceiling can be persuaded to leap into the jar. One should be careful not to crush the specimen or break legs, antennae or tails. These appendages are often necessary for species identification. Earthworms should be killed in alcohol. This requires only a few seconds, then the worm is removed, straightened by rolling it like a string of clay in the hand or on the thigh, then placed in diluted formaldehyde.

A small, inexpensive aquarium dip net is good for most aquatic collecting and will easily fit into a cave pack or pocket. Wrap it in a plastic bag to prevent tearing the netting. Tea strainers also make good nets. Many aquatic forms will be on the bottom or under rocks but can be shooed into open water where they can be netted.

The single jar technique represents a minimal effort but better scientific information is obtained by taking several jars and using each in a different habitat in the same cave: entrance area, guano deposit, organic detritus, etc. Also, it is best to put larger specimens (such as large crickets, beetles, millipedes and spiders) in a different jar than small specimens, which are often damaged by the larger ones kicking and squirming.

Usually, two or three specimens of each larger species and a dozen or so of the smaller ones will be enough for the specialist to identify. Often the collector will have insufficient time to collect that many anyway. Larger numbers should be collected only at the specific request of a qualified biologist.

At the end of the collecting trip, preferably as soon as you leave the cave, a small collecting label should be put inside each jar. The label should be on strong paper, in pencil (most inks will fade), and should have the following information:

1. Name and location of cave, including county (municipality, if in Mexico), state and other locating information such as direction and distance from county seat or prominent town, topo map coordinates, cave survey number, etc.
2. Date of collection (spell out the month or use a Roman numeral).
3. Collector's name.
4. Habitat where collected, temperature if known, etc.

It is at this point that some collectors ruin their own efforts. A collection with doubtful or missing data is useless and may have to be discarded by the biologist who receives it. Obviously, one should never put specimens from different caves in the same jar.

The habit of taking field notes, even on pleasure caving trips, should be encouraged. Observations on water and air temperatures, humidity, species associations, prime collecting areas, density of animals, hydrologic and meteorologic information, pollution, etc., can be invaluable later on and should be written down even if collecting is not your interest. Close-up photography of live specimens can be useful, but identification to species usually requires preserved specimens.

All areas of the cave should be checked. The entrance area is too often ignored, but nevertheless contains species of interest to the biospeleologist. Pay particular attention to organic materials such as feces (usually a rich source of collembola [Fig. 55], tiny hopping insects), rotting vegetation and thin films of mud and feces on flowstone. Even litter should be examined (I once found a very rare beetle under a moldy match box). Many tiny arthropods, such as beetles, pseudoscorpions and diplurans live under rocks. Spend at least a few minutes turning over rocks in each new area, especially if they are imbedded in mud (put them back if this defaces the floor). Look on the bottom of the rock and in the hole and be prepared to move fast as these secretive little guys will scurry away before you know it. A more thorough account of equipment and techniques may be found in Cooper and Poulson (1979).

Fig. 55. *Pseudosinella violenta*, a collembolan or springtail.

Much valuable collecting is done by cavers while they are mapping or exploring. There are many times on a caving trip when someone is waiting for someone else: while the sketchman is trying to catch up, while the novice is struggling up the rope, or while the photographer is setting up that big room shot. You may be surprised to find what is living under you. In fact, you may have crushed it and may as well collect it anyway, assuming you know a biologist to send it to (next section).

After The Trip

The collection should be sent off to the biologist with whom you are working as soon as possible. However, you should first make a list of all the collections and send it in a letter to the biologist, keeping a copy for your files. Make sure the lids are on tight (taping them is a good idea). Pad the jars with foam or crumpled paper and pack it all tightly in a strong box or mailing tube. Tape the box securely and wrap it in strong paper. This can be mailed by third class. The biologist should notify you when he has received the package. If he has not, you can ask the postal service to trace it.

Most biologists keep a good correspondence going with their collectors and are happy to send back identifications and interesting information on what was collected. When the information is published, they are glad to furnish collectors with copies of their articles. Addresses of biospeleologists who can help you get your collections to the right specialists are given at the end of this chapter.

Conserving Cave Life

There are several things that we can do in our own caving activities to conserve cave life:

1. Never dump carbide in a cave! It is poisonous. Carry all your trash out with you.
2. On the other hand, it is usually best to leave someone else's old organic litter (wood, paper, food, feces) in the dark zone of the cave, as it may be providing food and shelter to cave-adapted animals. Cave clean-up campaigns are becoming more popular and we should be thankful, but the thrill of ridding a cave of man-made trash should not blind us to the possibility that it already may have become part of the cave ecosystem. If such materials are removed, they should be thoroughly examined for animals, which should then be released in a similar habitat in the cave or collected for study.
3. Cave gates, if they are necessary, should allow access by bats and other normal cave visitors. See Hunt and Stitt (1975) and Tuttle (1977). More bat caves will need to be identified as "off-limits" during critical times of the year. This is especially true for the Gray Bat, *Myotis grisescens*, the Indiana Bat, *Myotis sodalis*, and the Virginia Big-eared Bat, *Plecotus townsendii virginianus*, all endangered species.

Every year more and more caves are polluted or destroyed by trash dumping, land development, quarrying and dam building. The loss of habitat and food resources that results from these activities is much more threatening to cave life than the most irresponsible collecting. To counteract this regrettable situation, many cavers have joined together in study groups, regional and state cave surveys and conservation task forces. These groups and you can make a real contribution to saving our caves and cave life by:

1. Studying the caves and their contents and documenting what is found in scientific bulletins and journals.
2. Attending public hearings held by government agencies on land use policies.
3. Petitioning government agencies and politicians

in a non-abrasive but forthright and well-informed manner to rectify intolerable situations.

4. Seeking publicity for particularly dire situations by writing articles for national magazines or communicating with large news media of good repute.

5. Buying land and caves for nature preserves, or supporting organizations like the NSS and the Nature Conservancy which do just that.

Cavers tend to be passive conservationists, that is, they conserve by not doing certain things. Cavers also tend to be poor (money wise). But it is not too late to change our ways and support active conservation as well. Whether we like it or not, economic power can make a difference.

The NSS Biology Section

The NSS Biology Section meets at least once a year (at the NSS convention) and hosts educational talks and scientific symposia on cave biology. It elects officers and publishes *The North American Biospeleology Newsletter* (NABN) several times a year. The NABN is an excellent source of information on current cave biology happenings in North America and the world. Members' names, addresses and interests are published, and a running bibliography of scientific papers is offered with each issue. Membership is open to all interested persons and the current (1981) subscription rate is $3 a year. Back issues are available. The officers will handle inquiries on specialists to work with and other matters. Consult the NSS office for names and addresses of current officers.

The following biospeleologists are willing to assist serious collectors in sorting problem materials for distribution and in providing advice and addresses:

East and Southeast
Dr. John E. Cooper
N.C. State Museum of Natural History
P.O. Box 27647
Raleigh, NC 27611

Southwest and California
Dr. William R. Elliott
12102 Grimsley Drive
Austin, TX 78759

West and Pacific
Dr. Ellen M. Benedict
Department of Biology
Portland State University
Portland, OR 97207

Midwest
Dr. Horton H. Hobbs III
Department of Biology
Wittenberg University
Springfield, OH 45501

Hawaii
Dr. Francis G. Howarth
Bishop Museum
P.O. Box 6037
Honolulu, HI 96818

Mexico and Central America
Mr. James R. Reddell
P.O. Box 7431
University of Texas Station
Austin, TX 78712

Dr. Cooper (above) is also head of the NSS Endangered Cave Fauna Conservation Task Force.

References

Barbour, R. W. and W. H. Davis (1969)—Bats of America:Univ. Press, Lexington, KY, 286pp, 20pl.

Cooper, J. E. and T. L. Poulson (1979)—A guide for biological collecting in caves:Caving Information Series, Natl. Speleol. Soc., Huntsville, AL, 14pp.

Hunt, G., and R. R. Stitt (1975)—Cave gating, a handbook:Natl. Speleol. Soc., Huntsville, AL, 42pp.

Mohr, C.E. and T. L. Poulson (1969)—The Life of the cave:McGraw-Hill Book Co., New York, NY, 232pp.

Moore, G. W. and G. H. Sullivan (1978)—Speleology, the study of caves:Zephyrus Press, Inc., Teaneck, NJ, 150pp.

Reddell, J. R. (1976)—Biological collecting made easy: Texas Caver **21**(3):40-46.

Tuttle, M. D. (1977)—Gating as a means of protecting cave-dwelling bats, pp. 72-82; IN T. Aley and D. Rhodes (Eds), National Cave Management Symp. Proc., Mountain View, AK, 1976:Speleobooks, Albuquerque, NM, 106pp. Reprinted in: NSS News **35**:175-180.

Vandel, A. (1965)—Biospeleology, the biology of cavernicolous animals:Pergamon Press, NY, 524pp.

CAVING LIABILITY

EVERYTHING YOU ALWAYS WANTED TO KNOW—AND MORE

Hugh W. Blanchard
NSS 4490F

Caver Liability

Let me discuss initially, very briefly, the risks of liability to the average caver. At the risk of oversimplification, liability ultimately depends on the caver's own negligence or absence of same. There are several common misconceptions in this area. One is that fellow club members of the negligent caver may also be liable simply by being members of the same club. **This is not correct**. Mere membership in the same organization does not make fellow club members liable for the negligent act. Liability attaches only to that person or persons who are actually responsible for the injury.

Another common misconception, sometimes known as the IBM syndrome, is that incorporating the caving club will somehow lessen the dangers of liability. Again this is not correct. Incorporation may be desirable for other reasons. For example, it is necessary in some states for an organization to be incorporated in order to receive legal title to land. However, **incorporation** of the caving club **does not affect** a member's or any of the club officers' **liability** for negligence in the slightest.

What type of acts constitute negligence in caving? To the best of my knowledge there are no actual cases that have ever decided this. Thus, I must go to a common sense determination of what an average jury might consider negligence. Let us assume a situation where an experienced caver takes a novice on a vertical caving trip and gives him little, if any, supervision. As a direct result the novice falls and is injured. A jury might decide there is negligence in such a situation.

Negligence on the part of a trip leader may occur in a different way. If the leader of a cave trip that involves vertical work delegates a lot of responsibility to a second caver, even though it is known that this second caver knows very little about vertical work, and as a result a third caver, a novice, is injured, a jury may find that both the second caver as well as the trip leader are guilty of negligence.

If a caving club has fairly frequent training sessions, including climbing practices, for its members and guests, it should consider having trainees sign waiver of liability forms. This, of course, will not remove all danger of liability especially when active negligence is a cause of the injury. Also a minor can subsequently disaffirm such a waiver. In most states today a minor is a person under 18 (moral—never trust anyone under 18). However, an intelligently drafted waiver signed both by the minor and his parents shows at least that the minor and his parents were put on notice concerning possible hazards and diminishes the prospects of future law suits. A typical waiver form is shown in Fig. 56.

I am not aware of any negligence insurance available for cavers at nominal cost. Doubtless, such insurance is obtainable, but only at a price which few cavers would be willing to pay.

For cavers planning international expeditions it is best to check with local cavers or, in the case of Mexico, to check with the Association of Mexican Cave Studies (address listed in Appendix C) since foreign law varies.

Landowner Liability

I will now attempt to summarize the main problems relating to landowners' liability. Fear of lawsuits is undoubtably the main reason why owners place their caves off-limits.

Traditionally, under the common law, a landowner owed varying degrees of care depending on who entered his land. The highest standard is owed to invitees. **Invitees** are business visitors who come on the land at the owner's invitation for a mutual business purpose. The owner has a duty not only to warn them of known dangerous conditions, but also to make a reasonable inspection of the property to discover unknown dangers. Visitors paying admission to visit a cave are invitees.

Licensees are persons who enter the property with the owner's consent only for their own purpose and not for the owner's benefit. The owner has a duty to carry on activities with reasonable care, but need not make any inspection to discover unknown dangers. Cavers exploring a wild cave with the owner's consent and not paying admission would be licensees.

The lowest standard of care is owed to **trespassers**. The owner need only refrain from intentional harm, such as

_________________________GROTTO
An affiliated organization of the National Speleological Society

I, _________________________ of
(Name)

____
(Address)
understand the risks involved in connection with caving and the caving-related activities of the

_________________________Grotto, and hereby agree to assume all responsibility for myself and my property and agree to indemnify and hold harmless the NATIONAL SPELOEOLGICAL SOCIETY

and the_________________________GROTTO and all members thereof, from any and all claims arising from risks which are hereby voluntarily assumed.

____
Name

____
Age and Birthdate

____
Date

____
Parents' Signature if Minor

____
Date

____
Witness to Signature

____
Date

____
Witness to Signature

____
Date

Fig. 56. Sample release form.

setting traps against trespassers entering his land without permission and has no duty to keep the land in a safe condition. There are several qualifications to this general rule of non-liability to trespassers. One, the so-called "attractive nuisance" doctrine, provides that trespassing children are legally viewed as licensees if the attraction, usually dangerous machinery, is an artificially created trap. This doctrine is not in effect in all states and, even in the states adopting it, it is not applicable to "natural" conditions of nature such as caves. The owner in some states also owes a duty of reasonable care to known or constant trespassers and is obligated to warn them of known dangers. Thus, in some states cavers entering a cave with the knowledge, but not the consent, of the owner would be legally classified as licensees.

In recent years courts in many states have abandoned the old classification of invitee, licensee and trespasser in favor of a simple rule of requiring reasonable care. Under this doctrine the landowner must maintain his property in a reasonably safe condition considering all the circumstances. I suspect that this change will be largely one of semantics and that only rarely will the legal result be different than under the old nomenclature.

A landowner's liability may be diminished by the installation of a gate on his cave, especially if locked and posted with no trespassing notices. Any person then found in the cave without the permission of the landowner could be considered a trespasser.

Within the past twenty years or so the state legislatures of most states have passed so-called "sportsmens laws." Such statutes limit the liability of landowners who permit the public to use their land for recreational purposes without charge. The landowners' duty of care under these statutes is similar to that owed a trespasser. These laws are not uniform and differ considerably in their language. Very few specifically mention cave exploring as one of the protected recreational activities. Some others include a general statement that all recreational activities are included. However, most contain a list of protected activities invariably including hunting, fishing and hiking, but do not mention cave exploring. This may cause problems as we will see.

It should be mentioned in passing that the federal government's liability for injuries occurring on federally-owned land is governed by local state law.

Let me now discuss a recent case which highlights the problems of landowners' liability and may contain some clues to possible solution. (Grateful acknowledgment is given to NSS Legal Committee member, James W. Harbison, Jr., who provided the writer with much of the information on this cave.) The so-called Knox Cave case started on May 3, 1975, with a trip to Knox Cave, New York, by six cavers led by two NSS members. Knox had been a commercial cave until 1958. Since then it had become the most popular wild sports cave in the northeast with literally thousands of cavers visiting it over the years. Its entrance lies at the bottom of a steep sinkhole and it was regarded as a safe cave with no reported injuries despite the large amount of traffic through it. However, on that tragic May morning, just after four cavers entered the cave, a one-ton block of ice fell 25 feet from the sinkhole edge squarely on the two remaining cavers about to enter the cave. One of the cavers, a young man, was killed instantly. His companion, a 19-year-old coed, was severely injured and rendered a paraplegic.

Several months later the injured caver, through her attorney, filed a $15 million damage suit against the cave owner alleging a breach of due care. The cave owner was a well-to-do New York physician who had acquired the cave along with 200 adjoining acres at a tax sale seven years before. The owner had enjoyed fine relations with northeast cavers and permitted them free access to the cave. Several years before, the cave had been briefly gated and "no trespassing" signs had been posted. However, both the gate and signs had long since disappeared by the time of the accident. Apparently, waiver forms had never been required to enter the cave.

The doctor had insurance on the 200 acres but, immediately after the filing of the law suit, his insurance company regretfully informed him that his insurance policy did not cover the accident since the coverage was only for "vacant land" and in their opinion "vacant land" did not include owning a cave frequented by substantial numbers of cavers. (Moral: you will never have any problems with insurance companies as long as you faithfully pay your premiums and never make any claims on the coverage.) Needless to say, the discovery that he was now uninsured came as a surprise to the doctor who immediately filed suit against the insurance company to determine the status of his coverage. A trial resulted with the New York Supreme Court finding in the doctor's favor by holding that the land was unoccupied and unused even though it included a cave. The Court also held that the fact that the doctor allowed experienced cavers to use his cave without charging admission and permitted them to install a platform and ladder in the cave did not alter the "vacant" quality of the land.

With this hurdle behind him, the doctor and his insurance company now prepared for trial on the question of his liability. However, just prior to the trial his insurance company felt it more prudent to settle the case out-of-court for a reported settlement of $325,000. Thus ended the Knox Cave case with no decision ever rendered as to whether the owner was negligent.

One cannot help but wonder what would have occurred had the case gone before a judge and jury. I personally regard the suit as quite weak since no one apparently had been aware of the falling ice hazard prior to the accident. However, it must be admitted that the jury would doubtless have been sympathetic to the plight of the paralyzed girl. Another complicating factor was whether cave exploring was included under the New York Sportsmens' Statute. The statute listed a number of recreational activities including hiking, but did not mention cave exploring. It would, of course, have been argued that the caving party was engaged in hiking, particularly since the accident actually occurred just outside the cave entrance. However, the counter argument would be that courts generally constru this type of statute narrowly since it is contrary to the common law. Under a narrow construction it is quite possible that the judge might have ruled that hiking is not the same as cave exploring.

At any rate, following the conclusion of the lawsuit, the doctor decided he would be happier without owning a cave and again offered it to the NSS. In October, 1979, the NSS was very concerned about the liability associated with owning caves and decided not to accept ownership but let the title pass to the Northeastern Cave Conservancy, a non-profit incorporated caving group. (The NSS currently owns two caves and is pursuing a cautious program to acquire more.) Like many other states, New York does not permit unincorporated organizations to receive title to land.

Are there any lessons to be learned from this sad story? I suggest there are several. One is that any landowner always faces a potential risk of being sued for injuries occurring on his land. Even if the injured person's case is very weak, it still needs to be defended and that involves attorney's fees. Also, even though a landowner has insurance, it does not necessarily mean that the insurance company will honor the policy when it is needed. Finally, a cave may be initially well protected with gates and "no trespassing" signs and within one or two years these may all have disappeared. The fact that almost all states have some type of sportsman's law may not be of much benefit unless it is clear that the particular statute includes cave exploring. Suitable amendments to specifically include cave exploration should be enacted when needed.

I have endeavored in this article to avoid legal citations and statute references. The interested reader may find references to additional articles dealing with caving liability in the May 1977 issue of the *NSS News*, page 112.

ELECTRONICS IN CAVING

Frank Reid

NSS 9086F

Many cavers are knowledgeable in electronics and would like to combine their seemingly incompatible interests.

Electronic aids to caving are gaining popularity in the United States. "Cave radio" is a powerful mapping aid. Underground and surface communication is vital to cave rescue. Electronic instrumentation and telemetry are used in cave related sciences, e.g., hydrology and bat study. The small, affordable electronic navigation receivers now available have numerous cave related uses. Caving electronics includes electric lights and battery charging systems (see the chapter on electric lighting).

Computers are increasingly important in cave study. The NSS Computer Applications Section[10] is primarily software-oriented with an interest in computer-assisted survey data reduction, map plotting, and cave data management.

Cave Radios

Magnetic induction "cave radios" can communicate through a few hundred meters of rock. More important, however, is their ability to precisely locate the surface point above an underground transmitter and measure depth. The technique is well developed and reliable. Besides mapping, cave radio is an aid to connection searches and rescue. It has located water well sites for landowners, surveyed property boundaries at commercial caves, and found places to dig new cave entrances.

Most cave radios operate at very low frequencies. Some transmit voice, others communicate only by Morse code. Cave radios are not available commercially. Plans have been published by the NSS Communication and Electronics Section[9], (one of many self-supporting special interest groups within the Society).

An underground transmitter passes low-frequency current through a coil of wire, creating a magnetic field which is detected on the surface by a receiver with a similar coil antenna. To home-in on the transmitter location, we use the directional properties of loop antennas. The received signal strength depends on the quantity of magnetic flux passing through the receiving loop. The nature of this dependence is shown in Fig. 1. The abrupt disappearance (null) of the signal when the plane of the loop is parallel to the field tells us when the antenna is pointing toward the transmitter. Note in Fig. 1 that the null is much more sharply defined than is the direction of maximum signal.

If the underground coil is level, then the axis of the magnetic field is vertical and the geometry of the field is as shown by dashed lines in Fig. 2 (from above) and Fig. 3 (from the side).

When within range and receiving the signal, hold the receiving loop in a vertical plane and rotate it around a vertical axis until the null is found. The plane of the loop at the null contains ground zero (the center of the magnetic field) but the direction is ambiguous. Move to a nearby point and repeat this procedure. The intersection of the two planes so determined gives the approximate location of ground zero, as shown in Fig. 2.

The ground zero location can be refined to within a few centimeters by holding the loop in a vertical plane with its axis aimed toward the expected location, and tilting it backward or forward to find the null. In the side view of the magnetic field, we see that the magnetic lines slant away from ground zero as they emerge from the ground nearby. Ground zero therefore lies in the direction opposite the tilt of the loop when the null is obtained. Move toward decreasing vertical angles until the null is straight down. Rotate the loop 90 degrees horizontally, and again seek a straight down null.

Repeat the turn-and-seek process as necessary. Ground zero is the one point where the null is exactly vertical, no matter which way the loop's axis is pointed. A spirit level should be mounted on the loop to indicate when it is vertical.

This technique is extremely sensitive. The null plane will differ measurably from vertical when the base of the loop is 10 to 20 centimeters from ground zero, even when the transmitter is 50 meters below. The main limit to the accuracy of this method is the precision with which the transmitting loop can be leveled. A leveling error of 1/2 degree will produce a ground-zero location error of about one percent of the transmitter depth.

Measuring Depth

The following procedure is from reference 1, which itself is from references 2 and 3. Since the closed curves of the magnetic field (side view) are ellipses, we cannot find depth by simple triangulation. The shape of the curves is well known, however, so we can still use this information to compute depth.

Using a simple but adequate approximation to the shape of the field, we can write the relation:

$$\text{Tan}\ \Theta = 3LD \ / \ (2D^2 - L^2)$$

This is the angle that the field makes with the vertical, at a distance L from ground zero when the trans-

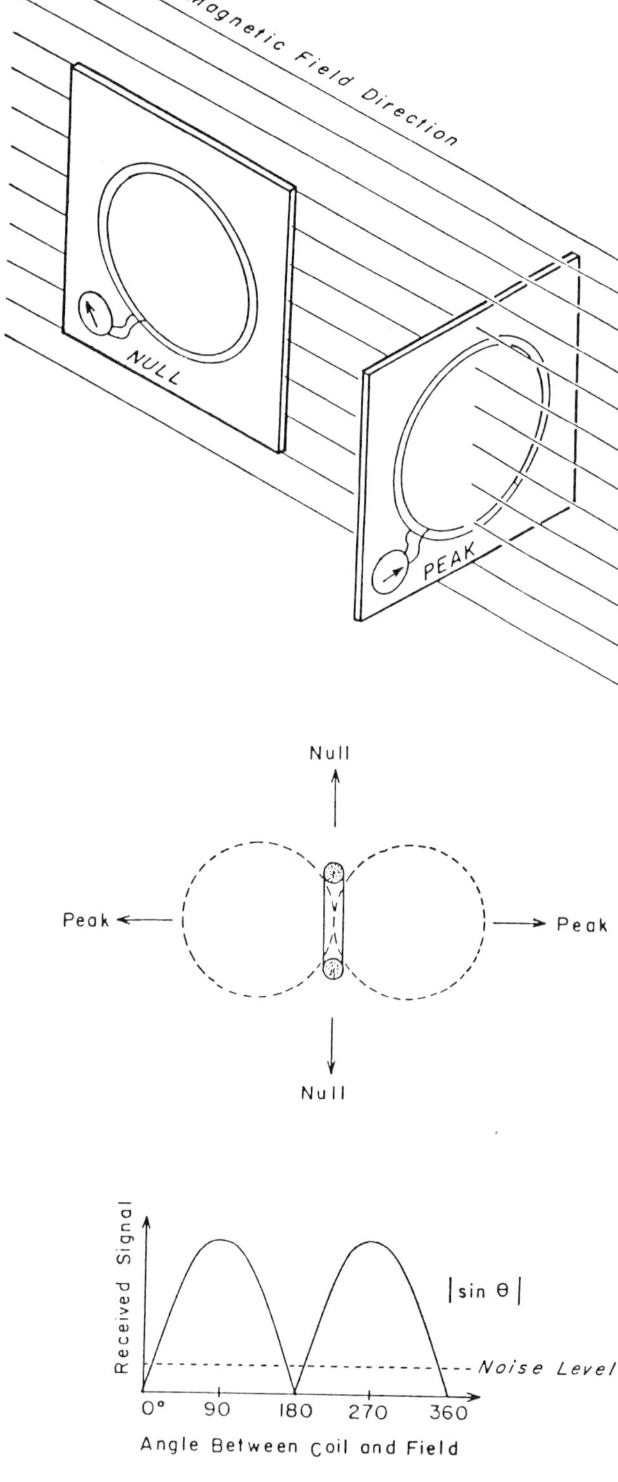

Fig. 1. Principle of direction finding. Received signal disappears when coil is parallel to magnetic field. Nulls are more sharply defined than peaks, but with very weak signals, you may have to seek peaks not nulls.

mitter is at depth D (the angle is measured in the plane containing ground zero). Fig. 4 is a set of curves of D versus the angle, for various values of the distance from ground zero. Larger charts are included in references 1 and 2.

Having such a diagram available, stretch a measuring tape in a straight line away from ground zero in some direction where it can be made to lie fairly level. Pick a set of distances along the tape which correspond to curves on the diagram (in meters or feet—the chart works with any distance units). Measure the angles Θ (Fig. 3) at these points. Do this by pointing the axis of the receiving loop toward ground zero, then tilting the loop forward or backward as needed to find the null in the signal. The resulting angle can be measured with an adjustable machinist's protractor or other inclinometer. Plot the data on the diagram as shown. The points should lie near a straight horizontal line corresponding to the depth of the underground station.

For best accuracy use enough points to give an accurate estimate of the best line; avoid parts of the diagram where the curves are steeply rising (Θ less than about 12 degrees). Measure vertical angles to at least the nearest 1/2 degree. If possible, take another set of depth data in the direction opposite the first.

The radio locating process has intrinsic error indicators. If the transmitting coil is not level, it will be impossible to find a unique ground zero. The receiver operator will keep searching around a small area. In such a case, check for proper alignment of the receiving loop's bubble level. If the problem persists, mark ground zero in the middle of the ambiguous area.

If the transmitting loop is not level or if ground zero has been improperly located, depth readings will have an increasing or decreasing trend as shown in the top half of Fig. 5. The curved lines of points approach the true depth as the distance from ground zero increases. If data have been gathered in opposite directions from ground zero as suggested, most of the error will be removed by averaging the two sets.

A programmable pocket calculator can be used to evaluate the above equation solved for depth:

$$D = \frac{L\left(3 + \sqrt{9 + 8\tan^2\Theta}\right)}{4\tan\Theta}$$

$$0^0 < \Theta < 90^0$$

Depths calculated from several pairs of data should be averaged. The calculator method does not require a copy of the special chart, and data may be taken at any convenient distance along the measuring tape. The chart method is least expensive and makes more obvious the effects of the errors discussed above. It should be possible to determine the depth of the transmitter within 3 percent.

Conductive or magnetic ore bodies that could distort magnetic fields seldom occur in limestone cave areas.

Cave Communication

Long duration underground camping expeditions, popular in many countries, are seldom used in the U.S.A. These require communication links with the surface for logistical support and weather warnings. Cavers, notably British Commonwealth and European, have developed sophisticated equipment for underground communication by telephone and wireless means.[7]

Pit Communication

Radio waves normally do not penetrate the earth, nor will they follow cave passages for any appreciable distance. Few radios can withstand the cave environment. Suitably protected CB and VHF radios have been used for communication in very deep pits. Even in line-of-sight conditions, radio waves reflected from walls may cancel each other, resulting in dead spots. Inexpensive 49 megahertz headset radios have been used successfully in pits. Their voice activated transmitters offer hands free operation.

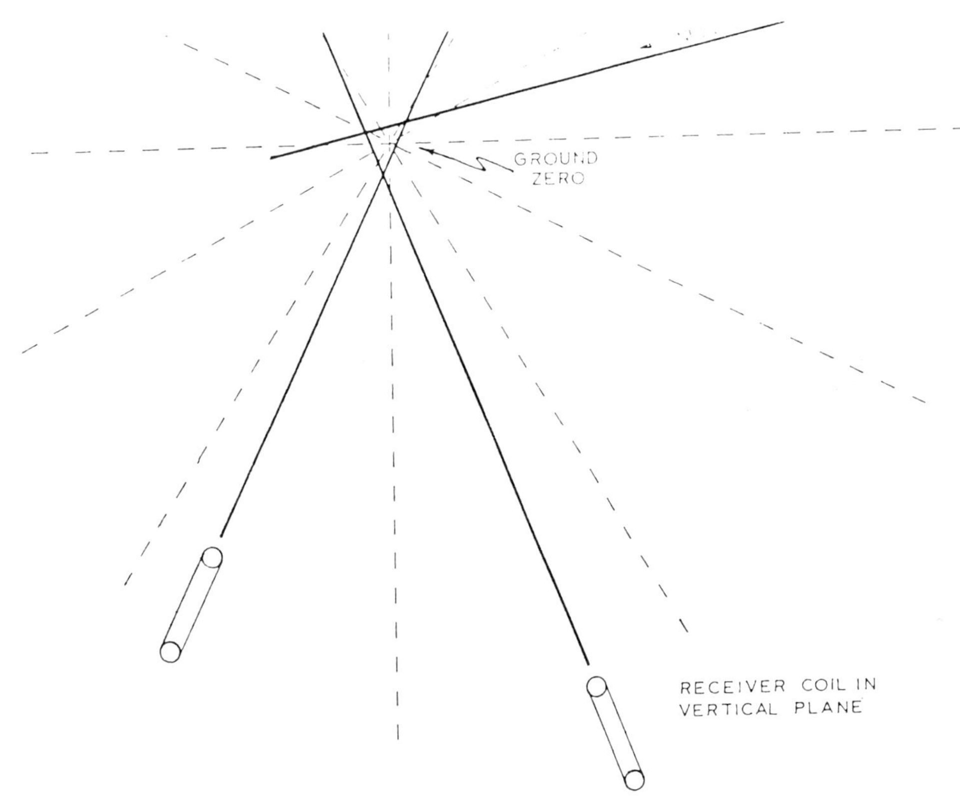

Fig. 2. Locating approximate surface point above the transmitter, viewed from above. Dashed lines in Figs. 2 and 3 and magnetic lines of force.

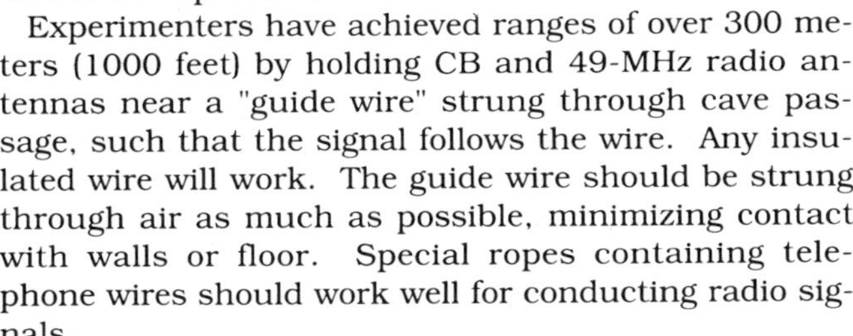

Experimenters have achieved ranges of over 300 meters (1000 feet) by holding CB and 49-MHz radio antennas near a "guide wire" strung through cave passage, such that the signal follows the wire. Any insulated wire will work. The guide wire should be strung through air as much as possible, minimizing contact with walls or floor. Special ropes containing telephone wires should work well for conducting radio signals.

Rescue Communication

Communication is vital in cave rescue. Cavers crawling back and forth with messages waste time and create extra traffic and confusion. Cave radios are not widely available, therefore we rely upon military surplus or other field telephones underground. Radio and telephones provide outside communication. The National Cave Rescue Commission (NCRC)[8] and NSS Electronics Section have developed special equipment for rescue communication.

Communication, of course, is not electronic equipment but the exchange of ideas and information. Problems often occur when cavers and other rescue participants do not understand each others terminology. Practice rescues should include communication with other emergency services (fire, rescue, ambulance, etc.) likely to be involved.

The easiest way to maintain clear and effective com-

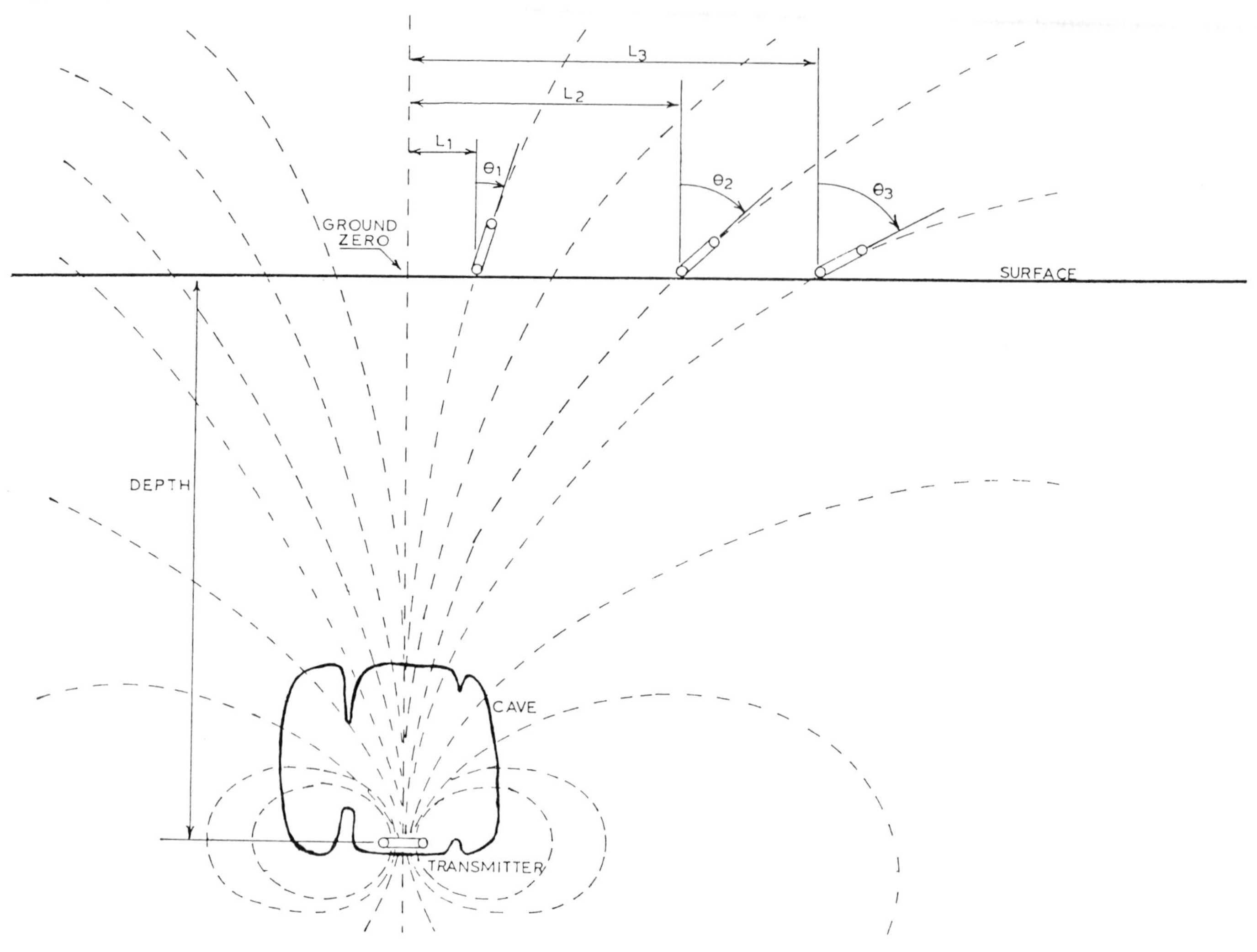

Fig. 3. Ground zero is the point where the field is vertical (see text). Distances (L) and vertical angles (θ) are used in calculating the depth of the transmitter.

munication is to decide upon message content before speaking. Listen before you transmit. The worst communication problems occur when inexperienced or excited operators all try to talk at once. Talking too loudly causes distortion and decreases intelligibility.

A field telephone circuit from the cave entrance to as near the patient as possible is the most critical link. It should be considered second only to getting the first medical team to the patient. This link expedites delivery of manpower and supplies, and will provide communication to a physician outside the cave. Phone and wire should immediately follow the first team if the patient's location has been found.

Test all telephones before deployment! The first wiring team should carry two phones, in case of failure or for an intermediate station at a critical point between patient and entrance. A telephone talker should accompany the team moving the patient.

For planning purposes, phone wire should be considered expendable. In real rescues it often becomes damaged or hopelessly tangled during retrieval, or is abandoned if rescuers are too exhausted. Telephones or radios may link the cave entrance to a staging area (perhaps the nearest parking area or shelter). Ideally, the various communication links should be able to interconnect as desired. A log keeper should record the times and contents of messages to prevent loss of vital information and for later analysis of the rescue.

A long range link ties the rescue site to the outside world (police, hospital, etc). This link speeds the dispatch of additional resources, and allows coordinators to activate or release the backup teams on standby.

The longer distance control circuit usually requires a commercial telephone or a ham radio link. Two-way radio can establish communication between the rescue site and the nearest available telephone.

Rescue communications equipment should include telephone directories, and a portable Bell-compatible telephone with a very long cord and various connectors. A telephone credit card allows charging long-distance calls to your home number when using another private or public telephone.

All phones and radios must be cleaned, dried and tested soon after each rescue, or else corrosion may do irreversible damage.

Radio Communication

All radios are delicate. Treat them as you would cameras. Do not use radios underground unless there is no alternative. Tie portable radios to climbers and people near pits.

Twenty-seven MHz Citizens' Band (CB) sets are the most common type of two-way radio. It is usually possible to amass several sets of CB equipment on short notice. However, CB has serious limitations: Interference can make CB unreliable or totally unusable. CB radio traffic concerning a cave rescue may attract unwanted attention. CB radios are not sturdily constructed, and often fail under field conditions. If you must depend upon CB at a rescue, try to procure as many spare radios as possible.

The radio requirements of each group will differ, depending upon group size, organization, operating area, and how the group interacts with other emergency services. There is presently no national standardization of two-way radio for cave rescue. The reasonably priced frequency-agile radios now available can meet a wide range of contingencies.

Radio security

Press and family should NOT be able to overhear cave rescue communications or discussions between

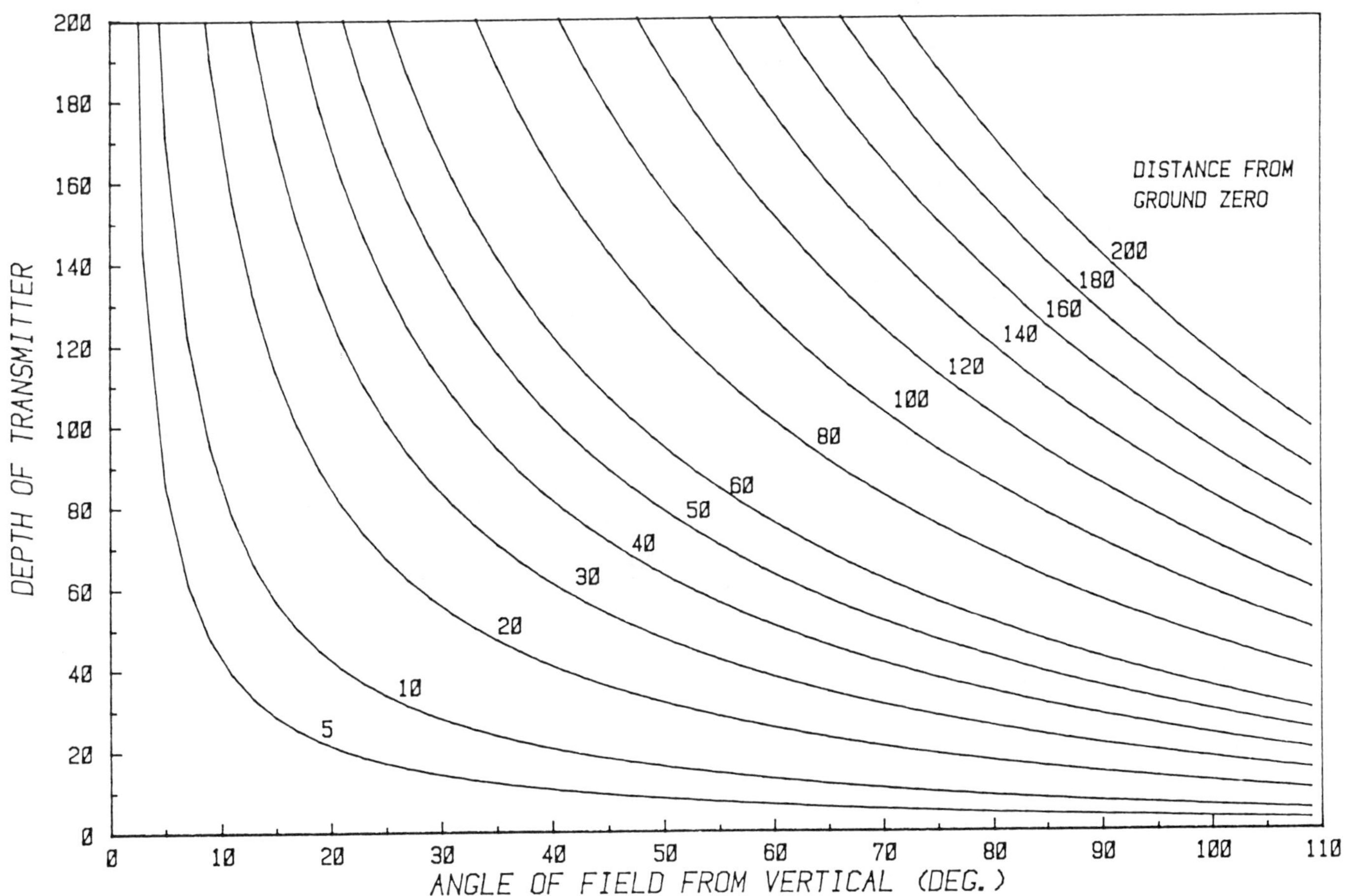

Fig. 4. Cave radio depth guage.

rescuers, lest they draw incorrect conclusions from fragments of conversation. News agencies often discover cave rescues by monitoring emergency frequencies. Crowds attracted by radio traffic can impede a rescue. The following will minimize eavesdropping:

Minimizing Eavesdropping

- Restrict unnecessary conversation.
- Use telephones instead of radios when possible.
- Avoid broadcasting names and locations unless necessary.
- Avoid CB radio.
- Use earphones.
- Use tape to cover frequency readouts on radios.
- Use short range radios for local communication.

Interconnected Communication Links

Connecting the various systems together saves time and preserves message integrity by eliminating the need to relay messages. For example, the field phone circuit inside the cave could be linked directly to a radio transceiver at the entrance, and by radio into commercial telephone. It is especially important to provide a direct voice link to a physician when medical treatment is required.

A phone patch connects radios and telephones together. Phone patches are available commercially, or can be home-built. Cave rescuers have designed a universal phone patch for linking field phones, commer-

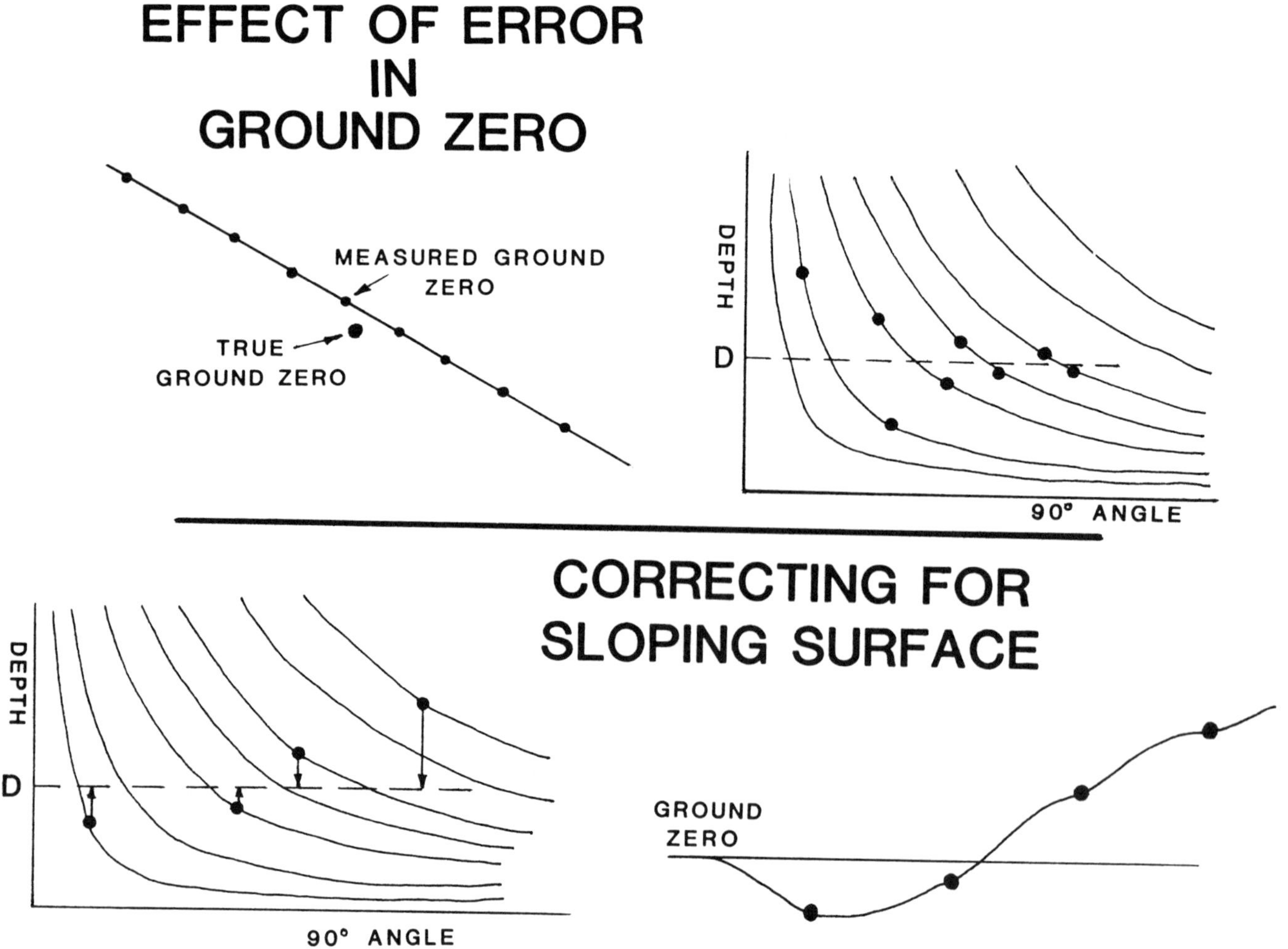

Fig. 5. Sources of error in depth measurement.

cial phones and radios in any combination.

Acoustic patch (holding a radio and telephone close together) is cumbersome and degrades voice quality but often works acceptably. It is worth trying when no direct-connect device is available.

VHF and UHF repeaters greatly extend the range of mobile and hand held transceivers by retransmitting their signals from high elevation at high power. Amateur radio repeaters cover most of the U.S.A. Many have an autopatch feature, allowing access into the telephone system via a Touch-Tone keyboard on the user's radio. Autopatch repeaters have proven invaluable during many cave rescues.

The National Cave Rescue Commission has tested a voice activated portable repeater made from field telephones, phone patches, and hand held radios. This system automatically links underground telephones to radios on the surface.

Amateur or ham radio operators (not to be confused with CB operators) freely offer valuable support during cave rescues and other emergencies. Hams can organize and man communications networks, freeing cavers to work underground. Cave rescue groups should contact a local ham-radio club and become familiar with their capabilities, which often exceed those of professional emergency services. These public service oriented groups build and maintain repeaters and emergency communication vehicles, conduct simulated emergency exercises, and hold training classes for people wishing to get amateur radio licenses. (The technician class license, which allows VHF and UHF voice operation, is quite easy to get.)

Future Caving Electronics

Portable earth-satellite communication equipment may become available for cave rescue operations. Rescue groups have experimented with biomedical telemetry (EKG) from cave to hospital via interconnected communication links.

Amateur radio packet-digital communication networks are being established which carry long-range, error-free, and relatively secure written messages. Their usefulness has been demonstrated in large-scale emergencies. Packet technology is also useful for transmitting scientific data from cave to surface. Cavers have demonstrated microprocessor-controlled instruments for underground data gathering.

Small, affordable receivers for the Loran-C electronic navigation system are becoming available. These are useful for surface karst studies, mapping, guidance to unfamiliar caves, and specifying locations for rescue helicopters.

There are presently no reliable ways of detecting caves electronically. Research in remote-sensing, geophysics, and antisubmarine warfare may someday yield useful methods.

References

1. National Speleological Society: *Caving Information Series #18*:. Use of the Cave Radio in Mapping.

2. Mixon, W. and Blenz, R: *Locating an Underground Transmitter by Surface Measurements*, Windy City Speleonews, December 1964, p. 61, reprinted in Speleo Digest, 1964. A revised, condensed version by W. Mixon appeared with the same title in the NSS News, April 1966, p. 61.

3. Plummer, W: *Depth Measurement with the Cave Radio*, Baltimore Grotto News, August 1964, p. 259. This and other cave radio articles by Plummer were reprinted in Speleo Digest, 1964.

4. Reid, F: *Cave Man Radio*, 73 magazine, February 1984.

5. Drummond, I: *Cave Radio Update*, NSS News, Dec. 1984, p. 366.

6. *The Radio Amateur's Handbook*, Newington, CT: American Radio Relay League, revised yearly.

7. Cave Research Group of Great Britain: *Manual of Caving Techniques*, C. Cullingford, ed., Routledge & Kegan Paul, London, 1969.

8. National Speleological Society: *Cave Rescue Techniques*, 1987.

9. NSS Communication and Electronics Section, PO Box 170274, Arlington, Texas 76003.

10. NSS Computer Applications Section, 6304 Kaypro St., Laurel, MD 20707.

WOMEN IN CAVING

Bernice Gottschalk
NSS 16581

The purpose of this chapter is to welcome new women cavers into the caving community and to discuss issues of special concern to women cavers.

There are many more men who try out caving than women. Perhaps it's the image of an adventure sport that appeals to more men. Or maybe it's the mud.... Even among NSS members, whose interests are not limited to sport caving, men outnumber women by almost four to one. Depending on where you live and who you cave with, you may feel somewhat isolated as a new woman caver.

But you are not alone! Though there are proportionally more men, there are many active women cavers, some of whom have made significant contributions to cave exploration, speleology, and conservation. Many of these contributions were made while carrying out roles of mothering, student and professional.

For example, Patricia Crowther was the first human to go through the "tight spot" connecting Mammoth Cave with the Flint Ridge system. She has also contributed in the cave cartography field. Jeanne Gurnee is a pioneer who explored and helped develop the Rio Camuy cave system in Puerto Rico. Carol Hill wrote *Cave Minerals* and co-authored the more recent *Cave Minerals of the World* (both published by the NSS). Patty Jo Watson is known for her archaeological studies in the Mammoth Cave area and several women are prominent biospeleologists. Sara Corrie, in her 50's and 60's, was a leader among vertical cave explorers. Many grottos have at least one female officer, and the NSS could never function as smoothly as it does without women like Evelyn Bradshaw, who has for many years coordinated the interaction between the NSS, its grottos and other internal organizations.

Women enjoy unique advantages as cavers. Most women are smaller and shorter than most men, so they usually have an easier time of it in crawlways, tight passages, and places that require twisty contortions. A man's chest is often the widest and thickest part of his body; he may have to exhale to squeeze through a constriction. Women's wider hips tend to be more compressible. Women may also have more natural cold tolerance and stamina than men, real advantages on long surveys and explorations.

It is, of course, dangerous to generalize about personality differences between men and women, but women tend to be socialized differently than men. They are less likely to have a macho attitude, and may be more cautious in potentially dangerous situations. Cooperation, essential in an activity where your life may depend on your companions, is generally valued by women more than competition. And women may place more value on appreciating the cave experience than on rushing through passages to blindly cover distance.

You may experience some difficulties on climbs or straddles where tallness or upper body strength is an advantage. Your socialization may work against you if you have not grown up with confidence in your abilities at sports or at roughing it, and particularly if you have not been prepared to take leadership roles in these activities. You may hesitate to assert yourself for fear of making a mistake or being criticized. However, all of these problems are solvable with some thought, practice, and encouragement.

Every caver must find his or her own best route through a cave. What's right for the six-footers in the group might not be right for you. Take the time to think it through and do it right. Accept help if you need it; offer help when others need it.

Just as it takes a measure of courage to push one's physical limits in a demanding cave, or to venture beyond known territory and traverse a new crawlway or attempt a new climb, it takes courage to try new roles. The support of camp followers, cave photographers, grotto officers, and newsletter writers/editors cannot be discounted. Taking on leadership responsibilities may seem particularly daunting, but many women have become successful and highly respected caving leaders.

The NSS is probably the best place for new women cavers to find support and fellowship. Members of the Vertical Section have lots of experience helping cavers of all shapes and sizes design comfortable and efficient climbing rigs. Women and men who are experienced in all phases of cave exploration and cave science are usually willing to help newcomers. The Women's Section of the NSS was created as a support network for women cavers confronting the challenge of new responsibilities and as a means of helping the NSS incorporate the changes in women's roles that have transformed society at large. We welcome you to the caving community!

WHY YOU SHOULD JOIN AN ORGANIZED CAVING GROUP*

David McClurg
NSS 4608F, OS

Organized caving clubs offer five things you can't provide for yourself– and for the most part you won't be able to find any other place. Here's what they are:

WHAT CAVING CLUBS OFFER

1. They know how to cave and can show you how.

2. They know where the caves are.

3. They have ropes and other special gear.

4. They go caving.

And in most cases—unless you're a complete klutz—

5. They'll welcome you, whether you're a beginner or an experienced caver.

Let's take these one at a time to see how important they are both to the neophyte and to the old timer who has recently moved to a new area.

1. They know how to cave and can show you how. Experienced cavers by definition know how to cave. Just as vital, they know the caves in their area and know what's needed to explore those caves.

Whether they have a formal training program or just take you out to some easy caves on your first trip, this is the way to learn. You're with other cavers, so that meets the proviso about not caving alone. And by following what they do and asking questions you can learn the basics much more safely than you can alone or with some other inexperienced recruits.

2. They know where the caves are. It doesn't matter what part of the country you live in, this is worth the price of admission all by itself. Every new caver soon finds out that the best way (sometimes the only way) to find a cave is to go there with some one who's been there before. Clubs have been there before. More on this later.

3. They have the specialized gear. This is why some groups got together in the first place. They wanted to share the cost of an expensive piece of equipment like a long rope, mechanical ascenders, or surveying equipment. One club I know passes the hard hat at every meeting to save up for new equipment.

4.They go caving. What this actually means is that they have regularly scheduled trips, probably once a month or more in good weather. Trips are often varied, some to horizontal caves, some to vertical, some for beginners, some more advanced.

Many clubs lay out the schedule in January for the whole year. This lets them make the most of holidays or three day weekends. Also, members can plan their time off to go on a Christmas trip to Mexico or a June excursion to the annual caving convention.

So strongly do cavers prize their three day weekends, that when my youngest daughter got married, she felt compelled to apologize to local cavers on two counts. Not only was she marrying a non-caver, she was getting married on Memorial Day Weekend. (It was the only time the college chapel was free.) Many cavers came anyway, three day weekend or not. It only proves that all cavers worth their weight in carbide will never turn down free food and beverage!

5. They will welcome you (usually). As I said, unless you're a complete klutz, most caving groups will welcome anyone with a real interest in the sport. Now, I know of some exceptions that prove the rule– but by and large it's true. However, I'll give you this warning gratis– if you're shy, you may be completely overlooked at your first meeting. Don't be afraid to speak up. Tell the group who you are and why you decided to come to their meeting instead of staying home to watch your favorite TV show.

Some clubs have an official meeter and greeter who watches for new people and hands out membership applications or new caver info sheets. If you're lucky, you may locate this kind of group . If not, don't be put off at first by the inside jokes and comments about activities that seem completely foreign. Stick with it for a meeting or two even if it seems like you're being treated like an outsider.

Whatever you do, don't start out by asking for a complete list of local caves, or for detailed directions on how to find them. I guarantee you that this will not endear you to the group. Many cavers are super sensitive about conservation and very protective of local caves.

If you've been caving elsewhere but are a newcomer to the area, you can usually expect to be welcomed too.

*Adapted from the author's book *Adventure of Caving*, copyright 1987, D&J Press.

By the way (if you'll pardon the commercial), this is one of the hidden benefits of being a member of the National Speleological Society. With an NSS membership list in hand you can chart your course to locate kindred caving spirits all over the country. Many will invite you to their meetings or on a cave trip. If you're on the road, you might get lucky and be asked into their homes to talk caving or to stay if you don't mind sleeping on the floor.

To sum it up, cave clubs offer fellowship and a framework for cave exploration. So the next question is how do you find a local club?

The National Speleological Society

As you might have guessed, a good place to start is to ask the NSS. It turns out that a lot of the action in the caving world takes place in and around the chapters and individual members of the National Speleological Society.

It has an active publications program designed to keep the membership up to date on developments in both the sport of caving and the science of speleology.

Besides grottos, the NSS has many special interest sections (geology, vertical caving, electronics, biology, photography, to mention a few) most of which have their own publications and sessions at the annual convention.

As of 1987, the Society has about 6,500 members and more than 100 local chapters or grottos. Most are in the United States, but Canada has a number of members too, as well as one or two grottos.

To find out if there is a grotto near you, address an inquiry to the:

National Speleological Society
Cave Avenue
Huntsville, AL 35810
Phone: 205/852-1300

Since they get a whole bunch of inquiries every month, a self addressed stamped envelope would be appreciated, even though it's not required.

The Society has some paid professionals in its Huntsville office, but the administration, committees, and local grottos are all run by volunteers. Be patient if things seem a little on the slow side.

Conventions

One of the most rewarding Society events is its annual convention, generally held in late June or mid-August. It rotates around the country, and is a tribute to the hard work and stamina of the local volunteers who put it on in their area.

The annual NSS convention is the one time of the year when the Society really comes together—cave trips, meetings, fellowship, technical sessions, papers, more fellowship, slide shows, seminars, films, workshops, a banquet, and even more fellowship.

I've always felt it's the best thing the Society does by a long shot. You meet friends old and new, and swap caving stories (some of them even true), during a week that's so full of activities that you just can't do everything you'd like to.

Regional Conventions

In addition to the summertime national convention, many NSS regional organizations hold weekend caving meets in their part of the country. Some of these are quite venerable affairs, with over 25 or 30 years of tradition behind them. They're usually held on the three day weekends in the Spring and Summer, like Memorial Day, July Fourth, or Labor Day.

Like the NSS Convention, many regional events have contests, papers, slide shows, and a banquet in addition to cave trips.

During the Winter, a number of regions also sponsor educational seminars, sometimes called papers or sessions regionals. These often take place on Washington's Birthday or around Easter, when many people have three day weekends.

All of these meetings are great fun—a real chance to see old friends and learn some new skills.

They're all part of the many benefits—publications, caving trips, meetings, fellowship, and more—that you get from joining organized caving .

APPENDIX A
SUGGESTED FURTHER READING

Prices, where available, are as of 1987, but vary with dealer. HB stands for hardback, PB for paperback, OP for out-of-print. Many books listed may be available in public libraries.

General

Caves
A.C. Waltham, 240 pp, 1974, $12.50. All about caves, their inhabitants, geology and exploration around the world.

Cavers, Caves and Caving
B. Sloane, Ed. 420 pp, 1977, $12.50 HB, $6.00 PB. About American caves and cavers.

The Caves Beyond
J. Lawrence, Jr. and R. W. Brucker, 290 pp, 1975 (Reprint of 1955 edition, HB OP, PB $6.50). Story of the 1954 week-long exploration in Crystal Cave, Ky., the first such a venture in the U.S.

Celebrated American Caves
C.E. Mohr and H.N. Sloane, ed. 339 pp, 1955, OP. A collection of 24 stories by 15 authors about caves in the western hemisphere.

Depths of the Earth
W.R. Halliday, 432 pp, 1976, $15. Hair-raising stories of American caving and a fair account of the history of caving in America.

Exploring American Caves
Franklin Folsom, 280 pp, 1956, OP. A general book touching on the geology and biology of caves, human use of caves, history of caving and how to get started in caving. A very good book that, in the mid-50's, presented the state of the art of caving.

The Jewel Cave Adventure
H. and J. Conn, 240 pp, 1977. PB $7. The fascinating story of two people exploring, and mapping in what is now the second largest cave in the U.S.

The Longest Cave
R.A. Watson and R.W. Brucker, 312 pp, 1976. OP. The story of the events leading to the connection of the Flint Ridge Cave System to Mammoth Cave to form the longest known cave in the world.

Speleo Digest Series
Series editor, William Mixon and others, annual since 1957, prices vary. A collection of the year's articles from grotto and regional newsletters. An excellent way to keep up with exploration, equipment, techniques, safety, speleology and humor in other parts of the country.

Trapped!
R.K. Murray and R.W. Brucker, 335 pp, 1979, $10. Story of the 1925 attempted rescue of Floyd Collins from Sand Cave, Kentucky.

Under Plowman's Floor
by R.A. Watson, 224 pp, 1978, $10. A fictional story of real persons and a real cave system. About a man who does far-out solo caving and the motivation behind his actions.

The World of Caves
A.C. Waltham, 128 pp, 1976. Color photographs and description of caves and caving around the world.

Safety

American Caving Accidents
Compiled annually by NSS American Caving Accidents Editor. Reports and analyzes cave incidents and accidents, including causes and what not to do.

Techniques and Equipment

Adventure of Caving
D. McClurg, 332 pp, 1986, $15. Complete guide for advanced and beginning cavers, covering safety and hazards, conservation, personal gear, horizontal techniques, rigging, and vertical caving.

American Caves and Caving
W.R. Halliday, 348 pp, 1974. A guide to caving covering types of caves, gear, communications, rescue, and more.

Caves
G. Laycock, 101 pp, 1976, $7. An introduction to caving for 10 to 14 year olds.

Exploring Caves
D. McClurg, 287 pp, 1980, OP. Covers conservation safety, finding caves, personal gear, ropes, vertical techniques, and equipment.

Manual of Caving Techniques
C. Cullingford, ed., The Cave Research Group of Great Britain, 416 pp, 1969 OP. British caving techniques. Good, but often different from U.S. techniques.

Prusiking
R. Thrun, 75 pp, 1973, OP NSS First book devoted to ascending a rope. Covers knot prusiking, early mechanical ascenders, and types of ropes

Single Rope Techniques: A Guide for Vertical Cavers
N.R. Montgomery, 122 pp, 1977, $15 PB. A comprehensive book (now a bit dated) dealing with most aspects of vertical caving (except for belaying).

Cave Sciences

Cave Minerals of the World
C. Hill and Paolo Forti, 283 pp, 1986, $30 HB, $25 PB. A description of cave minerals from all over the world, with over 100 photographs, plus bibliography with over 2000 references.

Karst, An Introduction to Systematic Geomorphology
J.N. Jennings, 252 pp, 1971, $12. A synthesis of European, Austral-Asian, African and American speleological theories and research.

Karst Landforms
M.M. Sweeting, ed, 448 pp, 1981, $56. World-wide review of karst, not only of landforms, but also water tracing, carbonate solution chemistry, karst hydrology and types of karst.

The Life of the Cave
C.E. Mohr and T.L. Poulson, 232 pp, 1966. OP. A popular book devoted to cave life. Many fine photographs and illustrations.

The Science of Speleology
T.S. Ford and C.H.D. Cullingford, eds. 593 pp, 1976. Chapters on surveying, chemistry of cave waters, cave minerals, geomorphology, fauna and flora and computer use for speleology.

Speleology, The Study of Caves
G.W. Moore and G.N. Sullivan, 150 pp, 1978, HB, PB. A very good introduction to speleology for the layman.

Surveying Caves
Bryan Ellis, 88 pp, 1976, $4. General mapping book on the principles of cave surveying with many unusual hints.

APPENDIX B

SOURCES OF EQUIPMENT AND BOOKS

This is a basic list of mail order firms who specialize in caving equipment and books. Many of them will send you a catalog upon request. If you're in a hurry (and have a credit card) some suppliers are happy to accept phone orders. But please remember– use 800 numbers only for orders, not just for free information.

A good place to locate beginning caving equipment is the army-navy or surplus stores found in almost every town. These are a good source of cave packs, camping equipment, and other small items useful to cavers. Inexpensive clothing suitable for caving can be obtained at second-hand stores such as those operated by Goodwill Industries or the Salvation Army.

For more specialized gear like carbide lamps, recommended hard hats and most vertical equipment, the caving suppliers shown here are probably your best bet.

Equipment

Blue Water LTD
209 Lovvorn Road
Carrollton, Georgia 30117
Caving rope and vertical equipment.

Bob & Bob
P.O. Box 441
Lewisburg, West Virginia 24901
Complete line of caving and vertical equipment
304/772-5049

Caving Supply
19 London Road
Buxton, Derbyshire SK17 9PA, Great Britain
European caving and vertical gear.
From USA: 44/0298-5040 (5 hours later than EST)

Custom Cave Gear
P.O. Box 7351
Charlottesville, Virginia 22906
Vertical caving equipment.

Donald G. Davis
5311 309 Road
Parachute, Colorado 81635
Premier carbide lamps and parts.

Gibbs Products
202 East Hampton Avenue
Salt Lake City, Utah 84111
Vertical caving equipment.

Inner Mountain Outfitters
102 Travis Circle
Seaford, VA 2696
804/898-2809 (evenings)
Caving and vertical equipment.

L & S Sporting Goods
P.O. Box 176
Philippi, West Virginia 26416
Caving and vertical equipment
304/457-2567

Mountain Safety Research
631 South 96th Street
Seattle, Washington 98108
MSR hard hats.

Pigeon Mountain Industries
P.O. Box 803
Lafayette, Georgia 30728
Caving rope, rescue, and vertical equipment.

The Speleoshoppe
P.O. Box 297
Fairdale, Kentucky 40118
Complete line of caving and vertical equipment.
800/626-5877

J.E. Weinel, Inc.
P.O. Box 213
Valencia, PA 16059
Caving, vertical, and rescue equipment.
800/346-7673

Wilderness Outfitters
800 Town Clock Plaza
Dubuque, Iowa 52001
Caving, camping, and climbing equipment.
319/556-1121

BOOKS

American Cave Conservation Association
P.O. Box 409
Attn: Publications
Horse Cave, KY 42749
Cave conservation and management publications.

Association for Mexican Cave Studies
P.O. Box 7037
University Station
Austin, TX 78712
Publications on Mexican caves and caving.

Cave Books
4700 Amberwood Drive
Dayton, OH 45424
Cave books and publications of the Cave Research Foundation.

Paul Damon
P.O. Box 302
Monroeville, Pennsylvania 15146
Out-of-print and current cave books, periodicals.

D & J Press
1610 Live Oak Drive
Carlsbad, NM 88220
Publisher of *Adventure of Caving*
505/887-5761

NSS Bookstore
Cave Avenue
Huntsville, Alabama 35810
Cave books, publications of the NSS, patches, symbolic devices.
205/852-1300

Anne and Tony Oldham
Rhychydwr, Crymych
Dyfed SA41 3RB, United Kingdom
Cave publications from around the world, current and out-of-print.

Speleobooks
P.O. Box 10
Schoharie, New York 12157
Current and out-of-print cave books and ephemera.
518/295-7978

U.S. Geological Survey
Branch of Distribution
Box 25286 Federal Center
Denver, Colorado 80225
Topographic and geological maps and reports. State index maps free on request.

APPENDIX C

GLOSSARY OF CAVING TERMS USED IN THIS MANUAL

aquifer—a pervious rock unit that is saturated with water and yields water to a well or spring.

aragonite—a mineral of calcium carbonate, $CaCO_3$, like calcite but of a different crystal form and higher specific gravity.

ascender—a mechanical device with a cam that grips a rope when downward pressure is applied to the device.

Association of Mexican Cave Studies (AMCS)—a group of active cavers who explore Mexican caves. Address: AMCS, P. O. Box 7037, Univ. Station, Austin, TX 78712.

bedding plane—a surface in a rock unit that separates individual layers or beds of rock.

belay—a safety rope tied to a climber that is played out or taken in by a second person as the climber moves. The purpose of the belay is to catch the climber in the event of a fall.

brake bar—a round bar about 2½ x ¾ inches that is placed on rappel racks or carabiners so that a rope can be threaded through the rack or carabiners for rappelling.

breakdown—rock slabs, blocks or chips on the floor of a cave that have fallen from the walls or ceiling.

cable ladder—a ladder made of two parallel cables with metal rungs held in place on the cables with metal tubes crimped to the cables.

calcite—a mineral composed of calcium carbonate, $CaCO_3$; the main mineral composing most common speleothems in limestone.

calcite raft—a thin sheet of calcite or aragonite that forms on the surface of still cave pools.

carabiner—an oval of steel or aluminum with movable spring-loaded gate on one side. Locking carabiner is one where the gate is threaded and has a ring that can be threaded over the gate opening to prevent it from opening.

carbide—calcium carbide, CaC_2, a gray material that reacts with water to produce acetylene gas and calcium hydroxide.

carbide lamp—see Fig. 1. in the Carbide Lamps chapter.

cave—a naturally formed void in the earth, generally large enough for a person to enter.

cave pearl—a calcite concretion that has formed in a shallow cave pool or floor depression.

Cave Research Foundation (CRF)—an organization of cavers united primarily for the scientific exploration and study of caves. Address: CRF, Box 26, Mammoth Cave, KY 42259.

cave system—a series of connecting caves or caves in an area that had been connected at one time.

caver—a person who explores caves in a safe manner while showing respect for the cave, other cavers and the land above the cave.

cavern—a large cave.

chert nodule—a nodule of silica, usually light-cream or gray to black in color.

crawlway—a cave passage large enough for a caver to traverse on hands and knees or small enough to squeeze through on back or belly.

dip—the slope of a bed, expressed as the angle made by a straight line along the bed with a horizontal line in the same direction.

dolomite—a rock or mineral composed of calcium magnesium carbonate, $CaMg(CO_3)_2$.

dome—a high shaft in a room or passage formed by solution.

double brake bars—a rappel device of two carabiners with a brake bar on each and connected together with another carabiner or a metal ring.

electric lamp—as used in caving, generally a helmet-mounted headpiece (bulb, reflector and lens) with a wire running to a battery carried elsewhere on the person.

flagging tape—thin plastic ribbon of any color about 1½ inches wide used for marking survey stations, trails, etc.

flowstone—mineral deposits that have accumulated as water slowly seeps over a wall or floor of a cave.

formation(s)—a rock unit with distinct characteristics within a sequence of rocks. Also an old term for mineral deposits in caves; see speleothem.

grotto—a local chapter of the NSS whose officers are NSS members.

guano—a rich manure of bat dung.

guano cave—a cave containing large amounts of guano.

gypsum—a common cave mineral composed of hydrous calcium sulfate, $CaSO_4 \cdot 2H_2O$.

gypsum flower—a fibrous speleothem of sulfate that radiates out from a common base in "petals."

hot-seat rappel—a method of rappelling with the rope running under one leg, up across the opposite shoulder and controlled with a hand. The friction of the rope on the body creates a lot of heat, hence its name.

joint—a fracture in a series of rock units, generally at an angle to the bedding.

karst—a terrain where the topography is formed by the dissolving of rock, usually limestone, and is characterized by solutional surface features, subterranean drainage and caves.

knots—various methods of securing or tying ropes or webbing material together. See prusik knots in vertical caving chapter.

limestone—a gray-blue rock composed of calcium carbonate, $CaCO_3$.

loess—a homogeneous deposit of mostly silt, usually deposited by wind.

mechanical ascender—same as ascender, but used to clarify the use of a mechanical device instead of a rope ascender knot.

middens—accumulations of animal droppings, other than guano; may be solidified.

newsletter—a publication written and published by grotto members, received by that grotto's membership and subscribers and exchanged for other grotto's newsletters.

NSS Bulletin—the quarterly journal of the NSS containing articles of scientific interest; received by all NSS members.

NSS News—the monthly publication of the NSS received by all members. Contains current and general articles of caver interest.

pahoehoe—lava flows with a smooth or billowy surface in which lava tubes are found.

pit—a hole in a passage or room of some depth which may require the use of vertical techniques to descend and ascend.

prusiking—the art of ascending a standing line with prusik knots.

prusik knot—a knot tied by looping a smaller diameter rope around a larger standing line that has the property of sliding with no load on the knot, but will hold when it is loaded.

rappel—the art of descending a rope using some sort of friction between the rope and the rappeller to control the rate of descent.

rappel rack—a long U-shaped steel bar that holds several brake bars and is used for rappelling.

rappel spool—one of the devices used to create friction between a rappeller and the rope that consists of a spool on which the rope can be wrapped around several times.

region(al)—generally used when talking about an NSS organization composed of several grottos in a common area and their meetings.

rimstone dam—a wall-shaped calcite deposit that impounds, or had impounded, pools of water.

scallops—formed on walls and in streambeds, these are oval hollows that have asymmetric cross sections and can be used to determine the direction of water flow.

selenite needles—a sulfate speleothem having the shape of a needle that grows from gypsiferous cave soils.

sinking stream—a stream that disappears underground, usually in a depression. Swallow hole is the preferred term to be used.

Speleo Digest—an annual publication that is a collection of articles selected from grotto newsletters; available only from the NSS Bookstore.

speleothem—secondary mineral deposit formed in caves such as stalactites or flowstone.

spelunker—usually used by non-cavers to mean a caver.

stalactite—a speleothem of cylindrical or conical shape hanging from the roof or a ledge.

stalagmite—a speleothem of cylindrical or conical shape rising from the floor or a ledge.

standing line—a rope of about 7/16-inch or 11 mm in diameter that is tied to a solid anchor and is used for descending and ascending.

stoping—the upward migration of the ceiling in a passage or room by the action of slabs falling.

stratigraphic column—a graphic means of representing the various rock types of an area in a geologic report.

stratigraphic sequence—the sequence of rock types in an area.

strike—a horizontal line on a bedding-plane. At any point the direction of strike is at right angles to the direction of maximum or true dip at that point.

sump—a place where the ceiling of a passage drops to and below water level, leaving no air space with the cave passage continuing underwater.

swallow hole—the place where a stream sinks in limestone terrain, usually in a closed depression.

topo map—short for topographic map. A map showing landforms by the use of contour lines (lines representing equal elevation on the earth's surface).

troglobite—a creature that is fully adapted to life in total darkness and can only complete its life cycle underground.

troglophile—a creature that may or may not live completely underground.

trogloxene—a creature that visits caves for a part of their activities.

vertical caver—a caver who enjoys and is competent doing vertical caving.

vertical caving—caving that includes a lot of ascending and descending.

virgin passage—a cave passage that has not previously been entered; a new discovery.